Riot!

Riot!

Civil Insurrection from
Peterloo to the Present Day

IAN HERNON

Pluto Press

LONDON • ANN ARBOR, MI

First published 2006 by Pluto Press
345 Archway Road, London N6 5AA
and 839 Greene Street, Ann Arbor, MI 48106

www.plutobooks.com

British Library Cataloguing in Publication Data
A catalogue record for this book is available from the British Library

ISBN-10 0 7453 2538 6 hardback
ISBN-13 978 0 7453 2538 5 hardback

Library of Congress Cataloging in Publication Data applied for

10 9 8 7 6 5 4 3 2 1

Designed and produced for Pluto Press by
Chase Publishing Services Ltd, Fortescue, Sidmouth, EX10 9QG, England
Typeset from disk by Stanford DTP Services, Northampton, England
Printed and bound in the European Union by Gutenberg Press, Malta

'A riot is at bottom the language of the unheard.'
Martin Luther King

Contents

List of Illustrations

Foreword

Paul Routledge

We read so much about Britain's foreign wars, not least because there were so many, that we sometimes forget ours is a nation often at war with itself. Quite apart from full-blown civil war, a class war has raged down the centuries, manifesting itself in riots, strikes, civil disobedience, conspiracies and public disorder of the most fearsome kind, France may have the better mob, but Britons are no strangers to mayhem on the streets.

Ian Hernon's book is a timely reminder of this overlooked dimension of the national character. For much of the last decade, presumably as an antidote to the quotidian dullness of life at Westminster where he works as a political correspondent, Hernon has patrolled the furthermost reaches of empire in search of forgotten imperial conflicts. He has now turned his attention to bloody, violent events at home, from the Luddites to the Stop the War campaign against the Iraq war. *Riot!* makes fascinating reading, and seeks to understand the positive results of law and order breakdown, as well as the unhappy human toll.

I have not been in many riots myself, but I do have some experience, including the people power revolt that brought down President Marcos of the Philippines, During the miners' strike of 1984/85, which I reported for *The Times*, I was on the front line at the time. Indeed, sometimes behind it. I recall a very cold November morning on the approach road to Brodsworth colliery, south Yorkshire, where half a dozen strikebreaking miners were being escorted into work by hundreds of police officers, many in riot gear.

Brodsworth was known as 'the Royal pit' because its coal warmed Buckingham Palace. There was little sign of the Queen's Peace that day. I travelled to the battleground with pit officials of the National Union of Mineworkers (NUM). It was quite clear what was going to happen. One of the young miners showed me his 'King Edward' – a large lump of concrete hidden inside his bomber jacket.

In the cold light of dawn, they confronted the police lines, throwing anything they could lay their hands on. A police Land-Rover, caught in a muddy field, drew an intense fusillade, which threatened to overwhelm its occupants. They were only saved by a determined recovery operation. Thereafter, the police charged the pickets, scattering them through a council estate. Officers hit out at anyone and anything, especially the windscreens of parked cars. It was a small riot, not many injured, typical of a 'normal' day's events as the strike moved inexorably to defeat. It achieved nothing, beyond venting the rage of the strikers. The scabs got through, but no coal was produced.

Incidents of this kind took place regularly in the dying months of that year-long confrontation. Hernon concentrates on what became known as the Battle of Orgreave, where NUM President Arthur Scargill and thousands of pickets laid siege to a coking plant near Sheffield. This operation was designed to replicate the Battle of Saltley Gate during the 1972 pit strike, when Scargill's flying pickets and striking local workers closed down a cokeworks in Birmingham, forcing the police to withdraw. Saltley was a victory for the forces of disorder, but, ultimately, a pyrrhic one. Conservative leaders engaged in a strategic rethink of policing policy and trade union law, which broke the back of organised labour a decade later when the party swept back into office.

It is the see-saw of power, now in the hands of a well-directed mob, now in the hands of the civil authorities, that has characterised the history of unrest. At every new manifestation of disorder, the authorities invest themselves with fresh powers to impose their hegemony. In the days of Peterloo, the Merthyr Rising and the Featherstone Riot, the military was routinely employed. In Featherstone, where the riot is still known locally as 'the Massacre', though only two died, soldiers of the South Staffordshire Regiment were despatched to put down a baying mob of striking miners. Ironically, the colliery manager, Alfred Holliday, is buried only yards from the victims in the local cemetery. Death levels the playing field.

In more recent times, the authorities – Parliament, the police and the legal establishment – have increasingly used the law to suppress unrest. In the 1980s strikers at Rupert Murdoch's Wapping plant found themselves and their unions tied down by a thousand Lilliputian legal knots, including sequestration of funds, curbs on so-called secondary picketing and court orders restraining individuals on pain of imprisonment. The legal route was first tried out in the dispute between print unions and Eddy Shah's Messenger Group, where it quelled a riotous siege of his Warrington production plant. Union leaders are actually a more conservative breed than is customarily acknowledged. A Victorian sense of probity gives high priority to the safeguarding of union funds, built up through generations of workers' pennies contributed by those with little enough to spare. By going for the financial jugular, the authorities knew how to cripple the directing brain of insurrection – where one was operating.

The process of legal control continues apace with New Labour's laws against terrorism, which give the police unprecedented new powers. Demonstrations have been banned in the environs of Parliament and Downing Street, minimising the risk of a televised repeat of the Poll Tax Riots which paralysed central London and accelerated the downfall of Margaret Thatcher. The ranks of MI5 have been boosted, giving the security services an information overload on who is planning what, and where. Briefly, the internet and the mobile phone made conspirational contact easier and surveillance harder, but the civil powers have invested massively in technological know-how and expert personnel to close that loophole.

All of which suggests that the day of the riot is no more. Even if they had radical instincts, which is debatable, the trade unions are in a legal straitjacket. And the root causes of unrest – unemployment, unfair or punitive taxation, the use of scab labour in industrial disputes – have diminished to the point where they do not easily offer a trigger for mayhem. Relative prosperity makes cowards of us all. A bottle of chardonnay on the table and a pizza in the oven are seductive deterrents to throwing bricks in the rain. Only the underclass, Marx's lumpenproletariat, could rightfully claim to have been left out of the prosperous society, and they are all too often steeped in drugs and alcohol, virtually immured in their sink estates and shackled with Anti-Social Behaviour Orders to have the energy for unrest.

Hernon recognises this historic social shift, arguing that 'riot as a weapon against degrees of poverty and exploitation which could and did kill the body became an expression of rage against a poverty of expectation which can kill the spirit. Whether violence can be justified in that ongoing struggle remains debatable.' For rioting to be justified, oppression must be real, tangible, and incapable of resolution by other, peaceful means. The trick of the British establishment has been to turn the spears of insurrection on one hand by bread and circuses and on the other by constructing a discreet security state whose mailed fist can be deployed at a moment's notice.

In such circumstances, it is small wonder that Hernon, ambivalent about the violence and dismissive of the efforts of trade union bureaucrats, should yearn for the passion of yesteryear's mob. Not for him Chairman Mao's view that it is too early to assess the impact of the French Revolution. Sometimes, he insists, there has been no alternative to taking to the streets. 'The brickbat may not be cricket, but Britain would be a different place without it.' Different, yes. But worse, or better? Hernon provides the evidence in these pages, which celebrate the civilians who took on the might of the Establishment. Unlike the heroes of Britain's imperial wars, they are not honoured in a single memorial in their own country. Perhaps they should be.

Paul Routledge is a columnist for the *Daily Mirror* and a biographer of Arthur Scargill, Peter Mandelson, Gordon Brown, Betty Boothroyd, John Hume, Airey Neave and Harold Wilson. He has personal experience of riots, having been a 'refusenik' in the Wapping dispute.

Preface

The broad purpose of this book is to catalogue almost two centuries of riot and disorder which show that Britain has had more in common with America's Wild West than our cosy self-image may allow. I have tried to show an unbroken link between the civil unrest caused by clear-cut injustices in the nineteenth century to the street violence of the twentieth, and the legacy left in the twenty-first. A secondary aim was to give a voice to those in the crowd who have not always been heard. In explaining the circumstances which led to civil violence it has also, inevitably, become a potted history of many other issues: the long battle for universal franchise, the growth of socialism and the trade union movement, immigration, social divisions, poverty, the changing role of the police, and the mechanics of both state repression and public protection.

These are not always edifying stories, and I have tried my best not to be too judgemental. The heroes are those who fought for rights which most now take for granted, but which are always under threat. The villains are easy enough to spot. But the vast majority on either side of the picket line or barricade were neither, just ordinary people caught up in the tumultuous tide of social history. Therefore the incidents I describe involve high-minded idealism, determination, courage and cowardice, official incompetence, savagery, stupidity, alcohol, bigotry, greed, self-interest, mob mentality and repression. Taken together they have helped shape modern Britain.

Some may question the inclusion of certain incidents, or complain about the exclusion of others, or question my focus on the violence itself, rather than wider social concerns. Such charges may be reasonable. My main motivation has been to recall battles which have largely dropped out of public consciousness. Schoolchildren may still be taught about Peterloo and the Suffragettes, but few people outside academia and the geographical locations themselves are very much aware of the Battle of Bristol or the police strike.

There are two glaring omissions, which makes this very much a history of insurrection in England and Wales. Too much has been written about Northern Ireland for me to make any valuable contribution in this volume, save to point out that the experiences of the Royal Ulster Constabulary in riots were closely monitored by the mainland police. And Scotland's social history has run a separate if parallel course for much of the period covered here. To include it, except in passing, would have made this book too unwieldy.

Finally, I must thank the following people who have given me much practical help and encouragement: Ian Craig, Raul de Vaux, Malcom Eidens, Bill Jacobs, Gary Kent, Mark Thomas and David Castle of Pluto Press. And, of course, my wife Pauline and my daughters, Joanna and Kim.

Introduction

'Always in demand to extinguish home fires'

Riots have always been with us. They have been a counterweight to oppression, or an opportunity for plunder, or a conduit for passion and anger, for as long as British history has been recorded. Fear of 'the mob' has gripped successive monarchs and Governments down the centuries. Calvin Coolidge pointed out that 'The only difference between a mob and a trained army is organisation.'

Rioting featured in all the British revolutions which overturned absolute rulers and created the earlier forms of a Parliamentary democracy. It was part of the great tidal waves of history and the smaller ripples of localised disputes. And the English in particular seemed to love it. A London mob marked the coronation of Richard the Lionheart in 1189 by massacring the Jewish community. In the eighteenth century the right to resistance against injustice, real or imagined, became an integral part of the national tradition. Lord North said that there were only two methods of changing a ministry: 'The King or the mob.'

In 1769 Benjamin Franklin wrote of his English visit: 'I have seen within a year riots in the country about corn; riots about elections; riots about workhouses; riots of collier; riots of weavers; riots of coal heavers; riots of sawyers; riots of Wilkesites; riots of government chairmen; riots of smugglers, in which custom-house officers and excisemen have been murdered and the King's armed vessels and troops fired at.' Ian Gilmour later added to the list of riots in the same year against 'turnpikes, enclosures and high food prices, Roman Catholics, the Irish and Dissenters, the naturalisation of Jews, the impeachment of politicians, press gangs, crimp houses and the Militia

1

Act, theatre prices, foreign actors, pimps, bawdy houses, surgeons, French footmen and alehouse keepers, the gibbets in Edgeware Road and public whippings, the Excise, the Cider Tax and the shops Tax, workhouses and industrial employers, the rumoured destruction of cathedral spires, even against a change in the calendar'.[1]

The most notorious riots were not sparked by high-minded principle. In 1749 Londoners rioted against the unpopular tax on gin. Playhouses off the Strand were attacked and the Gatehouse prison was stormed by armed ruffians. After much damage to property, the Government gave in and reduced both duties and penalties.

In 1789 Lord George Gordon, a retired navy lieutenant implacably opposed to Catholic emancipation, led a 50,000-strong mob to the House of Commons to demand the repeal of the Roman Catholic Relief Act. The demonstration turned into a riot which lasted five days. Numerous Catholic churches and private houses were destroyed. Other buildings attacked included the Bank of England and the King's Bench, Newgate and Fleet prisons. An observer described the attacks:

> The mob fired the gaol in many places before they were enabled to force their way through the massive bars and gates which guarded the entrance. The wild gestures of the mob without, and the shrieks of the prisoners within, expecting instantaneous death from the flames, the thundering descent of huge pieces of building, the deafening clangour of red-hot iron bars striking in terrible concussion on the pavement below, and the loud, triumphant yells and shouts of the demonic assailants on each new success, formed an awful and terrible scene.

The army was called in and in the resulting mayhem 285 rioters were killed, 173 wounded and 139 arrested. Lord Mansfield said that the military were called in 'not as soldiers, but as citizens. No matter whether their coats be red or brown, they were called in aid of the laws, not to subvert them, or to overthrow the constitution, but to preserve both.' Gordon was tried for high treason but acquitted. Twenty-five of his followers were hanged and twelve imprisoned.[2]

Violence was ever present during and after elections, which was no wonder given the venal and corrupt practices of the day. The Palace of Westminster, the law courts and other symbols of power and privilege were stormed on a regular basis. MPs, ministers, landowners, profiteers, nobles, magistrates, even princes, faced the constant threat of a mauling at the hands and feet of a disaffected crowd if they strayed too far from their heavily protected safe havens. The Adam screen outside the Admiralty in London was built to keep out sailors angrily demanding back-pay.

Such protest, however, was fragmented and, in the long run, ineffective. The poorest or the poor were too poor to travel to a good riot. If they did so, the obvious justification of extreme distress proved a poor defence. In 1796 Burke pointed out their dilemma: 'If the people are turbulent and riotous, nothing is to be done for them on account of their evil dispositions. If they are obedient and loyal, nothing is to be done for them, because their being quiet and contented is a proof that they feel no grievance.'

In addition, the panic engendered by the French Revolution, and the subsequent 'patriotic' wars against the old enemy, the French, set back the Radical Movement, allowing the ruling classes to equate demand change with treason.

In February 1803 Colonel Edward Marcus Despard and six working men were condemned to be hung, drawn and quartered for treason, having been caught in an alehouse planning to murder the King and lead an insurrection. The case was shocking to the ruling elite because Despard was one of their own, the youngest son of a family of Irish landed gentry and eminent soldiers. Despard had fought bravely alongside the young Horatio Nelson in the ill-fated San Juan expedition and had many friends of noble birth. The authorities blamed the bitterness he felt on his treatment after returning to Britain, including a spell in a debtor's prison. But his burning resentment was fuelled less by his own ill-treatment and more by his reading, while in prison, of Thomas Paine's *The Rights of Man*. It was a manifesto for general revolution, including the creation of a welfare state, the redistribution of wealth and no taxation without representation. Most controversially it called for the overthrow of the monarchy, an institution which he regarded as 'the master fraud, which shelters all others'. Paine was driven into exile but his tract sold over 200,000 copies, and each was lent, passed on or read aloud many times more. Despard said that it was the closest thing he possessed to a bible. It was a manifesto devoured by tradesmen, skilled workers, the self-taught and their more enlightened masters.

According to police spies and turncoats Despard plotted to kill the King on his way to Parliament by blasting the royal carriage with a

Turkish cannon captured from the French and on display in St James Park, and spark a general uprising. The plot was doomed from the start as the conspirators were riddled with informers. Nevertheless, the Establishment was determined to make an example of a renegade gentleman and his alleged followers. On the scaffold Despard addressed the crowd: 'Citizens, I hope and trust, notwithstanding my fate, and the fate of those who will no doubt soon follow me, that the principles of freedom, of humanity, and of justice, will finally triumph over falsehood, tyranny and delusion, and every principle inimical to the interests of the human race.'[3]

Soldiers, Bow Street Runners and other police officers were out in force, expecting a riot, but the crowd applauded a brave man and drifted sullenly away. For the ruling elite always had force behind them. There was the militia, created by a 1757 Act, selected by ballot from lists of men aged between 18 and 45 by parish constables. They served for five years, given limited training and liable to be called upon in civil emergency. They were organised in county regiments, officered by gentlemen selected by the Lords Lieutenants of each county, and funded by land tax. They were provided with uniforms and given a ten-guinea annual bounty, the equivalent of 20 weeks' wages for a farm labourer. Exemptions were granted to married men with more than three children, clergymen and Quakers. Their behaviour, as agents of law and order, was not always impeccable. The bounty was too often spent on drink, while uniforms were often used as a disguise to settle old grudges.

Then there were the Volunteers, regiments of part-time soldiers formed purely for civil defence, and county Yeomanry forces, cavalrymen who supplied their own horses in return for status and glittering uniforms. When the latter were formed in 1794 their duties specifically included 'the suppression of riots and tumult'.

And finally, there was the regular army. Over 11,000 troops were deployed in London to quell the Gordon Riots. Britain was divided into military districts and the Army could be called in provided there was a formal request from the civil authorities. An Act of 1714 had given magistrates the power to order rioters to disperse in the Sovereign's name, provided more than twelve people had been rioting for more than an hour. The penalty was life imprisonment. Too often, when the soldiers came, it meant immediate death.

1   Instructing the Volunteers
Engraving after John Leech, c.1860s

Richard Holmes wrote:

> The British army in the age of Brown Bess was the product of a society
> showing all the strains of population explosion coupled with radical changes
> in both industry and agriculture ... The men who filled the army's ranks
> came increasingly from an urban working class whose living conditions
> were only latterly improved by the burgeoning of the nation's wealth.
> They were led by scions of the ruling elite ... And while the army's most
> spectacular achievements were on foreign fields, it was always in demand
> to extinguish home fires, ignited by King Mob in the towns and Captain
> Swing in the countryside.[4]

Nevertheless, not all soldiers were willing to turn their weapons on
their civilian brothers, and the fear of mutiny was always present when
the authorities deployed them. In 1800 the Wolverhampton Volunteers
declared that they had not enlisted 'to give security to the inhuman
oppressor, whilst the poor are starving in the midst of plenty'. The vast
majority of soldiers and militia were denied the privileges, status and
political power of those they fought for. The authorities were well aware
of that. It is no accident that such care was taken to exclude volunteers
with supposed radical views, or that large numbers of labourers were
stood down from home defence duties when the threat of a French

invasion faded in 1805. Ministers appreciated the danger of arming and drilling the masses. That said, however, by 1814, 890,000 men were under arms – 250,000 in the regular army, 500,000 as part-time soldiers and 140,000 in the Royal Navy – a total proportionately only a little less than that mobilised during the First World War. Tradesmen in particular swelled the ranks of the militias, eager to protect their property against their customers.

The established order, enforced by arms, came under renewed pressure as the Industrial Revolution promised a new form of power for those who worked and created wealth rather than those who merely reaped the rewards of other people's toil. Riotous assembly, the stockpiling of arms, the creation of self-help societies and trade associations, radical new ideas openly expressed, organised vandalism, civic disobedience and the withdrawal of labour all became part of the common cause. From then on most public disorder or civil insurrection was motivated by the perception of extreme injustice. Burke famously told the Commons that the people would not seek illegal means of redress if they had legal ones. It was a point few Governments recognised. To them, any challenge to their authority or the status quo was the outcome of licentiousness or outside agitation. And the violence employed by the state could not be compared to the violence of the mob. Such double standards were eloquently summed up by James Mackintosh, writing of the early days of the French Revolution: 'The wild justice of the people has a naked and undisguised horror. Its slightest exertion awakens all our indignation, while murder and rapine if arrayed in the gorgeous disguise of acts of state, may with impunity stalk abroad.'

The last 200 years have seen the assassinations of Archdukes and Tsars, revolutions for good and evil abroad. Britain did not escape that turmoil, but its impact was slow rather than instant. The nation did not escape revolution, as most assume, but adapted to revolutionary ideas until they became the norm. Votes for men and women, workplace rights, the forging and dismantlement of an empire, the stresses and benefits of immigration, youth culture, industrial change, the lessening – if not eradication – of rule by a hereditary elite, the rise of socialism and fascism, all played a part in forging today's nation state. As Despard's biographer, Mike Jay, put it most succinctly: 'The ship of state inched through the shoals and reefs of popular unrest, adjusting its course as little and as late as possible and always bristling with force of arms.'[5]

1
Luddites and Blanketeers

'The sword is the worst argument that can be used'

From the turmoil of the Industrial Revolution a mythical figure emerged. General, or King, Ned Ludd was named after an eighteenth-century rebel industrial worker. Letters bearing his name began to circulate in 1811. They terrified both the traditional ruling elite and the new boss class of factory, foundry and mill owners. To them he represented the devilish nature inherent in the emerging class of industrial workers. And the orgy of rioting and destruction he inspired confirmed their fears. These were no spontaneous outpourings of passions, but a co-ordinated campaign of intimidation and violence which had to be put down with the utmost severity. The riot for defined political aims, until then regarded as a foreign concept, became a commonplace.

*   *   *

The eighteenth century had been a violent and tumultuous one, but one in which the power of a complacent ruling class had solidified. England was massively nationalistic and had grown used to winning foreign wars and – apart from the loss of the American colonies – was carving out a global empire second to none. It was one of the richest countries on earth, its wealth based on trade, slavery, speculation, foreign plunder, wool, farming and cottage manufacturing. But few of the benefits trickled down to a vast underclass, for whom the average life expectancy was rarely more than 35. Grinding poverty, gnawing hunger and dependency on Poor Relief was the norm. The workhouse, the debtors' prison and the gaol provided a spur to recruitment to the army and navy. Many women were forced into prostitution and petty crime which carried harsh penalties. The population was swelling – rising from 5.8 million in 1701 to 8.9 million in 1801 and 10.2 million in 1811 – and there were too many mouths to feed at home, while up to £50 million in the new income tax was swallowed up by the wars against Napoleon. Yet the rich and powerful continued to indulge themselves in feasting, drinking, gambling and whoring while condemning those of the labouring class who strove to follow their example in the rare periods of plenty. Successive administrations took the view that fear of foreign invasion, particularly by the detested French, would keep the populace in check, and for a long time they were right. Radical doctrine was patchy at best and rarely reached the illiterate poor. In the 1790s the Government boasted that the country was overflowing with patriotism. William Warburton believed that domestic peace at a time of the gravest social injustice was due to the 'special providence of God'. But the seeds of discontent, so long in the nurturing, began to flower as Napoleon's armies retreated.

It was no accident that dissent was focused in the mushrooming factory towns of the North of England. The invention of the steam engine meant that factories need no longer be built on rivers where the flowing waters powered machinery and could be erected at existing centres of population. The result was spectacular as rural workers were drawn into towns and villages where work was continuous, not dependent on the seasons. Historian Robert Reid wrote:

> The social upheaval created by this dramatic change from an agricultural to an industrial culture, from a rural to an urban environment – the consequences of this essentially uncomplicated technology – was to be immense. The flow of thought of the nation's leaders in both politics and religion would veer markedly, the intellectual thrust of its thinkers would have new aim, the lives of the mass of people in the country would change pattern and – though this unbelievably was scarcely noticed at the time – the centre of gravity of the nation would shift from south to north.

Manchester saw its population rise from 41,000 in 1774 to almost 200,000 within 40 years. Outlying hamlets like Bolton and Oldham swelled to 30,000 and 50,000.[1] Yet their representation in Parliament remained almost non-existent.

Furthermore, the huge advances in technology within two lifespans saw the creation of a free-enterprise economy which fed working families during times of plenty but which dismissed them as surplus when conditions changed. The dizzying speed of the Industrial Revolution created new millionaires alongside grinding poverty. The new cities and their factories belched fire, smoke and ash. Sir Charles Napier wrote: 'Manchester is the chimney of the world. Rich rascals, poor rogues, drunken ragamuffins and prostitutes form the moral; soot made into paste by the rain is the physical ... what a place! The entrance to hell realised.'[2] A *Times* correspondent wrote: 'It is occupied by spinners, weavers ... its present situation is truly heart-rending and over-powering. The streets are confined and dirty; the houses neglected, and the windows often without glass ... the miserable rags of the family hung out to dry.'[3]

The cruelty of the free market was magnified by the crippling cost of warfare and a series of crop failures. It was exacerbated by the hated Corn Law, introduced in 1804 by the landowners who dominated Parliament to impose a duty on all imported corn. It was most unpopular in the fastest-growing towns with no access to home-grown products. During the passing of the legislation Parliament was defended by mounted troopers against large, angry crowds. The cost of bread and other common goods rocketed just as wages were being cut and the new textile machines were putting more people out of work. Hargreaves' Spinning Jenny had been improved year on year until ultimately one man could spin 120 cops (conical rolls of thread wound on spindles) of cotton yarn simultaneously. Arkwright's new method of spinning cotton between rollers revolutionised the industry and threw numerous traditional weavers into penury. Whitney's gin, a cotton rotation machine, was introduced at the turn of the century and meant that one man could clean as much cotton as ten men before, while one man and a horse to turn the device could do the work of 50. Angry and redundant workers enjoyed widespread popular support, not only in their own communities but outside, where the poor quality of the first machine-made goods put many consumers on the side of the craftsmen who were being laid off.

The first threatening letters from Ned Ludd, almost certainly a group of militant workers rather than an individual, were sent early in 1811 to factory owners in Nottingham. They were warned to hire people instead of machines. Fury was stoked by wage reductions and the use of non-apprenticed workmen. After the warnings went unheeded, small

groups of masked men began to break into factories late at night to
smash the hated new machines. In a three-week period during March,
over 200 new stocking frames were broken, and several attacks were
recorded each night. The Nottingham burghers were forced to enrol
400 Special Constables to protect the factories. Even then the raids did
not cease. Britain's rulers grew fearful that the malaise would spread
and the Prince Regent himself offered £50 reward to anyone 'giving
information on any person or persons wickedly breaking the frames'.

Such fears were swiftly realised as Luddite attacks spread to Yorkshire,
Lancashire, Leicestershire and Derbyshire. In Yorkshire a small group
of highly skilled croppers, or cloth finishers, began to smash the new
shearing frames which they knew would eventually cost them their
livelihoods. In February and March 1812 more factories were attacked
in Huddersfield, Halifax, Wakefield and Leeds, and the government of
Spencer Perceval proposed that machine-breaking should be made an
offence punishable by death.

The move was eloquently opposed by Lord Byron. He said:

> The perseverance of these miserable men in their proceeding tends to
> prove that nothing but absolute want could have driven a large, and once
> honest and industrious body of the people, into the commission of excess
> so hazardous to themselves, their families and the community. They were
> not ashamed to beg, but there was none to relieve them. Their own means
> of subsistence were cut off, all other employment pre-occupied; and their
> excesses, however to be deplored and condemned, can hardly be subject
> to suprise.

He added: 'As the sword is the worst argument that can be used, so
it should be the last.'[4]

His appeal fell on deaf ears and the Frame Breaking Act made the
destruction of industrial machinery a capital offence. The Government
ordered 12,000 troops into those areas of Luddite operations. The
outcome was close to warfare.[5]

On 11 April 1812 George Mellor, a young Huddersfield cropper, led
a raid on Rawfolds Mill near Brighouse in Yorkshire. Its owner, William
Cartwright, had introduced cloth-finishing machinery the previous year
and laid off local croppers. The disaffected men met at a public house
before the attack and Cartwright, forewarned, called in armed guards
to protect his property. The raid was repulsed by gunfire and two
croppers died of their wounds. A week later another local mill owner,

William Horsfall was murdered, most probably in retaliation. Over 100 suspects were rounded up, and 64 of them were indicted by local courts. Three men were hung for the slaying of Horsfall and another 14 were executed for the attack on Rawfolds Mill. In his condemned cell Mellor, just 23, sent a letter to his cousin asking that his name be added to a petition demanding Parliamentary reform. The letter was intercepted by Government agents.[6]

Such savage countermeasures sparked outrage as well as fear and the violence on both sides intensified. Throughout 1812 there were attacks on Lancashire cotton mills by hand-loom weavers who objected to the introduction of power-looms. At the same time crop failures resulted in soaring wheat prices. Workers unable to afford to feed their families became increasingly desperate. Food riots erupted in Manchester, Oldham, Ashton, Rochdale, Stockport and Macclesfield.

On 20 April a large number of men attacked Burton's Mill at Middleton just outside Manchester. Volleys of stones smashed the windows 'to atoms'. The *Leeds Mercury* reported: 'A body of men, consisting of from one to two hundred, some of them armed with muskets with fixed bayonets, and others with colliers' picks, marched into the village in procession, and joined the rioters. At the head of the armed banditti a man o' straw was carried, representing the renowned General Ludd whose standard bearer waved a sort of red flag.'[7] Other reports denied the men had a single firearm. However, the mill owner, Emanuel Burton, had hired his own private army when he installed the new power-looms. They did not hesitate to use their muskets and three weavers were shot dead in the attack. The following day the crowd returned and, after failing a second time to destroy the mill, they burnt down Burton's house instead. Soldiers were called and another seven men were killed. Three days later the Wray and Duncroff Mill at nearby Westhoughton was set on fire. Archibald Prentice, a contemporary local author, wrote: 'The military rode at full speed to Westhoughton and on their arrival were suprised to find that the premises were entirely destroyed, while not an individual could be seen to whom attached any suspicion of having acted a part in this truly dreadful outrage.'[8] The 25-year-old High Sheriff of Lancashire, William Hulton, nevertheless ordered the arrest of twelve suspects. Of those, Job Fletcher, Thomas Kerfoot, James Smith and twelve-year-old Abraham Charlston were executed. The young Charlston cried for his mother on the scaffold.

Local journalist John Edward Taylor later claimed that the attack had been instigated by agents provocateurs employed by Colonel Ralph Fletcher, a Manchester magistrate. He asserted that the Westhoughton attack was planned 16 days before at a meeting on Dean Moor near Bolton, at which at least ten of the 40 present were Fletcher spies. He wrote: 'The occurrence of circumstances like these renders it not a matter of presumption, but of absolute certainty, that that alarming outrage might have been prevented, if to prevent it had been the inclination of either the spies or their employers.'[9] The use by the authorities of agents was later found to be widespread.

The authorities did not have it all their own way. In June John Knight organised a meeting of disaffected weavers at a Manchester inn, ironically called the Prince Regent's Arms. It was interrupted by James Nadin, the thuggish and despised Deputy Constable, who had the pub surrounded. He arrested Knight and 37 other weavers. Knight was charged with 'administering oaths to weavers pledging them to destroy steam looms'. The others were charged with attending a seditious meeting. The evidence proved particularly shaky, however, because Nadin had missed a man hidden under the stairs who gave evidence for the defendants. All were acquitted.[10]

Magistrates were not so scrupulous about evidence elsewhere. During the summer eight men were executed and 13 transported to Australia for attacks on cotton mills. A further 17 were hanged at York thanks to the vengeful zeal of Lt. Gen. Thomas Maitland, the officer commanding Government forces in the Midlands and the North. The ferocity of such sentences and a massive onslaught on civil rights destroyed the Luddite movement and further attacks petered out.

*   *   *

The draconian use of state power against individual liberty was masterminded by the Home Secretary, Lord Sidmouth, who rightly saw new dangers following the crushing of the Luddites at home and of Napoleon overseas.

The working man, thanks to Sunday schools, was becoming increasingly literate, and with books and pamphlets came radical ideas which were harder to contain with cudgels and shackles. The Luddites had been fighting a simple, visible enemy – the machines which

stole their livelihoods – but now the clamour was for Parliamentary
reform, voting rights and no taxation without representation. The
inequalities were clear to the eye at every level. Almost 2 million people
in Lancashire were represented at Westminster by two county members
and another two for Liverpool. Manchester, Bolton, Stockport, Oldham
and many other mill towns did not have a single voice. By contrast MPs
for rotten boroughs like Midhurst in Sussex represented just two voters,
while, most notoriously, Old Sarum in Wiltshire was a constituency
with a hill, no buildings and no voters. The inequalities of reward were
just as startling. While skilled craftsmen took home 15 shillings a week
and factory workers perhaps a third of that, Government sinecurists
like Lord Arden received £39,000 a year from the public purse and the
Bishop of Durham drew £24,000. The money set aside for the relief of
the poor across the entire country was a token £42,000.

Agitators for reform become vociferous, and not just from the working
class. Sir Francis Burdett, a patrician MP; Major John Cartwright, a
former officer in both the navy and the Nottinghamshire militia; Henry
Hunt, the hard-drinking Bristol Radical, and William Cobbett, the
self-educated pamphleteer, added their voices to the growing clamour
for both Parliamentary change, improved rights, freedoms for all and
the relief of poverty.

Waterloo and the end of a generation of warfare with France added
to the clamour. The wars of the previous 22 years had cost Britain
a staggering £800 million, a tenth of that spent in 1815 alone. The
war had sucked dry the profits of both the old industries and the new
technologies and the response of Government and employers was to
raise taxes and working hours while cutting wages and Poor Relief. In
addition, large numbers of soldiers and sailors returning home from
the wars faced nothing but unemployment, the workhouse and the
beggar's bowl.

In 1815, under further pressure to protect farmers and the big
landowners, Parliament passed a new Corn Law. Prices leapt upwards
and then, following a disastrous harvest in 1816, higher still. There were
riots in London against the legislation, followed by food riots across
Britain: in Bridport, the protest was against bread prices; in Bideford,
it was against the export of grain while families starved at home; in
Bury, the unemployed destroyed machinery; in Newcastle-upon-Tyne,
hungry miners went on the rampage; blood was shed in Glasgow in a

riot over the inadequacy of soup kitchens; unemployed weavers struck in Preston; 30 machines were destroyed in Nottingham by the remnants of the Luddites; in Merthyr Tydfil, the protest was against wage cuts; in Birmingham, the unemployed took to the streets.

The nation was fast turning into a powder keg and ministers feared that it would be the Radicals who would light the fuse.

They saw such evidence closer to home on 15 November 1816 when Henry Hunt addressed a massive and excitable crowd at Spa Fields in Southwark. A small portion went on the rampage and bogus rumours that the mob was besieging the Tower of London travelled by mail coach to Manchester and the North. Fuelled by drink, crowds of Manchester working men took to smashing windows to show solidarity. The word went back to London that armed insurrection was being planned.

Lord Sidmouth, a conscientious man who on occasions expressed sympathy for the plight of the poor and the conditions endured in the factories, believed above all in the rule of law. It was his job to keep a tight lid on the keg. Born Henry Addington in 1759, he was the son of a doctor who had grown rich running a lunatic asylum in Berkshire. Despite a stammer and no oratory skills, he became an MP and, due to the skill with which he courted powerful friends, held the great offices of state: Speaker of the Commons, briefly and unsuccessfully Prime Minister, and Chancellor of the Exchequer, when he introduced income tax at source. As Home Secretary in January 1813 the newly ennobled peer authorised the Special Commission into the 'rebellion' at York which had led to mass hangings. He continued to tighten the grip of the state, aided by his gluttonous brother Hiley, whom he appointed Under-Secretary. They shared with Lord Liverpool, the Prime Minister, the belief that good Government relied upon the strict maintenance of discipline upon the unruly lower orders.[11]

The outcome was a regime of growing repression. Public criticism of a system under which most Britons suffered taxation without representation was labelled 'sedition'. The freedom of the press was severely curtailed. Trade unions were outlawed. Postal services were intercepted and letters to and from Radicals or suspected agitators were routinely copied for the Home Office. Hiley Addington encouraged and extended the network of spies employed by local magistrates and constables. Joseph Nadin, for example, received extra cash to provide weekly payments for his 'secret agents' infiltrating meetings in Manchester, the outlying towns and Halifax in Yorkshire. Their ungrammatical reports were painstakingly transcribed by Home Office clerks.

Nadin came himself from the working classes and was hated the more for the zeal in which he pursued the interests of the masters. He was born in 1765 and was a spinner before becoming a thief-catcher. He was made Manchester's Deputy Constable in 1803 and grew rich on corruption. Every brothel in town was said to pay him to stay open. Radicals claimed that for 20 years he was 'the real ruler of Manchester'.[12] He took a cruel delight in that role and, at over six foot tall with a broad frame, he posed a terrifying figure to the weak and vulnerable. Samuel Bamford described him thus: 'His head was full sized, his complexion sallow, his hair dark and slightly grey; his features were broad and non-intellectual, his voice loud, his language coarse and illiterate, and his manner rude and overbearing to equals or inferiors.'[13] He was, in short, the well-paid strong arm of Manchester's propertied class, the brutal frontline tool in a chain of command which went from magistrates to Sidmouth to the Prime Minister and, ultimately, to the monarch.

Robert Reid summed up the overall repression:

> The result ... was to engender fear and hatred in the working people it was meant to control. Where civil liberties were already reduced to an unacceptable level and where by far the larger proportion of men and women had no proper representation in Parliament, the nation, by 1817, had come closer in spirit to that of the early years of the Third Reich than at any other time in modern history.[14]

*   *   *

By the end of 1816 the name of one working-class orator began to appear often in the clandestine reports sent to Sidmouth and his brother. The weaver John Bagguley was barely 18 but a powerful and inspiring speaker burning with the injustices he saw around him as he moved between the Lancashire manufacturing towns. Wherever there were meetings of the unemployed or disgruntled workers, he seemed to be there, inciting the dispossessed to take what was theirs. He appealed directly to the underfed and underprivileged and, rather than the flowery rhetoric of the more affluent Radicals, he spoke their language. His fame spread swiftly and his appearance alone could guarantee a crowd of 2,000 or more.

By early 1817 spies reported that Bagguley and his associates were planning a petition to Parliament backed up by the threat of more 'direct' action. Joseph Nadin warned Sidmouth: 'The lower orders are everywhere meeting in large bodies, and are very clamorous. Delegates from all quarters are moving about amongst them, as they were before the last disturbances, and they talk of a general union of lower orders throughout the kingdom.'[15]

Henry Hunt was also busy raising a huge petition which he intended to deliver to the State Opening of Parliament. It was to be a peaceful affair with the compliance of sympathetic MPs. Hunt drew massive crowds at Westminster which refused to cheer the corpulent 60-year-old Prince Regent. After delivering his speech, the Prince was returning home past the garden of Carlton House when a missile shattered a pane of glass in the royal carriage. Sidmouth told a shocked House of Lords that it was either a stone or a bullet from a gun. There was little or no evidence of a serious attempt on the Prince's life – Hunt later claimed that the missile was a potato – and no culprit was found. But it was enough for Sidmouth. He speedily pushed through bills which banned public meetings of any kind without the sanction of local magistrates and outlawed all societies which fraternised with other bodies. His aim was to prevent any concerted action by groups of workers or their sympathisers. Sidmouth made sure no one misunderstood. 'An organised system has been established in every quarter,' he said, 'under the semblance of demanding Parliamentary reform, but many of them, I am convinced, have that specious pretext in their mouths only, but revolution and rebellion in their hearts.'[16] He then dropped his bombshell. A further bill, rushed through within a month, suspended habeas corpus and allowed arrest and detention without trial.

Such measures, striking to the very heart of individual liberty, failed to dampen down the unrest. More meetings, planned and spontaneous, sprang up in Manchester and the Northern towns, often using the open spaces attached to churches and religious meeting halls. Bagguley's public performances became ever more frenzied. At one meeting he indicated that the English should be as ready as the Irish to spill blood in the cause of their freedom.[17] He called for a mass petition to the Prince Regent, demanding the rights of free men. If there was no response within 40 days, he declared, the people had the right to imprison the royal family.

This was indeed seditious stuff and Sidmouth, with the new powers open to him, was preparing a list of warrants against Manchester reformers. Bagguley's name was at the top. But General Sir John Byng, a Waterloo veteran who had replaced the bloodthirsty Maitland as commander of His Majesty's Northern Forces, was reluctant to act. After a lifetime soldiering abroad he had little time for the mill owners who had changed the face of the England he had known as a boy. He believed that the unrest would blow over and was more interested in his prized bloodstock and his new mansion at Campsmount.[18]

At Stockport Bagguley was advised of an archaic law which might circumvent the draconian new curbs on public demonstration. It allowed ten people to carry a petition to the monarch. Bagguley conceived the idea of thousands marching on London in groups of ten, each brandishing its own petition for the Prince Regent. A date was set, 10 March, with the starting point set at St Peter's Field, Manchester. Those in work would give part of their earnings to the unemployed who joined the march, which was estimated to take nine days each way. Each man was to carry a blanket on his back while shelter along the route would be provided in village halls, schools and the homes of sympathisers. Nadim sent an urgent message to his political masters warning that the march was much more than the Reformers claimed. 'As they go through the country,' he wrote, 'they will breed a commotion in the towns as they go along and by that they will have a heavy body together and try at a Revolution. I never saw people so dissatisfied and determined in my life ... I assure you there is something more amongst them than reform of Parliament.'[19]

After some delay in drafting, a simple petition was printed to draw attention to abject poverty, visible hunger and the distress suffered by workers and their families in the industrialised North. It said that their plight had been ignored 'so that now, when the waste of war is over, our sufferings are becoming more general and deeper than ever'.[20] It protested at the injustices of the Corn Laws and the suspension of habeas corpus and asked for Parliamentary reform. Each marcher was to wear it tied to their arm. Nadin arrested several of Bagguley's more prominent supporters. One of them, the printer William Ogden, was in his seventies. That did not stop Nadin having the old man dragged from his bed at night and clamped with a 30 lb iron manacle.

On 6 March a frightened magistrate sent a message to General Byng, who was taking the airs in Pontefract, calling for a large military force to be sent to Manchester. Byng was unable to dodge such a direct official appeal. He stirred himself into action, collecting troops along the road. The night before the meeting he wrote to a Home Office official: 'My private opinion is that you need not take any alarm for tomorrow's proceedings here.'[21] He had some reason to be confident. The forces at his disposal included a detachment of the King's Dragoon Guards, five mounted troops of the Cheshire Yeomanry and several others of infantry. More than enough to keep the peace against a bunch of rabble-rousers, as he saw it.

The men and women who walked towards St Peter's Fields were no rabble, however. They were instead fired by the enthusiasm of the youthful Bagguley and by the burning resentment of harsh experience. They were setting out on an adventure with right, not arms, at their side. By 10.00 a.m. on 10 March it was estimated that there were already 12,000 marchers on the streets and the final numbers were estimated at 40,000.[22] Soon afterwards Bagguley arrived in an open carriage and addressed the throng. He yelled at the marchers, by now known as Blanketeers for their back loads, urging them not to be dispirited as they headed for London. 'Can you leave your wives and children and tear yourselves from all friends to go and claim the rights your ancestors got for you?' 'Yes', they shouted back. 'Will you turn back when you get to Stockport, or when you come to face those high and cold hills of Derbyshire?' 'No, no, no', they roared back.[23]

Those with blankets on their backs were formed into files of ten, and then five to make absolutely sure they were within the letter of the law. After some confusion the first groups set off. Taking that as his cue, General Byng, still in leisurely mode, asked the Manchester magistrates observing the scene whether they wished him to arrest the orators stirring the crowd into action. When they answered yes he put his well-considered plan into action. Nadin and his Special Constables moved through the crowd to the hustings. He was instantly recognised but his step did not falter in the face of immense hostility. Nadin may have been a brute but his courage was never questioned. Colonel Teesdale's regiment of dragoons, highly professional and experienced horsemen, followed smartly behind. They divided the crowd without casualties, wheeled, turned and within a few minutes had the hustings surrounded.

Bagguley was handcuffed and taken away with his associate John Drummond.[24]

Those marchers who had already set off had no chance. Waiting for the vanguard at the Stockport bridge across the Mersey were tough special constables who quickly arrested 20. The main body of marchers were followed along the road by contingents who rounded up another 143 who joined their comrades in the yard of Stockport Castle. Constables under the ambitious solicitor's clerk John Lloyd raced ahead to Macclesfield, the next town on the London road, and arrested 180 more Blanketeers. Here real violence was used and several marchers were badly injured, run down and trampled by the horses of their pursuers. An elderly cabinet-maker, John James, heard the commotion and ran into his garden. He was sabred by a panicking young trooper and died after two days of great pain. More marchers arrived in other towns but by then they needed little persuading to turn back and go home.

Most of the prisoners, mainly young men, were sent to Chester Castle gaol for interrogation. Their statements gave little evidence of revolutionary ardour. One of them, John Shaw, explained the purpose of the march as he saw it: 'The most miserable looking of us was to kneel down and the other to take the petition and the Prince would then tell us why trade was so slack.' Byng reported to Lord Sidmouth that his forces suffered just one casualty, a cavalryman whose helmet was broken by a brick thrown in St Peter's Field.[25] The Prince Regent briefly broke off from waltzing at the farewell ball for Grand Duke Nicholas of Russia to send Byng his personal congratulations.

Eight days later just one Blanketeer who had evaded the roadblocks reached London. Abel Couldwell deposited the petition at the Home Office. It joined several other copies which had already been sent to Lord Sidmouth by spies.[26]

*   *   *

The hysteria continued. Spies claimed to have uncovered a plot to ignite 40 factories and 'make a Moscow out of Manchester'. Several supposed ringleaders were arrested, including Samuel Bamford, who had played no part in any of the recent events. He and the other prisoners were arraigned before the Privy Council. The prisoners were clearly incapable of fomenting revolution and half were released. Several, however, were incarcerated under Sidmouth's powers and found themselves detained for an unknown period. Inside Gloucester gaol they found the young Bagguley in solitary confinement.

Sidmouth and his brother Hiley continued to rely on a growing network of spies and agents who had a pecuniary interest in exaggerating or fomenting unrest. One such spy encouraged an unemployed Nottingham frame-worker, Jeremiah Brandreth, to call a general strike. The mass demonstration flopped, but a gentleman's manservant was killed in a raid on a house. Brandreth and two others were hanged outside Derby Castle gaol and eleven more were transported for life.

Lord Liverpool and his ministers were now confident that firm action would be followed by tranquillity. The spring rains followed by a warm summer ensured a bumper crop. England's enemies, both abroad and within, had seemingly been vanquished. To signal the Government's confidence Bagguley was let out from solitary confinement while Samuel Drummond and other Radicals imprisoned without trial were also freed. Shortly after the State Opening, Lord Sidmouth repealed the bill suspending habeas corpus.

But this period of relative calm was to prove only a lull in a continuing storm. The Government had learnt that a disaffected population could be controlled by disciplined troops and the powers of the judiciary. Rioting Luddites had paid a heavy price. So too had the wider working population. But that population was also outraged by the brutal and underhand tactics employed by Sidmouth against the largely peaceful Blanketeers. There would be one more attempt at non-violent agitation. The outcome would make the case for the most bloodthirsty revolutionaries amongst the 'mob'.

2
The Road to Peterloo

'The lords of the universe'

The Government's optimism was misplaced. The good harvest may have brought prosperity and full bellies to many, but the basic conditions of industrial workers in the North were unchanged and the beacon of Parliamentary reform was undimmed. Furthermore, there was a renewed, if cautious, militancy among workers' leaders. Within hours of John Bagguley's release he was out campaigning again. His language was even more extreme. The Blanketeers' March had been a peaceful affair but it was still broken by the violent action of the state. He now believed, as did many of his embittered colleagues, that state violence must be met with violent protest.

On 9 March 1818, a day less than a year after the Blanketeers' meeting, Bagguley was again addressing a massive crowd at St Peter's Field. He was joined by other ex-prisoners, including Samuel Drummond and Joseph Mitchell, recently released after spending 240 days detained without trial. Also present was John Lloyd, the Special Constable who had so enthusiastically broken Blanketeer heads and interrogated prisoners. He had long been a hated and feared figure. Even the ruthless General Maitland had despised him for his brutality, including the use of torture, during the Luddite uprising. Lloyd rode alone into the crowd until spotted by Mitchell who pointed him out to the multitude. Lloyd ignored cries of 'Turn him out' and stood his ground. He spent the rest of the meeting conspicuously taking notes on horseback but was unmolested.[1] As Nadin had proved earlier, courage is not the sole preserve of the good-hearted.

Magistrates in Oldham, Bolton, Stockport, Rochdale and Middleton protested that they could not guarantee the peace with only small contingents of constables and militia. Sidmouth, however, was preoccupied with other affairs. He was tired, ill and, when his brother Hiley succumbed to excessive drinking and eating and died in June, heart-broken. As a result the Home Office was effectively left in the hands of his new Permanent Under-Secretary, the young lawyer and poet Henry Hobhouse. He took the opportunity with relish. Five years earlier he had prosecuted Luddites with great zeal, ensuring the maximum sentences. He formed a close working relationship with the equally zealous John Lloyd, who sent him a regular flow of intelligence on Radical leaders. Lloyd was eager to destroy agitators but was equally contemptuous of profiteering employers whose greed fostered such dissent. In February he wrote to Hobhouse: 'It is known that the manufacturers do not pay their work people proper wages according to their present profits.' He pointed to the previous year when almost half a million bags of raw cotton from the Americas and East Indies worth £8 million had been converted into £32 million worth of cloth. He added: 'If the present system is continued much longer, the only difference between the work people of the cotton *planters* and the work people of the cotton manufacturers will be in the colour of their skin.' In other words, English men and women could be slaves. Such sentiments, however, would never undermine Lloyd's passion for the rule of law.

As 1818 progressed Britain was hit by a disastrous slump in trade, an aftershock from the end of the wars with France. The response from the manufacturing overlords was predictable – they again slashed wages. Weavers who in 1803 could expect to earn 15 shillings for a six-day week saw their pay cut to 5 shillings or even 4s 6d. The spinners, at the top end of the scale, saw their income cut by a third. The bosses quoted market forces and offered no relief for working families who could not feed themselves on such a pittance. The slump had a knock-on effect on the Lancashire towns created by the cotton industry and its technology. There was a rash of strikes. First out were the building workers, followed by the colliers, and then by spinners and weavers. Ten thousand spinners took to the streets of Manchester and in Stockport power-loom workers threatened factories kept operating by scab labour. General Byng saw something sinister in the way the Manchester spinners' strike was conducted. He wrote to Hobhouse: 'The peaceable demeanour of so many thousand unemployed men is

not natural; their regular meeting and then again dispersing shows a
system of organisation of their actions which has some appearance of
previous tuition.'

Not all the Manchester spinners displayed a peaceable demeanour,
however. Magistrate James Norris protested at the intimidation of
known or suspected blacklegs: 'The spinners take the names and
addresses of individuals who work, and prevent them leaving their
own houses. The mother of a child carrying breakfast to it at Mr
Houldsworth's mill was molested.' The Birley factory in Oxford Road
had its windows broken by unemployed spinners. On 17 July, when
a group of spinners surrounded another factory, Lloyd took eight
dismounted troopers into the crowd and came out with 20 hand-cuffed
prisoners. Shortly afterwards a troop of the Manchester Yeomanry
Cavalry rode down several Stockport workers, inflicting serious injuries
on at least one. The same day a Cheshire Yeoman fired his pistol
through the windows of a respectable Reformer, Dr Thomas Cheetham.
Relations between the working people of the area and the Yeomanry
were reaching new lows.

The Cheshire Yeomanry were well-established under the baronet
Sir John Fleming Leicester in their richly ornamented and laced blue
jackets. But it took the shock of the Blanketeers to see the formation
of the Manchester and Salford Regiment of Yeomanry Cavalry. They
were part-time, amateur soldiers who saw their job primarily as the
defence of property and the status quo. Initially comprised of 150
men and 20 officers, their commanders were the leading Manchester
manufacturers Thomas Trafford and Joseph Birley. The officers were
mainly merchants, the rank and file from several trades and professions.
The largest number of recruits were publicans – service with the
Yeomanry ensured the renewal of their licences. They tended to be
Tories with a deep hatred of Radicals. Their unpopularity with the
local populace grew every time they swaggered on parade or trotted
towards peaceful protesters.

As the unrest continued Lloyd was determined to arrest Bagguley for
sedition but was stymied by Home Office lawyers who had doubts over
whether a prosecution would stick. On 2 September Bagguley led his
supporters to Manchester to join an estimated 30,000 striking spinners.
A brick struck Manchester's new stipendary magistrate, James Norris,
on the knee. Another hit a soldier full in the face. Norris reported to

Sidmouth: 'If the thing continues a day longer it will be necessary to put every mill on its defence and many lives will be lost. In short I do look to some bloodshed in this affair and perhaps it may be for the best.' The following day Lloyd counted 1,222 men and 355 women in a weavers' procession in Stockport. Two pipers played fifes and this gave a peaceful demonstration a decidedly militaristic air. At another meeting in the town Bagguley addressed 3,000. Lloyd was close enough to note down 'words of sedition'. He applied for warrants against Bagguley, John Johnson and Samuel Drummond and five spinners for conspiracy to raise wages. The spinners were easily rounded up but Bagguley and his colleagues took flight, heading for the port of Liverpool and, it was later claimed, a passage to America. They were captured the following morning on the dockside, an hour before a boat was due to sail. Their captor was Joseph Nadin who took characteristic glee in shackling them. Bagguley and his two friends were sentenced to two years' imprisonment.

One striker wrote in the Radical newspaper the *Black Dwarf*:

> The whole of the acting magistrates in the district, with the exception of two worthy clergymen, are gentlemen who have sprung from the same source as the master cotton barons. These evils to the men have arisen from the dreadful monopoly which exists in those districts where wealth and power are got into the hands of the few, who, in the pride of their hearts, think themselves the lords of the universe.

The magistrates also ordered the arrest of John Doherty, a Radical whom they believed was behind a plan to form a General Union of Trades, on a trumped-up charge of assaulting a woman while on picket duty. He was sentenced to two years' hard labour. Deprived of their leaders and with no money to feed their families, the Manchester spinners called off their strike after ten weeks, in September, and were forced to swallow their wage cuts. Within weeks the even poorer Manchester weavers called their own strike, demanding a 13 shilling minimum weekly wage. The strike spread to Bolton, Bury and Burnley. Some bosses agreed to pay the proposed minimum but most refused and the strikers straggled back to work after a few weeks.

The strikes, skirmishing and unrest continued into the new year. In March 1819 Sir Francis Burdett's motion for Parliamentary reform was thrown out. Sir Robert Peel's bill to reduce and regulate the hours worked by children in the mills was bogged down at Westminster.

More factory owners and their property came under attack. Trade suffered another downturn. The country was polarising with workers increasingly agitated and the ruling classes becoming more ready to use the force at their disposal.

And Henry Hunt filled the political vacuum created when young John Bagguley was locked again in Chester gaol. Hunt was a 46-year-old braggart with a flair for public performance of any sort. He was physically big, bluff, bombastic, a charismatic chancer who was not a natural champion of the working class. But he was an effective performer and spoke eloquently for the underdog. He was born into a prosperous farming family in Uphavon, Wiltshire. As a boy he sneaked aboard the gunship *Prince of Wales* at Portsmouth in front of the King and Queen. When there was an attempt to eject him roughly an old admiral intervened and the crowd gave him three cheers for his pluck. The effect on the boy was startling and it may be said that he spent much of his life seeking out such heady applause from the crowd.[2] His father wanted him to take holy orders but instead he began working on the family farm at 16, while continuing to study the classics. He married at 22 and had two sons and a daughter but left them to elope with a friend's wife. As a young man he was a keen militia man but challenged Lord Bruce, colonel of the Marlborough troop, to a duel. The bout did not go ahead but Hunt refused to apologise and was fined £100 and given six weeks' imprisonment in the King's Bench gaol at the end of 1800. It was there that he began to form Radical views. That did not stop him speculating unwisely and he lost much of his fortune in a dodgy brewing enterprise at Clifton near Bristol. Despite such setbacks he began to make a mark in local politics. In 1807 he visited London to meet Radical leaders. And on his return formed the Bristol Patriotic and Constitutional Society to promote electoral reform. In 1810 he was again gaoled, this time for assaulting a gamekeeper, and during his three-month sentence shared the same rooms as William Cobbett. The following year he contested Bristol and complained that his opponents had used bribery and violence to sway the voters. It was not a frivolous charge. But it was the Spa Fields meeting in 1816 which propelled him to national prominence. Radicals, Reformers and the appalled Establishment came to respect or fear his crowd-pleasing oratory, fire and brimstone delivery and his trademark white hat. He actively opposed the election of Hobhouse

as MP for Westminster and published a pamphlet called 'The Green
Bag Plot' which accused the government of actively encouraging the
Derbyshire disturbances as an excuse for further repression.[3] Until then
Hunt had never visited the North and knew next to nothing about the
conditions of the industrial workers and their families. But his fame in
the South reached the ears of Joseph Johnson, a Stockport brush-maker
who feared that Bagguley's imprisonment would leave local Reformers
leaderless and uninspired. He invited Hunt to address a meeting on St
Peter's Field, which by now had become the North West's chief venue
for protest, on 18 January 1819.

His arrival was typically flambouyant. On stepping down from the
mail coach Hunt hired a barouche. On the outskirts of Manchester he
ordered the horses to be uncoupled and the shafts were taken instead
by enthusiastic supporters for a grand entrance to the city. At the
Exchange building he was barracked by a group of manufacturers.
To the delight of the crowd he doffed his white hat and bowed to
them with obvious contempt. Spotting the veteran campaigner John
Knight he stopped his carriage to take on the old man, called for a
glass of water and toasted him with the words 'Liberty or death'.[4] In
St Peter's Field he was given a rapturous welcome by 10,000 people.
Even the collapse of the barouche under his substantial weight as he
made his speech did not damp their ardour. After the meeting was
over, thousands followed him in triumph to the Spread Eagle Hotel.
John Lloyd's spies noted a young man in the crowd waving a 'Cap of
Liberty' banner, a potent symbol of revolution. Once inside Hunt and
the wealthier advocates of Reform enjoyed an expensive subscription
dinner. The rest were left to walk back through the cold night air to
their backstreet hovels.

As the months turned warm, so did the political temperature in
Manchester. The magistrate, James Norris, sent regular dispatches
to London warning, in feverish terms, of plots, conspiracies and the
prospect of a general uprising. John Lloyd and Nadin continued to
use strong-arm tactics against any dissenters. As the conditions of the
cotton workers slumped even further, mass meetings at Sandy Brow
and Blackburn attracted up to 40,000 people. Joseph Johnson, the
brush-maker, wrote: 'Nothing but ruin and starvation stare one in the
face, the state of this district is truly dreadful, and I believe nothing
but the greatest exertions can prevent an insurrection.'[5]

The greatest fear of the authorities was that Henry Hunt would be invited back to Manchester. It was an understandable concern. On 21 July 1819 Hunt addressed a vast meeting at Smithfield Market in London. Estimates of its size varied from 70,000 to twice that number. Those present passed a motion drafted by Hunt which gave notice that at the turn of the new year no one would have power over the common people other than those 'fully, freely and fairly' chosen by the majority. It was a direct challenge to the state.

A few days later the authorities were given evidence, to their satisfaction, of violent elements amongst the demonstrators. William Birch, a widely hated Stockport special constable, was walking at night to the home of a magistrate when he was surrounded by a crowd of angry workers. A man produced a pistol and shot Birch at point-blank range. John Lloyd, who was quickly on the scene, called in a troop of the 15th Hussars but the assailants had fled. Surgeons operated on Birch, but could not find a bullet inside him.[6] As Birch lay apparently dying – he later recovered – alarm spread throughout the country. Lord Sidmouth recommended that a reward of £200 be offered to anyone revealing the identity of Birch's attack, and a pardon for any accomplices. The Manchester Yeomanry Cavalry were put on full alert. A cutler, Daniel Kennedy, received a batch of 63 sabres and was ordered to make the blades 'very sharp.'

The Reformers reacted in a similar spirit. Bamford and others recruited retired soldiers to drill their army of spinners, weavers and other working men in isolated fields and hillsides. At the beginning of August a royal proclamation declared civilian drilling to be illegal, but it did not stop.

And the greatest fear of Hobhouse and local magistrates was realised. Henry Hunt was coming back to Manchester.

3
The Massacre

'Feather bed soldiers'

The mammoth meeting, organised by Joseph Johnson, was scheduled for 8 August. It was to be chaired by Henry Hunt and was intended to be entirely peaceable. The authorities found spurious legal reasons to ban it. The organisers reconvened it for 18 August, backed by the signatures of 700 householders, most of them weavers. The purpose, as posted in the *Manchester Observer*, was 'To consider the propriety of adopting the most LEGAL and EFFECTUAL means of obtaining a REFORM in the Commons House of Parliament.'

Unfortunately no one told Hunt of the change of date, as he was furious to discover when he arrived in Stockport on the 7th. Even the delirious crowds who greeted him failed to mollify him, but he filled his days writing letters to the press, raging at Johnson and having his portrait painted by the artist Henry Scott Tuke.[1]

Magistrate James Norris was thrown into a characteristic panic. His fears were deepened when he heard that his superiors all seemed to be on holiday. Lord Sidmouth was in Broadstairs enjoying the sea air, while General Byng, in charge of all the soldiers in the North, was at York races where his black colt Belianis came third in the King's Plate, and refused to return just to pander to Norris's supposed panic. Even Sir John Leicester, commander of the Cheshire Yeomanry, was at the seaside with his wife, leaving his regiment in the hands of Lt. Col. Townshend. On the other hand, the Manchester Yeoman Cavalry were under the immediate command of the city magistrates. Furthermore, Byng had left six troops of cavalry and seven of infantry in Manchester, with more in the surrounding towns within an hour's canter, under

the command of Lt. Col. Guy L'Estrange, a capable veteran of the
Peninsula War. Such substantial forces failed to ease Norris's troubled
mind. He wrote to Sidmouth: 'We are in a state of painful uncertainty.'
The Manchester magistrates, citing the threat of violence, issued a
notice forbidding women and children to attend the meeting. It was
largely ignored.

Joseph Bamford led the contingent from Middleton, 3,000 men,
women and children with banners and church band. Like others from
Stockport, Bolton, Saddleworth, Rochdale and elsewhere they began
their march early and in festive mood. They accepted Hunt's urging
that they should come 'armed with no other weapon but that of a
self-approving conscience'. Bamford described the orderly procession
which set off from the town:

> At the sound of the bugle not less than five thousand men formed a hollow
> square, with probably as many men around them, and an impressive silence
> having been obtained, I reminded them that they were going to attend the
> most important meeting that he ever been held for Parliamentary Reform,
> and I hoped their conduct would be marked by a steadiness and seriousness
> befitting the occasion, and such as would cast shame upon their enemies,
> who had always presented the reformers as a mob-like rabble.[2]

Up to 5,000 people from Saddleworth marched behind a banner
proclaiming 'Equal Representation or Death'. Men were told to leave
behind cudgels or staves, but some kept them, ostensibly as walking
sticks on the steep six-mile route. By mid morning every road into
Manchester was full of marchers.

Colonel L'Estrange was meanwhile gathering his forces – 250 men of
the 31st Foot, several companies of the 88th Regiment, two squadrons
of the 15th Hussars, another of the Cheshire Yeomanry and one troop
of the Manchester Yeomanry. He stationed the regular cavalry in Byrom
Street, a quarter of a mile from St Peter's Field. Alongside him was Lt.
Col. Leighton Dalrymple, who commanded the Hussars and who had
lost a leg at Waterloo. They were joined by 420 troopers of the Cheshire
Yeomanry under Lt. Col. Townshend. They included John Lloyd,
who had enlisted in the Stockport troop. The bulk of the Manchester
Yeomanry, 101-strong in their sky-blue jackets with white facings, were
stationed half a mile from the Field under their commanding officer,
Major Thomas Trafford, and his second-in-command, Captain Hugh
Hornby Birley, the brother of one of the city's biggest manufacturers.

The Manchester Yeomanry spent part of the morning in local taverns as their boots were cleaned and their horses curried. Many, if not all, were half drunk. And finally, the forces of law and order were topped up by burly Special Constables carrying staves and under the command of Jame Nadin. In total L'Estrange could call on more than 1,000 troops and up to 400 constables.

2   Henry Hunt and the St Peter's Field massacre
Illustrated London News

At noon Bamford's column marched into St Peter's Field. Bamford said it was like entering a 'chasm of human beings'. Estimates of the size of the crowd varied wildly, but given the dimensions of the open space it could easily have been 150,000.[3] There was not a soldier in sight and the event took on the air of a gala. Henry Hunt's open carriage was packed with the meeting's sponsor, Joseph Johnson, the old campaigner John Knight, Stockport reformer James Moorhouse, the pamphleteerer Richard Carlile, *Manchester Observer* managing editor John Thacker Saxton and Mrs Mary Fildes, the President of the Manchester Female

Reform Union. Behind the carriage were her committee of women, dressed in white. The carriage was decked out with blue and white bunting, Mrs Fildes was gaily dressed, and Hunt waved his white hat to gales of applause from the crowd. John Benjamin Smith, a prosperous young man watching from an upstairs window, noted: 'A number of women, boys, and even children, were in the procession, which had more the appearance of a large village party going to a merry making than that of a body of people advancing to the overthrow of the government of their country.'

The hustings from which Hunt and the rest were to speak was made from two wagons lashed together near the Windmill public house. Shortly after noon Edward Clayton, the city's borough reeve, appeared with several hundred Special Constables. They pushed their way through the crowd and formed a double line of men reaching from the Field's perimeter to the hustings themselves. The crowd quickly realised that this created a corridor by which the magistrates could send officers to arrest Hunt or any other speaker. To prevent that the hustings were pushed several yards deeper into the Field and the crowd circled around with linked arms. That effectively denied the constables easy access to the speakers. Joseph Nadin ominously walked up and down the corridor between his men but was subjected only to verbal abuse about the size of his belly.

Hunt made his way to the hustings to continuous cheering. The various bands joined together to play 'See the Conquering Hero Comes' and then, to underline the legal and loyal nature of the meeting, 'God Save the King'.

The magistrates observing from Mount Street did not see it that way. They counted five 'Caps of Liberty' being waved and took particular notice of the black Saddleworth banner. A quarter of a mile away L'Estrange took the great cheer which greeted Hunt as he stepped on the platform as his signal to stand by. His troopers loaded their pistols. It was 1.40 p.m.

The organisation of the meeting was chaotic and there was some confusion over who should speak first. But the crowd was there to hear Hunt and when he finally spoke the hubbub died down. Hunt appealed for calm but also called on the thousands gathered before him to 'exercise the all-powerful right of the people'.[4]

A hundred yards away, in the house of Mr Buxton, the Manchester magistrates strained to catch a single word, but could not because of the roars from the crowd. During the past hour their select committee chairman, the effeminate and nervous William Hulton, had received demands from over 60 manufacturers and merchants to take action before the meeting turned into a property-smashing riot. Hulton – the same man who seven years ago had approved the Westhoughton hangings – now handed Chief Constable Jonathan Andrews previously prepared warrants for Hunt and three other people on Joseph Nadin's hit list – Johnson, Knight and Moorhouse. Andrews said that without military help they could not be served. Hulton then scribbled two notes calling for the help of the Manchester Yeoman Cavalry. He later justified his action: 'I considered at that moment that the lives and properties of all the persons in Manchester were in the greatest possible danger. I took this into consideration, that the meeting was part of a great scheme carrying on throughout the country.'[5] The notes were handed to the manufacturer Joseph Birley, whose brother was waiting in uniform nearby, and Thomas Withington, who also had a relative serving in the Manchester Yeomanry. Both men galloped off in two directions to deliver the letters. Joseph Birley handed his copy to his brother who handed it on to Major Trafford.

Trafford immediately gave the order to draw swords and two troops of the Manchester Yeoman Cavalry galloped furiously down Nicholas Street and left into Cooper Street, towards St Peter's Field. It was then that Mrs Anne Fildes, no relation to the lady sharing a platform with Hunt, stepped into the road, thinking that the last horse had passed. She was bowled over by a trooper bringing up the rear. Her two-year-old son William was thrown from her arms and died instantly. The infant was the first casualty.[6]

The amateur troopers reached the corner of the Field in some disorder and reformed near to the magistrates' vantage point. Witnesses reported that they were 'rolling about' on their steeds through drink. Nadin went between the two lines of constables, telling them to be ready to pull back to let the Yeomanry through. Hulton decided it was time to read the Riot Act and gave the job to a preacher, the Reverend Mr Ethelston, because of his vocal abilities.[7] The preacher duly read it from the first-floor window, although it is doubtful whether more than a handful of the nearest heard his baritone proclamation.

Captain Hugh Birley received orders from the magistrates to surround the hustings so that the orators could be taken off the stage. Birley bellowed orders to his troops who responded by raising their sabres. Hunt, halfway through his speech, noticed the flash of steel in the corner of the Field and said something to the crowd. Quite what was lost in an almighty cheer.[8] The Yeomanry, perhaps interpreting that as a yell of defiance, gave a shout in return and spurred on their horses.

*   *   *

The deployment of the Manchester Yeomanry Cavalry was a major factor in the impending tragedy. They were all local men, many connected to the cotton industry by family or employment, who had long suffered the taunts of the Radicals. Donald Reid wrote:

> If experienced Hussars had been used instead, men skilled in manoeuvering into and breaking up a crowd without violence, there would probably even then have been no bloodshed, for as Bamford said, the Radicals had been instructed not to oppose the arrest of any of their leaders. Regular troops would therefore have had no occasion to use their sabres.[9]

Hugh Birley, flanked by two trumpeters on piebald horses, led his men down the corridor between the two lines of constables. For the first few yards they kept a rough order, five abreast. But as they got further into the crowd it was clear they had difficulty controlling their spooked mounts. Within moments a canter turned into an undisciplined charge. Hooves flew out and as the horsemen progressed the Reverend Stanley, from his second-floor observation post, saw the crushed body of a woman. The people closest to the Yeomanry, unable to pull back, screamed in terror. Those further back, and unaware of the danger, hurled such taunts as 'Feather bed soldiers'.[10] The Yeomanry, either enraged by the insults or unable to rein in, increased their pace, half-blinded by clouds of swirling dust. Another observer recalled that the part-time soldiers acted with 'a zeal and ardour which might naturally be expected from men acting with delegated power against a foe by whom they had long been insulted with taunts of cowardice'. They 'continued their course, seeming to vie individually with each other which should be first'.

The platform was quickly surrounded. When the Yeomanry reached the hustings 'a scene of dreadful confusion ensued. The orators fell or were forced off the scaffold in quick succession, fortunately for them the stage being rather elevated, they were in great degree beyond the reach of the many swords which gleamed around them.' Hugh Birley pressed up against the wagons, sword waving, and shouted to Hunt: 'Sir, I have a warrant against you, and arrest you as my prisoner.' Hunt replied: 'I willingly surrender myself to any civil officer who will show me his warrant.'[11] Astonishingly, Nadin, who had narrowly escaped being ridden down by the cavalry, was close at hand with the necessary piece of paper. James Moorhouse and John Knight were not on the hustings, but Hunt and Joseph Johnson were available for arrest. They both jumped to the ground to accept the inevitable. Nadin grabbed Johnson's legs but was promptly hit on the arm by a thrown brick. Within moments there was mayhem.

John Tyas, the *Times* correspondent who was standing on the platform, heard the Yeomanry cry 'Have at their flags!' He reported: 'The Manchester Yeomanry Cavalry lost all command of temper.'[12] The cavalrymen plunged in different directions to seize the banners on the hustings and in the thick of the crowd, intending to take them as battle trophies. The result was frenzied carnage.[13]

A shoemaker, George Swift, jumped back to avoid the chopping sabres. He dragged an unconscious and bleeding woman through the chaos. People ran in every direction to avoid the blades and hooves. Not everyone thought only of escape, however, and the Yeomanry provoked a shower of bricks and stones. Tyas witnessed a deliberate attack on Saxton of the *Manchester Observer*, identified by one trooper as 'that villain ... run him through the body'. Tyas wrote:

> The man immediately made a lunge at Saxton, and it was only by slipping aside the blow missed his life. As it was, it cut his coat and waistcoat, but fortunately did him no other injury. A man within five yards of us in another direction had his nose completely taken off by a blow of a sabre; whilst another was laid prostrate, but whether he was dead or had merely thrown himself down to obtain protection we cannot say.

There were numerous reports of women being sabred as they crouched over the bodies of their children. Bamford, who had left the hustings to 'seek some refreshment' before the speech had begun, observed the Yeomanry from a distance:

> On breaking the crowd they wheeled and, dashing whenever there was an opening, they followed, pressing and wounding. Many females appeared

as the crowd opened; and striplings or mere youths also were found. The cries were piteous and heart-rending, and would, one might have supposed, have disarmed any human resentment, but here their appeals were in vain. Women, white-vested maids, and tender youths, were indiscriminately sabred or trampled ...[14]

William Marsh suffered a sabre cut to the back of his head while his leg bone was splintered and his ribs crushed as he was trampled by a horseman. He survived. So did 27-year-old John Leigh who was sabred on the hip after being knocked to the ground. He later claimed that Captain Birley had passed him, then returned to inflict the cut. An old man, Thomas Blinstone, was flattened by a galloping cavalryman and suffered both arms badly broken. His main concern, as he later attested, was his lost spectacles. In tragedy there was farce: a man who had bought a cheese for his family put it in his hat and it took the full force of a sabre cut, saving his life.[15]

Meanwhile L'Estrange cantered towards St Peter's Field with the 15th Hussars and other units of the Manchester and Cheshire Yeomanries. When he reached the edge of the Field he could make nothing of the dust-shrouded confusion ahead of him. He rode to the house where the magistrates were stationed and shouted to Hulton for orders. Hulton, who had earlier expressed a horror of all violence, shouted back: 'Good God, Sir! Do you not see how they are attacking the Yeomanry? Disperse the crowd.'[16] Colonel Dalrymple's four troops of 15th Hussars arrived on the scene. The troopers wheeled into line abreast along the entire east side of the Field and the trumpeter sounded the charge. At the same time the Cheshire Yeomanry, in good order, moved along the southern edge behind the hustings and they too moved forward. The crowd was caught in a vice of thundering horseflesh and flashing steel.

L'Estrange's later defenders pointed out that he had little option but to throw his men into the Field's hellish melee. He had direct orders from the proper civic authority and initially may well have believed, as Hulton did at one point, that the Yeomanry were being engulfed. Whatever the motivation, the combination of regular cavalry and a panic-stricken and crushed multitude created more corpses than the charge of the amateurs.

Some of the regular troopers, like Cornet William Jolliffe, used only the flat of their swords, but given the number of cut wounds inflicted on people, they were in the minority. One observer, the city tradesman William Buckley, said: 'The carnage seemed to be indiscriminate.' Another, John Jones, said that the soldiers were 'cutting at everyone they could reach'.[17] Some troopers, and especially Yeomen, appeared to go beserk. One in particular was Trumpeteer Edward Meagher, easily identifiable on his piebald steed, who was later blamed for some of the worst injuries. He was seen twice striking at 71-year-old Alice Kearsley whose ear was almost completely severed. Edward Dwyer, a 67-year-old weaver, was sabred to the head while William Alcock, a Stockport iron founder, almost lost an arm.

As much damage was done by the weight of horseflesh and iron-shod hooves. An Oldham weaver and Waterloo veteran, 22-year-old John Lees, suffered cuts to his head and elbow and was truncheoned across the back. He fell against his mate Joseph Wrigley and both found themselves being trampled by cavalry horses. Wrigley only managed to scramble away when an unknown officer cried to his men: 'For shame, won't you give the people time to get away. Don't you see them down?' Lees was not so lucky. Neither was Ann Barlow, a mother of seven, who had her breastbone broken in the crush.

Cornet Joliffe reached the end of the Field and noted that bodies were 'literally piled up to a considerable elevation above the level of the ground'.[18] He wheeled about and saw a cavalryman chasing workers into a walled graveyard. Blood and sabre slashes were later found on the trees between the headstones.

Several Hussars were brought down, not by protesters, but by piles of logs on the ground hidden by the press of bodies in the crowd. L'Estrange was struck by a brick but kept in his saddle. John Hulme of the Manchester Yeomanry twice sabred a fleeing worker, William Butterworth, before he was knocked from his horse by a brick thrown by a woman. He was then trampled by the horses of his colleagues. William Rooke of the 15th had his horse slashed by a two-handed sickle. Lieutenant Charles O'Donnell was confronted by a worker brandishing an iron railing. Subaltern William Buckley was lunged at with a bent iron rail. Buckley cut his assailant down.[19] The soldiers were also fired on by at least one marksman from behind the chimney of a half-built house. Foot solders of the 88th Regiment cleared the sniper from the roof.

Meanwhile Joseph Nadin and a colleague were trying to get the arrested Hunt and Johnson clear. Two cavalrymen struck blows at Hunt but missed. The staves of three constables connected, however, and Nadin was forced to lash out at his own men to protect his prisoner. As they reached the step of the magistrates' house the retired General Clay, who had played a bloody part in suppressing the Luddites, brought his stick down with both hands on Hunt's hat. Nadin shouted 'Shame!' and managed to get Hunt inside, having first replaced the famous white hat on his head. 'By this means Nadin saved my life,' Hunt wrote later.[20]

The prisoners were secure and the centre of the Field cleared, but the bloodshed continued as soldiers and cavalrymen scrambled to capture standards and the 'Caps of Liberty'. Middleton worker Thomas Redford was slashed between the shoulder blades as he tried to escape with a green banner.

For the main body of the crowd the horror was not yet over. They tried to flee in every direction but found the main exits blocked by Yeomanry and the 88th Infantry Regiment who stood and used fixed bayonets. Captain Richard Withington threatened to shoot dead any protester who tried to escape. The iron railings in front of a house in Windmill Street were flattened by the weight of humanity.

The worst pile-up was near the Friends' Meeting House on the Field's perimeter. A female householder described how people were trapped by the sweep of the Hussars and the frenzy of the Manchester Yeomanry:

> The people came in great crowds past my door, and a parcel of them beat down the fence. The stumps were all down on the ground, and also the stones were out of their places. There was a large stone with a stump at the bottom. The people were so pressed against it that they could not get away. They (the Yeomanry) kept cutting them in the corner, and the shrieks would astonish you, and they were laying on them all the time as hard as they could.

The press of panicked people tumbled into her cellar, crushing the life out of Mrs Martha Partington of Eccles.

The panic-stricken crowd squeezed into narrow alleys in their desperation, but for some there was still no escape. Cavalrymen pursed them into the confined spaces with shocking results. Sixty-year-old Margaret Goodwin recognised her pursuer, whom she had known since he was a child. She cried out: 'Tom Shelmerdine, thee will not hurt me, I know.' She was wrong. He rode her down and slashed her scalp with his sabre. A young woman was also slashed by Yeoman Edward Tebbutt, her neighbour.

Householders whose property flanked the Field and its exits took in scores of terrified and injured people to save them from hoof and sabre. A charwoman, Mary Dowlan, saved 14 injured people and dressed their wounds. She said: 'My house was liker to a slaughterhouse than to a Christian's house, with human blood.' Ann Jones was also 'fully employed in pulling people into my house'. A Special Constable forced his way in and shouted in triumph: 'This is Waterloo for you – this is Waterloo.'[21]

Samuel Bamford's wife Mima took refuge in a deserted vault but her hiding was interrupted by several men carrying the corpse of a middle-aged woman. Archibald Prentice, who had left the meeting to return to Salford just as Hunt was about to speak, recalled: 'I had not been at home more than a quarter of an hour when a wailing sound was heard from the main street and, rushing out, I saw people running in the direction of Pendleton, their faces pale as death, and some with blood trickling down their cheeks.'[22]

The one-legged Colonel Dalrymple decided that enough was enough and sent Jolliffe to find a trumpeter to sound the recall. When Jolliffe returned to the Field with the required man he was presented with 'an extraordinary sight'. He later wrote: 'The ground was quite covered with hats, shoes, musical instruments and other things. Here and there lay the unfortunates who were too much injured to move away, and this sight was rendered the more distressing, by observing some women among the sufferers.'[23]

Bamford's account of the same scene said:

> The yeomanry had dismouted – some were easing their horses' girths, others adjusting their accoutrements, and some were wiping their sabres. Several mounds of human beings still remained where they had fallen, crushed down and smothered. Some of these still groaning, others with staring eyes were gasping for breath, and others would never breath more. All was silent save those low moans, and the occasional snorting and pawing of steeds. Persons might sometimes be noticed peeping from attics and over the tall ridgings of houses, but they quickly withdrew, as if fearful of being observed.[24]

It was barely 15 minutes since Henry Hunt had started to address a peaceful crowd.

4

The Reckoning

'The extreme forbearance of the military'

The violence was far from over. During the afternoon there was a lull as the injured were cared for and distraught families searched for their loved ones, alive and dead. Hunt and Johnson were handed to L'Estrange who marched them through the city to the prison yard of the New Bailey. But anger and outrage quickly resurfaced as the scale of the disaster became all too obvious. Bamford wrote: 'All the working people were athirst for revenge.' Later he added:

> Many of the young men had been preparing arms and seeking out articles to convert into such. Some had been grinding scythes, others old hatchets, others screw-drivers, rusty swords, pikels and mop-nails; anything which could be made to cut and stab was pronounced fit for service. But no plan was defined – nothing was arranged – and the arms were afterwards reserved for any event that might occur.

In the tough district of New Cross a rumour spread that the grocer Tate, a Special Constable, had taken one of the women Reformers' banners as a souvenir. His shop front was smashed by a furious crowd. Elsewhere a troop of the 15th Hussars tried to clear the streets with minimum force. Their captain, Booth, first ordered that neither swords nor guns should be used because the Riot Act had not been read in the vicinity. The troopers charged repeatedly into a hail of bricks and stones. Each time the crowd fell back but swiftly returned when the horses passed. Booth lost his temper and told magistrate Norris that unless the Act was read he would return his men to barracks. Norris agreed and Booth ordered an infantry officer to form a hollow square. The infantry discharged their muskets into the crowd, killing at least two, and then opened up to let the cavalry through. Many more were trampled. That night the Reverend Ethelston wrote to Lord Sidmouth: 'The town is in great confusion and alarm.'[1]

Sporadic rioting and disturbances continued through a very long night, but the following day it was replaced with grief and sullen despair. The streets of Manchester were by now empty, with all shops closed by order. Jolliffe visited the Infirmary with some medical officer friends and saw scores of civilians with crushed bodies and severe sabre wounds. He saw two women he reckoned could not recover, a man with a gunshot to the head, and another with his leg newly amputated.[2]

The men who had inflicted such damage were in a mood of post-battle euphoria. The Cheshire Yeomanry displayed captured banners with as much pride as if they had been taken from Napoleon's crack regiments. John Lloyd, in a triumphant dispatch to Henry Hobhouse, wrote: 'We have come back with much honour today, having with out troop done essential service ...' He added: 'We remain on duty and now is the time to make a good finish.'[3]

There was no need. The people of the cotton towns were overwhelmed by grief and a sense of failure. They had taken on the power of the state with words and been crushed by military force. They were surly, but subdued. Sidmouth initially wrote congratulating the magistrates on the 'deliberated and spirited manner' in which they had carried out their duty. He also passed on the thanks of the Prince Regent, who had been enjoying the cool sea breezes on his yacht off Christchurch, to the Manchester and Cheshire Yeomanry. But as more dispatches arrived he quickly realised the scale of the violent over-reaction to a peaceful demonstration. He was also very much aware of the presence of reporters, not all of whom could be relied upon to follow the Government line. The *Times* correspondent Tyas had been arrested but local reporters pooled their copy and sent it to London, where it was published within 24 hours of the tragic events. Five days later crowds swarmed around the offices of the *Manchester Observer* to buy copies of a special edition. In its reports a new term, ironic and apt, was coined – 'Peter-Loo'.[4]

* * *

Manchester's manufacturers took revenge for the scare they had suffered. As William Marsh recovered from gruesome injuries he heard that three of his children working in Birley's Mill had been sacked because of his presence on St Peter's Field. That was repeated amongst many families. And any workers who went to work the following day with suspicious cuts or injuries were dismissed just as swiftly.

John Lees suffered horrific injuries of the sort he had witnessed four years earlier when he fought unscathed throughout the three-day Battle of Waterloo. His clothes were cut to shreds. There was a sabre gash to his left shoulder, another deep cut to his arm had separated the shoulder bone, the skin was cut from his right hip in two places, one foot was crushed and the whole of his back and loins was one vivid bruise from the batterings of hooves and truncheons. With the help of his stepbrother he hobbled the eight hilly miles to Oldham, stopping off for a drink on the way. The following day he arrived promptly for work at 8.00 a.m. His shirt was soaked with blood and his father sent him home before his condition was reported to the boss. Later that day he saw a doctor who advised rest and poultices. He lay shivering and in agony on his bed for several weeks. By 3 September he had lost the use of his left arm and the sight of his right eye. His elbow bone protruded horribly white from his arm. He could no longer move from the bed and leeches were applied. Finally, at 1.30 a.m. on 7 September, he died.

The scale of the carnage at Peterloo is still a matter of controversy. The *Times* reported eleven dead and up to 500 wounded.[5] Subsequent reports, as some of the wounded perished, put the fatalities much higher. Local research has confirmed at least 15 dead and most causes of death: John Lees of Oldham, sabred; two-year-old William Fildes, trampled; Thomas Ashworth, Manchester, sabred and trampled; John Ashton, Oldham, sabred and trampled; Thomas Buckley, Chadderton, sabred and trampled; James Crompton, Barton, trampled; Mary Heys, Manchester, trampled; Sarah Jones, Manchester, not recorded; Arthur O'Neill, Manchester, trampled; Martha Partington, Manchester, trampled; John Rhodes, Hopwood, not recorded; Joseph Ashworth, Manchester, shot; William Bradshaw, Bury, not recorded; William Dawson, Saddleworth, sabred and trampled; Edmund Dawson, Saddleworth, sabred.

The Manchester authorities did their best to disguise the full horror. Initial reports to the Home Office said that the Infirmary had taken in 29 injured, of whom two died, although by the following week the number of patients increased to 71. William Hulton wrote that such small numbers was 'proof of the extreme forebearance of the military'. But a solicitor, Charles Pearson, was determined to reach a more realistic count of the injured. Touring the area he personally found 200. Eighteen months later, a Relief Fund set up by manufacturers whose consciences had been pricked by the massacre paid out small amounts of compensation to 420 Peterloo victims.[6]

In the days following the slaughter the press reports stirred up a hornets' nest. Led by *The Times* and the *Leeds Mercury*, editorials accused magistrates and military of mass murder. A series of inquests, including one demanded by John Lees's father, were reported in precise detail, as several journalists were ejected and official witnesses refused to give evidence beyond the classic defence of 'only obeying orders'. At Lees's inquest a succession of working-class witnesses gave compelling evidence of the savagery of the soldiers. But crucially the trooper who had sabred Lees could not be identified. The inquest was halted on a technicality. The Radical MP Sir Francis Burdett wrote to his constituents expressing 'shame, grief and indignation at the account of the blood spilt at Manchester'. He added of the soldiers involved: 'Would to heaven that they had been Dutchmen or Switzers or Hessians or Hanoverians, or anything rather than Englishmen who had done such deeds. What kill men unarmed, unresisting and Gracious God! Women too, disfigured, maimed, cut down and trampled by dragoons.'

Hulton rightly sensed that he would carry much of the blame for the bloody events, and appealed to Lord Sidmouth for a more fulsome expression of support. The wily Home Secretary dodged the issue. However, Sidmouth wrote home about the fatal day: 'The proceedings were not of an ordinary character, but they will, I trust, prove a salutory lesson to modern reformers. Hunt and his associates are in custody, and their flags etc. have been seized and destroyed by the special constables and soldiery, all of whom have behaved with the greatest spirit and temper ...'

Hulton and his fellow magistrates convened a public meeting at the Star Inn so that decent, law-abiding citizens could express their approval for the stern action taken against the mob. The meeting, clearly rigged, was a farce. As a direct response the Radical manufacturer Archibald Prentice organised a petition to invalidate the magistrates' meeting and to condemn the violence used at Peterloo. Within three days he had 4,800 signatures, including many from the 'respectable classes'.

On 5 September a large crowd gathered outside the Queen's Street lodgings of the Yeoman Trumpeteer Edward Meagher. Several survivors bore the scars of his sabre. Meagher, half drunk from a Saturday night's boozing, fired several shots from his window into the crowd, wounding two men in the legs. A month later he was acquitted of assault by the Manchester magistrates he had served so enthusiastically.

From then on, supported by a reactionary Cabinet and the Prince Regent, Lord Sidmouth fulsomely backed Hulton and the magistrates and offered no concessions to anyone, or any class, who aimed to present Peterloo as anything other than a legitimate response to public disorder. He convinced the Prime Minister, Lord Liverpool, that even more stern measures must be taken to suppress dissent amongst the general populace. He argued that Britain was close to anarchy or revolution. By the end of 1819 Sidmouth laid before Parliament legislation which became known as the Six Acts. They prevented drilling by civilian groups; gave magistrates wider powers to search for arms; streamlined the administration of justice; prevented public meetings of more than 50 people; gave courts new powers to seize newspapers and pamphlets; and imposed stamp duty on a wider range of cheaper periodicals, effectively putting many out of business. Taken together with the pre-Peterloo legislation, they gave the Government legal powers of repression on a scale never seen before.[7]

*   *   *

Henry Hunt and nine other prisoners were indicted for conspiracy and unlawful assembly at Lancaster Assizes on 4 September 1819. All were bailed with £200 sureties raised by wealthier supporters. Hunt returned to Manchester, regaled by the cheers of crowds who gathered in every town and village he passed through. At Pendleton up to 80,000 people were said to surround his carriage. He reached Manchester on the 9th to another rapturous reception, and when he eventually reached London there were 300,000 people on the streets to greet him.

But by the time of his trial, and that of the other nine, at York on 16 March 1820, time and distance had dulled public interest. There was little uproar when Hunt was found guilty of seditious assembly and sentenced to two years in Ilchester gaol. Joseph Johson, Samuel Bamford, who had not even been on St Peter's Field at the crucial time, and Joseph Healy, a working-class Radical, were given one year's imprisonment in Lincoln gaol. John Knight was found guilty of another offence and sentenced to two years in prison. The rest were acquitted.[8]

That was not quite the end of the legal proceedings from Peterloo. The Reformers mounted a test case against four members of the Manchester Yeomanry Cavalry – Captain Hugh Birley, Captain Richard Withington, Trumpeter Edward Meagher and Private Alexander Oliver. It was brought by the Middleton hatter Thomas Redford who had been severely slashed while holding close his contingent's banner. The trial began at Lancaster on 4 April 1822 and familiar evidence of military savagery was retold. It suprised no one when all four were acquitted. The Government paid their defence costs.

*   *   *

Henry Hunt never again enjoyed the heady delirium of mass adulation following his release from gaol at the end of October 1820. His motives became increasingly suspect to the new generation of Reformers. His vainglorious boasting following such an awful tragedy became tiresome. He was successfully elected MP for Preston in 1830 but was badly defeated three years later. During his brief time at Westminster he presented the first petition in favour of women's rights and he demanded the ballot and universal suffrage. But he alienated old friends and allies, including William Cobbett. He refused to join the Chartists and criticised old allies for advocating piecemeal reform as the only realistic way forward. He retired from public life to make money as a manufacturer of blacking. While travelling to pick up orders on 15 February 1835 he suffered a paralysing seizure and died at Alresford, Hampshire. He was buried at Parham in the family vault of his mistress, Mrs Vince. His obituaries described him in turn as gentlemanly, vivacious, energetic, a violent but impressive speaker, vain, domineering, capricious and jealous of the popularity of colleagues. One added: 'He made the wearing of a white hat the badge of a Radical.'

On their release from prison, genuine working-class champions like John Bagguley and Joseph Johnson faded from public view. Not so

Samuel Bamford, whose self-regarding writings on Peterloo resulted in considerable fame. He was always feuding with fellow Reformers, however, and he denounced the leaders of the new Chartist Movement, even though their aims were virtually identical to his own. In middle age he became a Special Constable and, on his retirement, he was appointed doorman of Somerset House.

Those most directly responsible for the massacre were never held to account: neither Hulton, Norris nor the other magistrates whose panic sparked mayhem. Nor Colonel L'Estrange, whose inexperience compounded the tragedy. Nor General Byng who left such inexperienced officers in charge because he could not drag himself away from York Races.

Captain Hugh Birley, who led the death charge at Peterloo, always claimed that he had never once swung his sabre on the Field. Neither did he ever admit that he had allowed his amateur soldiers to run amok, motivated either by their own fright or by vindictive hatred of the demonstrators. He later became a magistrate and a deputy lieutenant of Lancashire. He helped Sir Robert Peel introduce Saturday half-holidays for workers.

Joseph Nadin made a fortune out of his duties as Manchester's Deputy Police Chief. He retired in 1821 and used his ill-gotten gains to set himself up as a master cotton-spinner with a big house in Cheshire. He died aged 83 in 1848, a very rich man.

William Hulton, the jittery magistrate who had ordered the Yeomen's bloody charge, claimed that 16 August 1819 was 'the proudest day of my life'. His unpopularity increased as public anger and official disquiet over the massacre increased. While campaigning in Bolton for the Conservative candidate, Hulton was physically attacked by a crowd chanting 'Peterloo' and was rescued by party members. He died in 1864.

John Lloyd, the Stockport Special Constable and solicitor's clerk who had terrorised so many working men, was rewarded with the post of Prothonotary at Chester. He set up soup kitchens for starving families and castigated unscrupulous employers. He believed in caring for the 'lower orders' provided they appreciated it and obeyed the strict laws of their betters. His son, John Horatio, was elected Stockport's first MP – as a Radical. John Horatio's granddaughter married Oscar Wilde.

Lord Sidmouth continued to rule the domestic affairs of Britain with an iron will. In 1821 when he attempted to retire, the former Prince Regent, now King George VI, persuaded him to remain for another three years. On one occasion he rejected the new monarch's attempt to give clemency to 77 convicted felons. All were hanged. Soon after his actual retirement, Sidmouth married a rich wife 30 years younger than him. He enjoyed a further 21 years of marital bliss until his death, aged 86, in 1844.

The sacrifice at Peterloo achieved nothing in the short term but greater repression. However, it became a potent symbol of the aspirations of the working class and the brutality of a state determined to suppress them. J.E. Taylor, the first editor of the new *Manchester Guardian*, wrote: 'In one brief hour it has done more for the sacred cause of liberty than the slow but certain progress of opinion could have operated in half a century.'[9] Peterloo also awakened the rest of the country to the plight of the industrialised North.

Above all, Peterloo gave working men and women the heroes and villains they needed to sustain a mass movement for real change.

One such hero was John Lees. A few hours before he died he whispered to his friend William Harrison that he had never been in such danger as on St Peter's Field. 'At Waterloo,' he said, 'it was man to man, but there it was downright murder.'

5
Captain Swing and the Rural War

'Dogs and hogs and horses are treated with more civility'

On 24 November 1830 the court of North Walsham in Norfolk issued
a joint statement:

> The Magistrates are determined to enforce the Laws against all tumultuous
> Rioters and Incendaries, and they look for support to all the respectable
> and well disposed part of the Community; at the same time they feel a full
> conviction that *no severe measures will be necessary*, if the proprietors of
> Land will give proper employment to the Poor on their own Occupations,
> and encourage their Tenant to do the same.[1]

It was good advice but too late. The flames which consumed the
countryside across southern and eastern England during that tumultuous
year cost the lives of 19 executed farm labourers and almost 1,400
more transported or imprisoned.

*   *   *

The plight of the urban poor during the Industrial Revolution sparked
near-revolution in the North, but the distress of the rural poor was
felt throughout the country. Both groups had no Parliamentary vote
and neither did farm labourers enjoy any rights at all in the running of
their parishes or the farms and estates on which they laboured. After
the Enclosure Acts those who held land by custom were dispossessed
if they could not prove legal ownership. Few could. Traditional access
to common land for firewood, fruit and pig fodder was lost, and small
farms, unable to compete with larger holdings, were forced to sell
up. The meagre rights of the very poor were stolen from them. Farm

owners hired labourers on a casual, short-term basis for harvesting, sheep-shearing, ditching, threshing and other temporary jobs. For many, living on the farm was no longer an option. New threshing machines increased rural unemployment, and food riots followed poor harvests. One, at Beaminster in Dorset in 1764, occurred because of the 'exorbitant and unnecessary price of corn'. The following year a bunting mill was destroyed at Stalbridge and another attacked at Marnhull in the same county. Farmers refused to pay better wages during the boom in demand during the Napoleonic Wars, arguing that they would not be able to maintain such pay levels in less prosperous times. When food prices were high and wages below subsistence levels, starvation was only avoided by subsidies from local rates – Poor Relief. This put the feeding of families first, which was humanitarian, but also ended the distinction between workers and paupers.

Rural deprivation was massively increased when the wars came to a close in 1815 and the labour market was swamped by 250,000 demobilised soldiers and sailors. During the 1820s an agricultural recession and a series of poor harvests saw wages slashed and spending on Poor Relief cut by a quarter as a deterrent against idleness. At Stalbridge in 1826 a coroner's jury found parish officers guilty of causing the death of one young woman, Mary Coles, by neglect. It emerged that she was one of three women and a child who shared a single bed in a hovel attached to the poorhouse, with only a shilling a week provided for their food and upkeep. In the southern and eastern counties the response of many landowners was to buy more of the new threshing machines and make more labourers redundant and more families dependant on erratic and meanly distributed welfare. Rural crime soared between 1820 and 1830, even though the mere suspicion of poaching could result in transportation.[2]

When William Cobbett visited the Avon Valley and Pewsey Vale in August 1826 he recorded:

> In taking my leave of this beautiful vale I have to express my deep shame, as an Englishman, at beholding the general extreme poverty of those who cause this vale to produce such quantities of food and raiment. This is, I verily believe it, the worst used labouring people upon the face of the earth. Dogs and hogs and horses are treated with more civility; and as to board and lodging, how gladly would the labourers change with them! This state

of things never can continue many years! By some means or other there must be an end to it; and my firm belief is, that the end will be dreadful.[3]

But the fury of farm labourers did not boil up into arson and machine-breaking until the end of August 1830. Hobsbawm and Rude summed up the climate:

The conditions of the southern labourer was such that he required only some special stimulus – admittedly it would probably have to be exceptionally powerful to overcome his demoralised passivity – to produce a very widespread movement. The economic conditions of 1828–30 produced a situation which made his already bad situation worse, and almost certainly increased both rural unemployment, the attempts to diminish in some way or another the financial burden of poor relief on the rate payers, and the discontent of farmers and all those who depended on agriculture. The combined effect of continental revolution and British political crisis produced at atmosphere of expectation, of tension, of hope and potential action. They did not provide the actual spark. In north and east Kent it might have been Irish labourers and threshing machines, in the Weald the cut in poor relief, elsewhere in the country other local factors may have revived action here and there in those occasional villages where, for one reason or another, a tradition of resistance and action survived.[4]

It began in Kent when farmer Mosyer's ricks and barn at Orpington were burnt on 1 June 1830. More fires followed across the county until the labourers turned their attention to machinery. Around 100 threshing machines – the first on a farm at Lower Hadres near Canterbury – were smashed between 28 August and the end of October. Conservative periodicals sneered that most of the damage was done on Saturday nights after the local inns had shut. The attacks were generally carried out by gangs of between 20 and 50 masked men. Even though some passions may have been aroused by that June's revolution in France, they made no political demands but simply wanted a rise in wages from the average of 8s 4d weekly to 13s 6d in winter months and 15 shillings in summer, and a reduction in rents and tithes. Most trouble was noted in cereal-growing parts of the county where the lowest wages were paid to labourers, and in recently enclosed villages. Initially the attacks were treated as a joke and it was suspected that some owners were destroying their own machines for insurance or as an excuse to fire more labourers.

No leaders emerged, publicly at least, and most action was covert, sporadic and disorganised. But the rural protest movement, slow to start, swiftly gained momentum, bursting through the Kent borders and spreading to Sussex, Surrey, Hampshire and Wiltshire. Dissent spread by word of mouth, from village to village, and arson provided the beacons of revolt. Burning hayricks stained the skies and local constabularies worked overtime filling county gaols. In Hampshire and Wiltshire alone there were over 300 prisoners taken within a week. Having destroyed threshers the protesters turned their fury on other agricultural and industrial machinery.

A report sent to the commander of the Salisbury troop detailed events on 22 November in Wiltshire:

> A mob gathered at Great Bedwin today and visited a number of farms. One farmer, Thomas Gale, was forced to hand over a sovereign. At about noon the mob visited the farm of Mr William Randall, where they broke two machines, a winnowing machine and two sowing machines, almost all the pieces of the machines were carried away by the mob. Some of them got into the house and demanded victuals and money. One of them, Charles Pizzie, is reported to have demanded ten shillings, which he said Mr Randall owed him. The man is said to have threatened to knock Mr Randall's brains out if he did not get the money. Mr Randall handed over the money and gave the mob food and drink. The mob left but returned shortly after and Pizzie is said to have demanded more money, to have threatened to split Mr Randall's head open and to come in the night to set fire to his house ... Mr Randall borrowed half a sovereign from one of his servants and gave it to Pizzie after he repeated his threats and held an iron bar up to Mr Randall's head, in a menacing manner.[5]

The following day 25 towns and villages were affected across Wiltshire. Around 800 people smashed machines at Shalbourne and more cash was obtained with menaces. Solitary women were not safe from extortion. Miss Elizabeth Penruddock of Fifield confronted 400 men who threatened to smash the windows of her cottage and tear down the chimney if she did not hand over 5 shillings. An isolated farm at South Savernake was invaded by 80 men demanding 'Beer and a sovereign'. The farmer, Robert Lyne, tried to satisfy them with beer only, but they took the money as well. Another report from Wiltshire concerned an arson attack on a house and farm buildings at Oare:

> It was found necessary to place 12 Pewsey men to guard the water pipes after it was found that one of them had been cut. One of those fighting the fire has stated the belief that if it had not been for the Pewsey men there would not have been a house left standing at Oare and it is believed that the

fire was the work of the labourers of the village. As soon as the fire was put out those watching were heard to mutter threats against other farmers, and one of them, Charles Kimber, told Mr Edmonds to his face that his property would be the next to go. This fellow was instantly taken into custody and is now in prison. He was apparently very active in endeavouring to intimidate the Pewsey men and in throwing, and encouraging his companions to throw, brickbats at those putting out the fire. He is also accused of knocking James Self off a rick into the fire.[6]

Rioting in Wiltshire reached a climax on 25 November with fighting between rioters and Yeomanry in the Wylye Valley. John Harding of Tisbury was shot dead, several other labourers were wounded and 25 men were arrested. The inquest later heard: 'The Hinton troop of Yeomanry caught up with some rioters and a vicious fight ensued during which Harding caught hold of a yeomen's horse and proceeded to club the rider. After five minutes the soldier could take no more so he drew his pistol and shot his assailant.'[7] The Yeomanry had been called by Mr Bennett, MP for Wiltshire, whose own efforts to disperse the mob had been met with a shower of stones. Another contemporary report stated:

> At that moment the Hindon troop accidentally came up; and, the mob still persisting in throwing stones, the cavalry were ordered to fire blank-cartridges over their heads; but the mob only laughed at them, and asked them why they did not do their duty. The cavalry then attempted to charge; but the mob rushed into the plantations which surrounded the house, where they continued pelting the cavalry, who at last effected the charge; where several of the rioters were wounded and some mortally; one man was shot dead on the spot. A great number were taken prisoner, 25 of whom were taken to Fisherton gaol the same night. Several were severely wounded; one man had a cut across the back of the hand, which separated the muscles; another had three fingers cut off his left hand, and two off his right; another had a piece of his skull cut off; another received a severe cut across one of his elbows; another had his head cut open.

A verdict of 'justifiable homicide' was recorded on the slaying of Harding.

As the attacks spread further afield, engulfing much of southern and eastern England, mysterious letters began to appear, signed in different hands by 'Captain Swing'. They were addressed to local landowners, farmers and periodicals, and they were first mentioned in *The Times* on 21 October. Most threatened arson and other reprisals. It will never be known how many were from real protesters and how many were hoaxes. The genuine ones, sent by local ringleaders, appear to have been designed to spread alarm, fear and puzzlement. The name 'Captain Swing' was meant to invoke the terror of hanging.

Some of the most serious, and sometimes comic, clashes occurred in Dorset. James Frampton, the unpopular magistrate at Bere Regis, read the Riot Act, harangued a sullen crowd and ordered the arrest of a man and two boys. Threshing machines were destroyed in Blackmore Vale even though there was not enough corn grown to provide labourers with work through winter, with or without the machines. At Stour Provosts the farmer and constable Walter Snook was attacked. He responded by arresting several men and taking them to Shaftesbury as prisoners. The keys to the lock-up were mislaid and sympathisers rescued the prisoners.[8]

Rioters from Stoke Wake and Mappowder destroyed William Coward's thresher at Woolland on 26 November. The following day they demanded 1s 6d from a small farmer and blacksmith, Christopher Morey, who gave them 3 shillings. They went on to smash a machine 'with great noise and blowing of horns' at John Pount's farm at Buckland Newton. William James, a churchwarden and farmer who rented half the land in Mappowder parish, refused to pay protection money and later helped to condemn several labourers to transportation. A nearby farmer, John Young, gave the same crowd six half-crowns and his neighbour Matthew Galpin added £2 to persuade them to go away. On one night alone, 29 November, riots were reported in the Dorset parishes of Castle Hill, Lulworth, Preston, Winfrith and Wool. A few nights later there were serious assaults at Stalbridge, Sherbourne and Lytchett Maltravers.[9]

As the violence in Dorset died down, it flared just across the Somerset border. On 1 December two threshing machines were shattered at Henstridge and Yenston. A mounted group of farmers, members of the local hunt, rode into a crowd they believed to be responsible for the damage and took six prisoners. The horsemen later formed the nucleus of a troop of the North Somerset Yeomanry.

At Selborne in Hampshire several hundred attacked the village workhouse, turned out the occupants, broke the fittings and pulled down the roof with ropes. The following day, their numbers swollen, they did the same to the workhouse at Headley, seven miles away. The parsons in both villages were forced to promise to halve the income they took from tithes.

Not all the riots concerned wages or machines. In the Forest of Dean 200 miners equipped with axes cleared trees and freed animals in protest at the Enclosures. Their ringleader, Warren James, was transported for life. In East Anglia parsons were attacked if they refused to reduce tithes, At Ottmoor in Oxfordshire smaller farmers resisted drainage schemes, which they claimed cut them off from water supplies, by hacking down embankments erected at the time of the Enclosures. Troops were sent to the area but when they brought prisoners back to Oxford they were released by an angry crowd. In East Sussex the hated workhouses were the principal targets.

Despite the lurid and outraged reports in the press, the Swing Riots were marked by the discipline and ceremony with which most were carried out. Arms were rarely carried and, although there were bloodcurdling threats, no one was murdered or even accidentally killed. In many cases the main body was preceded by a warning flag or horn. Labourers used to working in gangs were well able to maintain discipline among themselves. Often mobs had their own treasurer who kept all 'fines' on landowners until the time came to share the booty out equally, too often in an alehouse.

It was the contagious nature of the disturbances, however, spreading from county to county, which most frightened the authorities. By December the 'Rural War' had spread to every county south of a line from Norfolk to Worcestershire, and there were sporadic eruptions of arson, damage and rioting as far north as Carlisle. Over 1,000 separate incidents of arson, machine-breaking and other disturbances were recorded. By then, however, Government tactics had changed. Partly because of the mayhem, Wellington's Tory administration fell, and with it the Home Secretary, Sir Robert Peel, who had preferred to leave matters to local magistrates. His successor in Earl Grey's new Whig administration was Viscount Melbourne. In a Parliamentary debate on the rural turmoil he said: 'With regard to this war ... it is my determined resolution, wherever outrages are perpetrated, or excesses committed, to suppress them with severity and vigour.'

Melbourne immediately mobilised all troops of Yeomanry with orders to aid the gentry and farmers whenever and wherever the trouble flared. Troops were generally stationed in or near such cities as Norwich,

Bristol and Leicester, and the larger manufacturing towns. From there small mobile squads were sent out to crush disturbances whenever the need arose. The gentry had meanwhile also got themselves better organised, swearing in more Special Constables and mustering their loyal tenants and servants into Home Guards.

Melbourne sent local magistrates strict instructions not to offer any sympathy to the rioters and to 'deem it their duty to maintain and uphold the Rights of Property, of every description, against violence and aggression'. Local courts offered rewards of up to £400 for the apprehension and conviction of anyone engaged in arson or machine-smashing. Such measures were effective and by the turn of the year 2,000 men and women were awaiting trial across the southern counties.

The Marlborough troop of the Wiltshire Yeomanry were especially active in hunting down malcontents. On one occasion, the troop, along with 200 mounted farmers, swept through Aldbourne and Ramsbury and apprehended 32 people suspected of rioting earlier. At Milton they dispersed a crowd of 300 and captured the leaders. Such clashes were inevitably violent. Although the official death count across the South was limited to the hapless John Harding, it is reasonable to assume that some of the dispossessed did not warrant the expense and trouble of an inquest. In other cases the wounded were secretly nursed and eventually buried in unmarked graves to avoid reprisals against their families.

The aristocracy adopted almost feudal measures to protect their property. At Carlisle 'all Masters and Heads of Families' were told to impose a curfew on servants, apprentices and children. In Norfolk Lord Suffield enrolled a private army of 100 men, a third of them old soldiers. The Duke of Buckingham set up a similar feudal force of labourers and tenants near Winchester. The Duke of Wellington boasted of hunting down Hampshire rioters like foxes:

> I induced the magistrates to put themselves on horseback, each at the head of his own servants and retainers, grooms, huntsmen, game-keepers, armed with horsewhips, pistols, fowling pieces and what they could get, and to attack in concert, if necessary, or singly, these mobs, disperse them and take and put in confinement those who could not escape. This was done in a spirited manner, in many instances, and it is astonishing how soon the country was tranquilised, and that in the best way, by the activity and spirit of the gentlemen.

In the new year the trials began. The Government, believing that the magistrates of Kent had been too lenient during the early days of the outbreaks, set up a special commission to deal with the worst affected 'Swing' counties of Hampshire, Berkshire, Buckinghamshire, Dorset and Wiltshire. These tribunals, run by Crown lawyers, were harsh and resulted in the hanging of nine men and boys, the transportation of 400 more – 200 for life – and the imprisonment of a further 400. Later trials in assize and county courts raised the totals to 19 executed, 644 gaoled and 505 transported to Australia for terms of seven years, 14 years or life. In all, 1,976 prisoners were tried by 90 courts sitting in 34 counties.[10]

The Annual Register recorded the hanging on Penenden Heath near Maidstone of three convicted of arson: Henry Packman, his brother William, and James Dyke.

> The two latter were boys, about 18 or 19, and looked much younger. Dyke invariably protested his innocence after his conviction; the other prisoners did not deny having set fire to a stack and barn, but said that an accomplice, Goodman, had urged them to do it for the sake of a reward. They paid little attention to their religious duties and, in consequence, the sacrament was not administered to any of the three on the morning of their execution. On their arrival at the Heath, one of the Packmans remarked to the crowd, 'That (the gallows) looks an awful thing!' and he and his brother regarded the appalling preparations for tying up Dyke with attention – the first symptom of feeling they had displayed. The Chaplain said, in a low voice, to Dyke, 'Now you have come to the worst, and there is no chance of escape, do tell the truth.' He answered, 'I am innocent.'[11]

The elder Packman turned to William and said: 'Brother let us shake hands before we die.' The teenager, when all was ready, raised the cap above his eyes and refused to pull it down, saying he wished to see the people who were witnessing his death.

Transportation to the hostile, unknown land of Australia was widely feared. Most Swing rioters survived the convict ships despite storms, bad food, crowded and insanitary shipboard accommodation, and the continuous threat of the lash for the smallest transgressions. Their fate when they arrived was a lottery: Government work-gangs were considered the hardest labour, assigned work to local settlers could be easier. It all depended on the character of the officer or master in charge. The Swing transportees were generally older and more experienced than the average criminal convicts, and could bring more skills to a penal colony fast turning into a Dominion, and then a nation.

In 1834 public pressure forced the Government to review certain cases, and the following year 264 pardons were issued. By the 1840s most of the transportees were freed but few returned to England. Some of those who did later returned to Australia with their families as fully-fledged colonists.

Many of their descendants can be traced. James Lush, convicted of the armed robbery of the farmer Pinninger, saw his death sentence commuted to transportation for life following a successful petition to the King. He was transported on the *Proteus* on 18 March 1831 and arrived at Hobart 138 days later. He left behind a wife and six children but his 17-year-old son James followed him to New South Wales. Lush was eventually pardoned and moved to Victoria. He died in that state in 1854, aged 66. His son died in the Liverpool Asylum of senile decay in 1889, also aged 66. Robert Holdaway, a 37-year-old carpenter and ex-publican, was accused of being the ringleader of the Selborne workhouse riots. His death sentence was also commuted and he was transported on the *Eleanor* to New South Wales. He worked as a convict labourer at Penrith and received a conditional pardon in 1837. He died in Camperdown, Sydney, in 1853. Aaron Harding, another Selborne rioter, was transported to New South Wales and kept in the hulk *Phoenix* for eleven months after his arrival. He was eventually released and married a woman who already had nine children. They had two more before he died in 1851.[12]

Government sanctions against Radicals, whom they blamed for inciting the labouring classes, were largely ineffectual. Richard Carlile, the former shoemaker whose Radical tracts were said to have inflamed the labourers, was sentenced to two years' imprisonment and fined £200, but served only eight months and never paid the fine. William Cobbett was acquitted of incitement after conducting his own defence.

Cobbett's alleged offence concerned his attempt, in a November edition of his *Political Register*, to pin the blame for the violence on those who lived off unearned income at the expense of their workers. He wrote:

Forty-five years ago, the labourers brewed their own beer, and that none of them do it; that formerly they ate meat, cheese and bread, and they now live almost wholly on potatoes; that formerly it was a rare thing for a girl to be with child before she was married, and that now is as rare that she is not, the parties being so poor that they are compelled to throw the expense of the wedding on the parish; that the felons in the jails and hulks live better than the honest labouring people; that men are set to draw waggons and carts like beasts of burden; that they are shut up like Negroes in Jamaica; that married men are forcibly separated from their wives to prevent them from breeding ... It is no temporary cause, it is no new feeling of discontent that is at work; it is a deep sense of grievous wrongs; it is a long harboured resentment; it is an accumulation of revenge for unwarranted punishment ... it is a natural effect of a cause which is as obvious as that ricks are consumed by fire ...[13]

The 'Swing' riots shocked many landowners, if only because total damage was estimated at £121,600. The disturbances did result in a heated debate on the causes of poverty, and that led to the 1834 Poor Law Amendment Act. In the short term many labourers saw their wages increased to 10 shillings a week, but that did not last. By 1850 the average had slipped to 9s 6d while rents, tithes and other living costs had risen.

The suppression of 'Swing' did not end rural protest; there was a series of disturbances running through several decades. They achieved little. Agricultural labourers continued to be the worst-paid, worst-fed and worst-housed of all working people.

6

The Reform Riots and the Battle of Bristol

'Drink or blood'

William Cobbett, analysing the causes of the Rural War concluded: 'What is to the result of all this? Why, a violent destruction of the whole fabric of the Government, or a timely, that is, an immediate and effectual remedy, and there is no remedy but a *radical reform* of the Parliament ...' [1]

The clamour for a reform bill to end the injustices represented by rotten boroughs, previously heard at Peterloo, was becoming too loud to ignore.

Earl Grey won power in November 1830 partly on a promise of reform and he told King William IV that such reform was long overdue. The fast-growing industrial towns of Manchester, Birmingham, Bradford and Leeds had no Parliamentary representation at all, while dwindling hamlets with a handful of voters returned their own MPs. Bristol had long been represented in Parliament but only a little over 6,000 people out of a population of 104,000 had the vote. The proposed Reform Bill was designed to extend suffrage to more men, to see that new and growing towns were properly represented, to redraw boundaries to abolish rotten boroughs and to curb the bribery extensively employed by some candidates.

Earl Grey steered the bill through the House of Commons on 22 September 1831. But the Tories dominated the House of Lords and, after a long and heated debate over five days and nights, the Upper Chamber rejected it by a majority of 41. John Hobhouse recalled seeing a placard in a shoemaker's window with the inscription '199 versus 22,000,000'. The newspapers reported the defeat of the legislation with black borders on the front pages.

The response of people who had come so close to real reform, only to have it snatched away at the eleventh hour, was predictably violent. In Nottingham the unoccupied castle was burnt down and the interior of a mansion wrecked. In Derby 23 prisoners were set free from the city gaol, but not before a bystander had been killed by gunfire from the gaolers. The crowd moved on to the county gaol but were repulsed by gunfire which killed one man and wounded three. There were serious riots in Worcester and Bath, and less serious disturbances in Leicester, Tiverton, Yeovil, Blandford, Sherborne and Exeter. Lord Tankerville, who had voted against the Bill, was attacked in his carriage at Darlington by a 100-strong mob. A double line of men ranged along the main street hurled paving stones, glass bottles and other missiles which they had earlier gathered into small piles. His Lordship and other noble occupants of the carriage escaped serious injury, but they were badly shaken.

3   Cruikshank's 'The Reformers' attack on the Old Rotten Tree'
Illustrated London News

On 10 October the inhabitants of London's Bond Street were thrown into a panic by reports of several thousand rioters hell-bent on booty. All shops were shuttered and the proprietors resisted petitions by demonstrators to put on display emblems of revolution. The following day a crowd rescued a prisoner from three constables. When more police arrived they were pelted into retreat by a mob who took advantage of a heap of macadamised stones in Waterloo Place. A large assembly gathered in Hyde Park. Nearby houses owned by the Duke of Wellington and bishops who had voted against the bill were attacked. The Duke's property was saved by a servant who fired two blunderbusses into the air from an upstairs balcony, although 30 windows were shattered by stones. Constables clashed violently with the crowd in and around Hyde Park. The Marquis of Londonderry, riding on horseback to the house of Lords, was surrounded by 4,000 people. At first he was not recognised but his luck did not hold. As soon as he heard a cry of recognition, he was hit by several pebbles. The Marquis pulled up his horse, drew a brace of pistols and declared that he would shoot anyone who again dared to molest him. The crowd pulled back, allowing him to trot towards Horse Guards, but then decided he was bluffing and followed him. 'The showers of stones were now thicker than ever,' said a witness, 'and one stone, hurled with considerable force, struck the noble marquis immediately over the right temple, cut through his hat, and inflicted a serious wound on his head, which rendered his lordship nearly insensible. The military here interposed, and the marquis was placed in a hackney-coach and conveyed home.'

New police squads from Scotland Yard formed themselves into a line at the end of King Street to protect the House of Commons. A general fight now ensued, in which the police were assisted by several respectable-looking men who used every endeavour to put the mob to the rout. The following day triple rows of policemen flanked the Westminster side of Temple Bar, ready for another attack. Workmen were employed to remove temporary gas-pipes. As dusk fell 400 protesters, mainly boys and vagabonds, rushed from the City and taunted soldiers and police officers with the cry 'Down with the raw lobsters!' The crowd moved towards Charing Cross, 'the whole of them yelling, shouting, groaning and breaking windows in their progress'.

They were charged by a strong body of E Division police who used their staves to rain down blows on heads, shoulders and arms.

By the evening the City was full of a tumultuous throng who stopped all traffic and blocked off Fleet Street. The police station there was rushed several times in attempts to break open the gate. Clashes between stave-wielding police officers and rioters with bottles and brickbats caused many serious injuries. A correspondent noted: 'The mob amused themselves by throwing stones and large pieces of wood among the police in Pickett Place; they obtained these missiles from the new Law Institution at Chancery Lane, the scaffolding at which was broken down and carried off, amidst loud cheers.' A separate crowd went down Piccadilly at a trot but were dispersed by men of D Division. Another carried tricolour flags to Spitalfields where they destroyed a gas lamp and smashed the windows of the local police station and Chapple's fruiterers.

The Duke of Wellington wrote to a friend:

> Matters appear to be going as badly as possible. It may be relied upon that we shall have a revolution. I have never doubted the inclination and disposition of the lower orders of the people. I told you years ago that they were rotten to the core. They are not bloodthirsty, but they are desirous of plunder. They will plunder, annihilate all property in the country. The majority of them will starve, and we shall witness scenes such as have never yet occurred in any part of the world.[2]

Whatever the unruliness of the capital, there was much worse to come in the West.

* * *

The old slaving port of Bristol had a long history of riotous behaviour. In 1709, 200 coalminers raised a riot over the price of bread. In 1714 two people were killed when 500 went on the rampage after Tories attacked Whigs and Dissenters at a political meeting. In 1729, weavers rioted and in one incident stormed the house of manufacturer Stephen Freacham. He fired into the crowd, killing seven people. Soldiers were sent to disperse the rioters and Freacham accidentally shot dead one of them. He only escaped hanging for the murder of the soldier by applying for a pardon. For 20 years up to 1749 there were numerous disturbances over the imposition of turnpikes on the local populace.

Tollbooths were frequently burnt down until the Turnpike Trustees and 50 sailors armed with cutlasses attacked a band of rioters and arrested 28 of them. Two were hanged, five died of smallpox in prison awaiting trial and the remainder were acquitted by sympathetic juries. Four food rioters were killed in 1753 and 50 injured by constables and a troop of the Scots Greys cavalry who charged after five citizens were captured by the mob. And in 1793, rioters destroyed the tollbooth on Bristol Bridge in protest at high charges levied by a private company. The Herefordshire militia fired warning shots over the heads of the crowd but 60-year-old plasterer John Abbot, on his way home, was killed by a stray shot. New tollbooths were erected and these too were destroyed. In a series of stand-offs the Riot Act was read six times. After the last reading soldiers fired, without any other warning, into the crowd, killing ten people, most of them innocent bystanders. The soldiers' commander, Lord Bateman, was given a reward of 10 guineas. What was to occur in response to the blocking of the Reform Bill was graver still.[3]

Local passions had already been inflamed during the passage of the bill because one of its most outspoken opponents in the Commons was the Recorder of Bristol, Sir Charles Wetherall. On 24 October there was a taste of things to come when civil disorder erupted in Bedminster as the Bishop of Bath and Wells, another opponent, arrived to consecrate the new church. On Saturday the 29th Wetherall arrived in Bristol to open the assize court. His carriage, pulled by four greys and flanked by protective outriders, was pelted with stones every yard of his route through the city. The Annual Register reported:

> As the procession moved onward, the crowd continued to increase. In Temple street the windows of the houses were crowded with spectators, and the lower orders of females were particularly vociferous, frequently charging the men with cowardice and want of spirit. In passing from the bridge to High Street one of the constables received a dangerous contusion on the head ...[4]

Wetherall reached the court safely but proceedings were halted due to frequent interruptions from the public galleries. He was driven to the Mansion House in Queen Square under a constant hail of stones, jeers and shouted obscenities.

Once the Recorder was inside lines of constables repeatedly charged the crowd, seeking to pluck out stone-throwers. By then the crowd had swelled to several thousand and some groups of constables were surrounded, disarmed and beaten.

Two troops of the 14th Light Dragoons and a troop of the 3rd Dragoon Guards under the command of Lt. Col. Brereton, a semi-retired officer who lived in the area, were called to the scene to protect the life of Wetherall. The Light Dragoons were known and hated as the 'Bloody Blues' because of their zealousness in quelling previous riots. The cavalry totalled 93 men and the forces of authority could also call on 100 constables and 119 'Specials'. Brereton found the Mansion House under siege. All the windows were smashed, every piece of furniture on the ground floor was broken and rioters were pulling up railings and paving stones around the square. Straw and stacks of firewood were piled against the walls. The Riot Act was read but the Mayor of Bristol, Charles Pinney, would not give Brereton permission to fire into the crowd. Sir Charles escaped ingloriously by scrambling over the rooftops.

The Annual Register reported:

> The soldiers trotted their horses backward and forward amidst the cheers of the mob, but not the slightest disposition was shewn to disperse. The Colonel cautioned them of the consequences which their conduct would infallibly draw upon them. He was everywhere received with the greatest cordiality, and with loud cheers.[5]

At dusk the troopers drew their swords and charged across the square. It was a short, sharp engagement which swiftly cleared the open space. One rioter, Stephen Bush, was left dead on the ground. Troopers pursued some rioters down side street and alleys, slashing at them as they fled, to prevent them reforming. The soldiers and constables withdrew 'for refreshment' and the next morning the mob returned, more determined than ever. This time it was Mayor Pinney who was forced to flee for his life over the rooftops. The rioters broke into the Mansion House and looted its extensive wine cellars. A contemporary report said:

> The result was that they became madly infuriated, and regardless alike of what mischief they committed or what risk they incurred. All ages, of both sexes, were to be seen greedily swallowing the intoxicating liquors, while upon the ground the bodies of scores were to be found dead with drunkenness.[6]

The troopers returned but were reduced to impotent onlookers without orders to fire. The soldiers were pelted with bricks and empty wine bottles and the Light Dragoons – whose hated uniforms inflamed the protesters – were ordered to withdraw. A portion of the mob followed them and on at least three occasions – at St Augustine's Back, College Green and Boar's Head Yard – troopers stopped, turned and fired on their pursuers. At least three rioters were killed and many wounded in these running clashes. Colonel Brereton rode through Queen's Square assuring the crowd that the 'Bloody Blues' would be sent out of the city.

By the evening the Mansion House, Excise Office, Customs House and the fine houses on the north and west sides of the square were stripped of valuables and on fire, the melted lead on their roofs pouring in hellfire streams down the gutters. There were reports of several looters being engulfed in flames which could be seen across the Bristol Channel in Wales. One report noted: 'The customs house was a large building, and the expertise of the wretches in lighting it up proven the destruction of many of them who were ranging the upper apartments. Some of them were seen to drop into the flames, and others in desperation threw themselves from the windows.' Another reported the scene in the Mansion House:

> The apartments in the front rooms [were] occupied by wretches facilitating the destruction of the building by fire. The infatuated creatures pressed forward to the windows and waved their hankerchiefs, in exultation of the final accomplishment of their designs. From the rapidity of the progress of the flames, it is supposed that some were cut off from retreat, and that they thus met with an untimely end.[7]

Householders lining the square were given 30 minutes to clear out by an arsonist band, comprised chiefly of boys. A rioter climbed the statue of King William in the square and fixed a tricolour 'Cap of Liberty' to it on a long pole.

Meanwhile, other rioters, armed with sledgehammers from the nearest blacksmith's, forced their way into Bridewell and Lawford's Gate gaols and released the prisoners before torching the buildings. At New Gaol rioters spent 45 minutes battering a hole in the gate big enough for a boy to squirm through and release the bolt. Around 170 inmates threw away their prison clothes and enthusiastically joined the mob, parading themselves, both men and women, 'almost in a state of nudity' to the delight of their new comrades. The *Annual Register* described the destruction of the prison:

> A black hankerchief was tied to the weathercock on the top of the porter's lodge, over the gateway, as a signal for commencing operations. Immediately dense clouds of smoke issued from every part of the building. The flames were first seen to break out from the tread-mill, which burnt with fury until it was quite consumed. In about an hour the governor's house was completely enveloped in flames; the wings, however, being built almost exclusively of stone and iron, with iron roofs, were but little injured.

The city gallows was thrown into New Cut ditch. Twenty men of the Dragoon Guards under Cornet Kelson watched the crowd for a few minutes but, faced by several thousand, turned and trotted away. Several tollbooths were also devoured by fire.

The Bishop's Palace near the Cathedral was also attacked because of Bishop Gray's opposition to the Reform Bill. He had been forewarned and fled to Stapleton. His armed servants and some city constables held the assailants back with brutal use of their batons. When Brereton arrived he was appalled by the violence being employed by the forces of law and order and warned that if they continued he would ride the constables down. It was not the only time that soldiers restrained the police. On another occasion a trooper warned a policeman that if he didn't stop assaulting protesters he would use his sword on him. Outside the Bishop's Palace the constables heeded the warning and the mob calmed down. Brereton withdrew his troops – and the palace was duly burnt down.

The crowd then turned to the Chapter House and made a bonfire of valuable books and ancient documents. The main cathedral building was broken into but the mob were held back by the Sub-Sacrist, Mr Phillips, who waved an iron bar and told them they should be protecting their heritage, not destroying it.

Isambard Kingdom Brunel, having secured the Clifton suspension bridge contract, was celebrating with friends in the city and got caught up in the events of that night. At one point he helped to rescue the Town Hall's silver plate from fire and pillage by carrying it across the roof of the building.

The *Annual Register* described a hellfire night:

> All seemed panic-struck. And but few cared except for their own personal safety. The city seemed given up to plunder; young fellows, in parties of

four, five and six, repaired to liquor-shops and public houses, knocked at the doors, and demanded drink or blood. When morning dawned, the flames were subsiding but the appearance of Queen's Square was appalling in the extreme. Numerous buildings were reduced to a heap of smoking ruins, and others were momentarily falling in; while around lay several of the rioters, in the last stages of senseless intoxication, and with countenances more resembling fiends than men.[8]

On Monday 31 October the anarchy turned into a pitched battle. Mayor Pinney finally equipped Brereton with the order to take the most vigorous, effective and decisive measures to quell the riot. Brereton, whose sympathies appear to have been mixed, still could not bring himself to sanction slaughter. It was left to Major Mackworth to order the attack. The troopers swept across Queen Square like a scythe, leaving slashed and trampled bodies in their wake. It was later claimed that over 250 people were killed or injured in this charge alone, although there are few contemporary eye-witness accounts. One report said: 'Nothing was to be seen on every side but women and children, running and screaming in every direction, many were severely wounded and some killed.'

The 14th Dragoons, who the day before had been sent to Keynsham by Brereton to placate the mob, were recalled, and more reinforcements came from Gloucester. Hundreds more were trotting towards the city under the command of General Sir Richard Jackson. The rioters, reeling from the carnage in Queen's Square, dispersed in every direction and some were pursued by the cavalry. Charles Greville, clerk of the Privy Council, wrote: 'More punishment was inflicted by them than has been generally known, and some hundreds were killed or severely wounded by the sabre. One body of dragoons pursued a rabble of colliers into the country, and covered the fields and roads with the bodies of wounded wretches, making a severe example of them.'

Towards that evening the pavement in Bristol's King Street was forced up by the heat of brandy burning in the vaults beneath.

The full attrition rate will never be known for sure. It was reckoned that up to 10,000 people were involved in the rioting. Estimates of the total death toll went as high as 500, according to Radicals. The Government, with its own agenda, claimed that the dead and wounded did not exceed 100. Of those killed, according to an official report, six were burnt, two were shot, two died of sword cuts and two from excessive drinking; of the wounded, ten were injured by shots, 48 by swords, two from drinking and 34 from other causes. The truth must lie between the two extreme estimates. Some of Bristol's finest buildings and around 100 houses owned by unpopular grandees were destroyed.

Colonel Brereton was court-martialled, charged with failing to do his duty, by being too cautious and compassionate during the early stages of the rioting, sending the Blues out of the city to placate the rioters, and failing to turn out the local militia to protect the city. On the fourth day of the hearing Brereton shot himself.

The anger of the Establishment was turned on the civil authorities in Bristol. Greville wrote: 'Nothing could exceed the ferocity of the populace, the imbecility of the magistracy, or the good conduct of the troops.'[9] The Reverend J.L. Jackson wrote: 'The magistrates, police and constables were wholly inefficient. It is a fact that the Bishop's Palace was plundered and fired by not more than 10 men and a rabble of mere boys.'[10] Mayor Charles Pinney was put on trial for neglect of duty and acquitted.

Five rioters were sentenced to death, but one was reprieved on the grounds of mental deficiency. The remaining four were hanged above the gate of the Old Gaol on the New Cut where the gallows had been dumped by the mob. A further 88 – all local people rather than outside agitators – were transported or imprisoned.

Charles Greville recorded his own verdict which was widely circulated within the Government:

> The country was beginning to slumber after the fatigues of Reform, when it was rattled up by the business of Bristol, which for brutal ferocity and wanton, unprovoked violence may vie with some of the worst scenes of the French Revolution, and may act to damper our national pride. The spirit which produced these atrocities was generated by Reform, but no pretext was afforded for their actual commission; it was a premature outbreaking of the thirst for plunder, and longing after havoc and destruction, which is the essence of Reform in the mind of the mob.[11]

He added: 'In London there would probably have been great uproar and riot, but fortunately Melbourne, who was frightened to death at the Bristol affair, made such provision of military force in addition to the civil power that the malcontents were paralysed.'

*   *   *

The Reform Riots were not over, however. At Bath a mob tried to prevent the Yeomanry leaving their city to help in crushing the Bristol rioters. The inn where the captain of the corps stayed was partially demolished. The Bishop of Exeter complained that inflammatory leaflets were circulating, calling on the people of his city to 'arm themselves and emulate the heroic acts of the Bristol men'.[12] A troop of Yeomanry were stationed on the bridge at Wareham to block the progress of a Poole mob who intended to sack Lord Eldon's home at Encombe. In Coventry a factory was burnt down and the military called in.

At Worcester on 3 November a crowd attacked the Bishop's Palace but were deterred by 25 Special Constables. The Riot Act was read but about 200 'itinerant thimble-and-peamen and low thieves excited the mob', according to the official report. Soldiers were summoned who at first merely paraded up and down the streets. When the mob started pelting them they waded in using the flats of their swords. The rioters set up a defensive position in Bull Court, which could only be approached down six stone steps which men and women defended with missiles. Two troopers were ordered to fire down the court but one of them preferred to charge it. His horse first refused to descend the steps, to shouts of 'Hurrah!' from the defenders. On the second attempt the horse negotiated the steps 'with the safety of a cat or a dog' and others followed. This so suprised the mob that they retreated in confusion. It was a moment of farce which capped such tragic events elsewhere.

*   *   *

A new Reform Bill was prepared in secret by Lord John Russell, author of the earlier drafts, and the ink was still damp when he presented it to the House of Commons. On 26 March 1832 the Lords again threatened to reject it. In May Earl Grey asked the King to create a host of new Whig peers in order to get the Reform Bill through the House of Lords. William refused and Grey, together with his Government, resigned. William asked the Duke of Wellington to form a new Tory administration. Wellington did his best but several prominent Tories, most notably Sir Robert Peel, refused to join a Cabinet set up to block the wishes of the vast majority of British people. Peel warned that if the Reform Bill was again killed there was a real danger of civil war. Moreover, William's own early popularity with the people had been severely undermined. William was forced to ask Grey to re-form his Government. He did so and this time William had no option but to give him a large number of new Whig peers. The Tories now knew they were beaten and Wellington, anxious to avoid further bloodshed, ordered his party's peers to either vote for the bill or abstain. Over 200 Tories were absent when the bill passed through the House of Lords on 7 June 1832.

The terms of the Great Reform Act, as it became known, were considered far-reaching at the time but now appear modest. Voting in the boroughs was restricted to men who occupied homes with an annual rental value of £10, and there were property qualifications in rural areas which kept the poor well and truly excluded from the democratic process. Broadly, only one in seven adult males had the vote. Fifty-six rotten boroughs returning 111 MPs were abolished and 30 boroughs with less than 4,000 inhabitants lost one MP each. But there were still vast differences in constituency sizes. Thirty-five seats were left with less than 300 electors, whereas Liverpool had a constituency of over 11,000. On the other hand, 44 seats were distributed to 22 larger towns, including Birmingham, Manchester, Leeds, Sheffield and the new London metropolitan districts.

It was a start, albeit a hard-won one.

7
The Merthyr Rising

'Oh Lord, what an injustice'

John Hughes, an old soldier who had seen six battles in the service of the British Army, lay on a cot in his friend's house. He had been shot in the centre of the back by a Highlander and the ball had emerged just above his navel. He told witnesses that he had been running away when the soldier took aim. He added that he had never been wounded before and 'should have died a better death'.

He expired 90 minutes later, one of the many casualties of an extraordinary battle barely remembered outside Wales.

*   *   *

The Principality was not immune from the troubles and dissent which swept through Britain in the fight for social and political reform. In 1793 several hundred copper and colliery workers from the Rhondda Valley marched on Swansea demanding higher wages to counter the exorbitant price of grain, cheese and butter. Three Merthyr men were sentenced to death for rioting in 1801. There was further widespread unrest over the Corn Laws. And at the Abbey Works in Neath during the 1820s, 50 men were sacked for trying to form a union.

But broadly Wales escaped much of the tumult which saw troops and protesters clashing bloodily on the streets of English towns and cities. One factor was the influence of the Calvinist Methodists who urged all church members to avoid such 'devilish' activity as union-forming and public protest. Robert Jones, writing in the *Mirror of the Times* in 1820, stated: 'There has been riot and commotion in England, Scotland

and Ireland, because they neither feared God nor honoured the King ... but our nation remains wonderfully faithful to the Government in all troubles'.

That was to change dramatically in 1831 when a popular protest over unjust work practices and living conditions saw the red flag of revolution raised. On its staff was impaled a loaf of bread. John Davies described it as 'the most ferocious and bloody event in the history of industrialised Britain'.[1]

The great depression of 1829 had hit South Wales hard, causing mass unemployment and spiralling debts among both working men and trades people. At Merthyr ironmaster William Crawshay lowered wages and the crisis was felt by local shopkeepers, while the debtors' court precipitated the widespread confiscation of working men's property. No cheap stick of furniture was safe from the bailiffs.

On 1 May 1831 a demonstration demanding compensation was led by a Cyfartha miner, Thomas Llewelyn. A breakaway mob of workers, traders and townspeople freed the inmates of the local prison and marched to Aberdare. At the same time, a few miles away at Hirwaun, when the court seized a cart belonging to local man Lewis Lewis, miners and ironworkers joined the protest.

The crowd, many full of cheap beer, swarmed into the streets of Merthyr. They raided shops and houses to snatch previously confiscated goods and return them to their owners. The mob appeared to disperse during the night, but on the 2nd they assembled in considerable numbers and paraded the streets throughout the day. In the evening they marched to the house of a Mr Coffin, an official at the debtors' court, and demanded the books belonging to it. Coffin refused and appeals for calm by magistrates standing on chairs to be seen and heard failed to cool the temper of the crowd. They broke into Coffin's house, smashed all the windows and carried off every item of furniture, which they burnt, as an act of revenge, on a bonfire in the middle of the street. The magistrates, by now panic-stricken, sent for an 80-strong troop of 93rd Regiment Scots Highlanders stationed at Brecon Barracks to restore order. The result was carnage.

The soldiers arrived on Friday the 3rd at about noon on an oppressively hot and thundery day and marched to the Castle Inn, in the town centre, where the magistrates had taken lodgings together for safety and where the town's Special Constables and ironmasters also gathered. Outside, according to witnesses, 'a large mob, a great proportion of which was armed with bludgeons, some with the handles of mandrels, others with parts of miner's pickaxes; a man amongst them had a red flag on a pole'. Some estimates put the total crowd as high as 10,000. They included ironworkers, colliers, women, children and curious bystanders and they massed around their red flag. They demanded better wages, the return of confiscated property and cheaper food. Crawshay the ironmaster came to a window and did little to ease the tension by shouting: 'So help me God, I will not listen to people coming in arms in this violent manner.' Within hours an erroneous report spread across the Valleys that Crawshay had fired a pistol into the crowd.[2]

A party of soldiers was ordered inside the tavern and the remainder kept guard outside, where they were supplied with lunch and liquid refreshment. By mid afternoon both sides had drunk well but the protesters were hungry. Their apparent leader, Lewis Lewis 'the huntsman', threatened the magistrates that unless they were given something to eat as well as the soldiers, within an hour they would kill every person in the inn. Lewis took out his watch to mark the time. When some bread was offered the crowd roared: 'Cheese with the bread! Cheese with the bread!' It was a symbolic rather than a practical demand. After 50 minutes Lewis repeated the death threats. When that met with no further response, Lewis was hauled by eager hands up an iron lamp-post and told the crowd in Welsh: 'We are met here to have our wages raised, instead of which the masters have brought the soldiers against us. Now, boys, if you are of the same mind as I am, let us fall upon them and take their arms away. Off with their guns!' A volley of missiles, some thrown from rooftops opposite, shattered the inn's windows. A heavy swell of men moved forward, as if pressed by those behind. An observer likened it to 'a great wave of the sea'.[3]

The crowd began to press upon the soldiers left outside, pushing them against the wall and jamming them so closely that their muskets were useless and they were hard-pressed to defend themselves. The mob then began to snatch the soldiers' muskets and sidearms. In the confused, close-quarter struggle at least two rioters were bayoneted to death and many were wounded on both sides. One soldier was hit so hard with a captured musket that the stock broke. A Highlander was twice pierced by a bayonet. A witness at the subsequent inquest,

William Roberts, was standing in a nearby doorway and reported seeing 'three or four upon a soldier, wrestling for their muskets'.

He continued:

> Four or five of the soldiers were upon the ground and at the same time a volley of stones, cinders, sticks, was sent against the windows. No firing had taken place at this moment. There was a conflict on the steps, the mob three or four times making their way into the inn, and being as often repulsed by two soldiers in the passage, and the special constables behind them. The soldiers in the passage had been able to bring down their muskets to the charge; a firing commenced from the windows above, but not 'til several of the soldiers had been struck down. Someone in the passage then gave the alarm that the mob were coming in at the rear of the house.

Roberts led an officer and three soldiers into the yard behind the inn.

> The yard is very narrow, the mob had by then advanced half way up it, and were within a very few yards of the back door; they fell back a little and then assailed the soldiers with a shower of stones and brick-bats; the soldiers fired, two or three of the mob fell and then drew back, and were driven through the stable-yard into the street by the end of the house.[4]

Roberts then heard that a portion of the mob was approaching from nearby fields. He went to see and came face to face with Lewis Lewis, who was holding a captured musket. Lewis called on his comrades to stop and stand their ground but by then it had turned into a series of running battles. Soldiers pursued rioters through the streets, and it was here that Hughes was shot in the back. Some did turn and fire before running on. Others mounted ambushes of soldiers in the confused battle. John Petherick, one of the Castle Inn's defenders, saw a rioter aim a musket directly at him, but it misfired. In the yard behind the inn the fighting was so close that a rioter smashed a soldier with a hand-held stone before he was shot. Another group snatched a soldier and dragged him 100 yards, beating him with the butt of his own musket. The soldier escaped and ran back to the inn. An invalid, Rowland Thomas, was by chance passing the spot and picked up the Highlander's cap. Another soldier shot him.

The main body of the crowd had run in panic as the first volleys of musket balls from the inn's upstairs windows tore into their packed ranks. But determined men, now armed with at least 30 captured muskets, rallied. They charged the doorway and windows of the inn several times, and more were cut down by volleys from within. Others broke into Thomas Lewis's store and demanded powder and shot. The terrified storekeeper could provide the powder, but all he could offer as ammunition was marbles. They took them and, crouched upon high ground known as the Tip, kept up regular sniping on the rear of the inn and its defenders. When they ran out of shot after several minutes, they fired the marbles.

In the Castle Inn one officer, Major Falls, was wounded and appeared demented. He screamed at his men to cease firing. A lone rioter was seen in a field firing at them. The soldiers returned fire and the man fell. He was the last casualty that afternoon.

Some weeks later one of the magistrates, Evan Thomas, wrote:

> The circumstances and duration of the conflict with the soldiers were such as seldom, I believe, never occurred in England before. It is certainly difficult to think of anything comparable. The determination and sheer blind courage of many in the crowd were matched by the bravery and discipline of the soldiers, who no doubt shared their desperation.

By the end of the day 24 rioters lay dead and scores more were wounded. Sixteen of the soldiers were wounded, six of them severely. Eight bodies – six men, a woman and a boy of about twelve – were removed from the front of the Castle Inn and laid in the coach-house to the rear of the premises. Many of the most badly injured were carried off by their comrades, or dragged themselves away, to die later in hideaways. The *Cambrian* reported: 'The dead have been buried in the most quiet and silent ways by their friends ... Bodies are daily found in the fields and hedges of the place ...'[5] It later emerged that one woman was killed by a musket ball as she sat in her room knitting. A pauper was killed on his way to collect his Poor Relief.

At the inquest on John Hughes and others the jury unanimously delivered a verdict of 'justifiable homicide' by soldiers unknown. They were heavily swayed by the evidence that no shots were fired before several soldiers had been beaten to the ground and their weapons stolen.[6]

The soldiers had not won, however, and had suffered numerous casualties which forced them to retire. Anthony Hill, the High Sheriff of Glamorgan, galloped from the Castle Inn to gather reinforcements. At Cardiff he despatched letters to every commanding officer within reach. He spurred his horse on to Newport and persuaded the senior officer to cram 28 men into coaches to speed up the Valley to aid their comrades in Merthyr. He then headed for London where he gave Lord Melbourne a breathless report, warning that there were up to 150,000 working people within a 14-mile radius of Merthyr and all could join the revolt. When the Royal Glamorgan Militia, the 3rd Dragoons and 150 men of the 98th Foot based in Plymouth converged at Merthyr, the town was largely empty. Even the defenders of the Castle Inn had pulled back to a more defensible position at Penydarren House, a mansion set well back from the main north–south road.

As their friends and relations succumbed to their wounds, the protest leaders fanned through much of North Glamorgan calling men to arms. They raided shops for pikes and axes, farms for fowling-pieces, and stores for ammunition. Within a few days their arsenal grew to over 200 firearms. The hard core, mainly men from Crawshay's ironworks re-formed in a camp near Cefn Coed further up the valley. There they defied all authority, drilling with newly acquired arms. Evan Thomas, chairman of the Glamorgan magistrates, noted: 'The Ringleaders of the Tumult up to Friday were mainly daring and profligate characters, but on the Saturday they were joined by most respectable workmen as to character ... men of good and quiet character earning 20 shillings a week.' The men organised themselves into detachments with their own commanders and flags. More pikes were manufactured in caves. They agreed an effective system of signalling. Road-blocks were set up, cutting the Brecon and Swansea roads. Foraging parties were sent out. The Marquis of Bute declared: 'The workmen to the number of some thousands are in a much more organized state than had been supposed.' The spectre of rebellion seemed very real.

The forces of the King were not idle either, but hampered by unknown terrain and a sullenly hostile local populace. Their main task was to keep the Cardiff road open, maintain Penydarren House as the temporary seat of Glamorgan governance, and supply themselves. But the Swansea Yeomanry suffered a disaster.

When the call for help came from Merthyr, the Yeomanry's horses were out to grass on the Gower peninsula. Their commander, Major Penrice, nevertheless set off at once with 34 men, telling the rest to follow as quickly as they could. Penrice's party was spotted long before he saw the enemy. The Yeomen entered the Defiles at Waun Coed Meyrick, a warren of slagheaps. Workmen appeared on the tips and appeared to be friendly. Penrice stepped forward with a companion.

The officer suddenly found himself surrounded by armed men, a musket pointed at his right ear and pistols aimed at his chest. His troop immediately surrendered. They were stripped of pistols, swords and carbines and sent back to Neath in disgrace.

The ignominious defeat sent shockwaves through the military and civil authorities. Colonel Brotherton, the new military commander at Merthyr, suspected treason by the Yeomanry. He wrote of their 'vile conduct ... not a single plea or excuse in extenuation ... more a willing than a compulsory surrender ...they were influenced by a worst feeling than intimidation'. Penrice claimed he had been surrounded by 1,200 armed men. Few believed that there were more than 50, not all of them armed.

However, regular troops, militia and loyal armed citizens were gathering in strength around Penydarren House. Negotiations were opened between Crawshay and the other ironmasters and the protesters. In the shadows solicitors, informers and officials aimed to break the unity of the workmen by offering separate deals. On the Sunday a great crowd marched on Cyfartha Castle, cheering and brandishing the captured Yeomanry weapons. The troops stood to arms as various deputations argued. The multitude were clearly divided between those who wanted to accept vague offers of wage increases, and those who wanted to fight on. Many began to slip quietly away. Suddenly, when the uprising appeared to be at its strongest, the initiative swung back in favour of the authorities.

With hindsight the ringleaders failed to co-ordinate the Merthyr revolt with strikes and other protest actions in Monmouthshire and the Neath and Swansea valleys. The initial enthusiasm of working people was also tempered at Sunday services when all the ministers, Welsh and English, preached sermons against rebellion.

On Monday 6 June over 500 men and boys did cross into Monmouthshire to march on the works at Nant-y-Glo and down the valley to Abersychan to recruit followers. They attracted crowds of 10,000 people and headed back towards Merthyr. Lt. Col. Richard Morgan of the Royal Glamorgan Militia decided to stop them linking up with the armed men at Cefn Coed and mobilised a strike force of 110 Highlanders, 53 militia men and over 300 Yeomanry. They met the oncoming crowd at Dowlais Top and the Riot Act was read. After a tense stand-off Morgan ordered his men to advance with fixed bayonets.

The crowd slowly gave way, clambering over stone walls lining the road. Some did filter through to Cefn but most went home.

There was still some fight left in the rebels. That morning the Yeomanry, determined to restore their honour, moved into Merthyr, clearing the streets of crowds and disarming men with clubs. But watchers at Cyfartha reported seeing vast numbers of men exercising in line with the muskets of the 93rd and the carbines of the Yeomanry. Most ominously, two black flags - the symbol of 'No quarter' - appeared at the Fdaren toll-gate. What happened next has never been fully explained.

At lunchtime the entire movement collapsed. Rebels began to disperse in large numbers. Some could be seen burying or breaking their weapons. The hard core of intransigents argued fiercely amongst each other. The military commanders took advantage of the unexpected situation and sent out strong patrols to break up the remaining groups on the hillside. Two rebel leaders were captured. During the night huge police raids swept through Merthyr, netting 14 known militants. The revolt petered out as first the forge and furnace men, then the miners and colliers, streamed back to work.

The manhunt continued into Tuesday and William Williams, who had carried the red flag, was caught in a poor relief queue. By that night 18 of the most notorious insurgents were in custody. Lewis Lewis escaped a search party in Hirwaun but was tracked down by two constables a few hours later in the woods of Hendrebolon near his home. They captured him after a ferocious struggle. Constables spent several weeks scouring as far afield as Carmarthenshire and Pembrokeshire.

Retribution was swift but, given the times, not that severe. The Glamorgan Summer Assizes opened at Cardiff on 9 July. A total of 28 people, including two women, were charged; 14 of them for raids on houses, eleven for seizing arms from soldiers, and others for assaults outside Merthyr. Lewis Lewis was sentenced to death but that was commuted after Constable John Thomas testified that he had stopped the mob beating him to death in the riot outside Coffin's house. Instead he was transported for life to Australia. David Thomas, Thomas Vaughan and David Hughes were also found guilty, and all four set off for New South Wales on the convict ship *John*. But others were found not guilty and, with one exception, Mr Justice Bosanquet halted the remaining trials. The exception gave the Welsh working-class movement its first martyr.[7]

During the fighting a Highlander called Donald Black was stabbed in the leg but could not identify his assailant. Two local men, James Abbot and his workmate James Drew, came forward and claimed that they had seen Richard Lewis, also known as Dic Penderyn, stab the soldier through 'the thick part of his thigh, somewhere above the knee'. Abbot said that he had taken Black into the brew-house, which served as a clearing station, bleeding like a pig. Abbott 'had no the slightest doubt as to the stab being given by Richard Lewis'. It was said that Abbot had sworn revenge on the defendant after losing a fight with him, and Drew was merely supporting his friend. Others said that the assailant was wearing a brown jacket, while Lewis was wearing a blue one. Still more witnesses claimed, but not until after his trial for attempted murder, that Lewis was nowhere near the scene when Black fell wounded.

On the eve of his execution Richard Lewis wrote to his sister:

> I ask you to come at once to fetch my body, since there is no likelihood of anything else at present. Come to Philip Lewis and get him to bring down a cart tonight and as many men as he can manage to bring with him. I believe the Lord has forgiven me my divers sins and transgressions, but since I am accused, I am not guilty and for that I have reason to be grateful.

Dic Penderyn was hanged in Cardiff gaol on 31 July 1831 despite appeals for clemency signed by many thousands. The last words he spoke on the scaffold were: 'Oh Lord, what an injustice.'[8] A popular Welsh ballad ran:

> I saw the Merthyr riots,
> And the great oppression of the workers;
> And some of the soldiers wounded,
> But dear heaven! The worst trick
> Was the hanging of Dic Penderyn.

Forty years later, Ieuan Parker of Cwmafan, who had emigrated to America, confessed on his death-bed to the stabbing of Black.

The Merthyr Rising and the martyrdom of Dic Penderyn is still remembered in Wales, but even at the time both made little impact on English popular opinion. That was, and remains, a matter of great resentment. A Mrs Arbuthnot, underplaying earlier events across the English border, wrote in her diary:

> [H]ere has been a great riot in Wales and the soldiers have killed 24 people. When two or three were killed at Manchester, it was called the Peterloo Massacre and the newspapers for weeks wrote it up as the most outrageous and wicked proceeding ever heard of. But that was in Tory times; now this Welsh riot is scarcely mentioned.'[9]

At Westminster, however, Lord Melbourne recognised the severity of the Welsh riots. He called for repression of all workers' organisations as 'unlawful assemblages of armed individuals' and said that South Wales was 'the worst and most formidable district in the kingdom.'[10]

Later he confided to a friend that 'the affair we had there in 1831 was the most like a fight of anything that took place'.

*   *   *

Peace did not come to the Valleys. The hanging of Dic Penderyn and the repression of embryonic trade unions forced desperate men to take desperate measures. In Monmouthshire a shadowy group calling themselves Scotch Cattle declared war on the ironmasters and colliery owners. They destroyed property in the night, threatened gaffers and intimidated ordinary workers who refused to condone their tactics. It was a short reign of terror in the Valleys, and was brought to an end with the hanging of one of their leaders, Edward Morgan. He was not considered a martyr.

By then the focus of dissent across the UK had switched to the rights of workers to organise. A miner in Merthyr told his magistrate: 'My Lord, the union is so important to me that I would live on sixpence a week rather than give it up.'

8

The Chartists and the Newport Insurrection

'An excellent republic'

During the 1830s Chartism was born out of failed movements. The working class had massively supported the largely middle-class campaign for the Reform Act – but still found themselves without a vote. The Whig administration, in power from 1830 to 1840, was a bitter disappointment, focusing as it did on aid to the more affluent at a time of economic crisis. The 1833 Factory Act regulated child labour but not adult hours and, in any case, applied only to the textile industry. The 1834 Poor Law Amendment Act reduced poor rates and forced more families into the hated workhouses. Resistance to it failed. Early trade unions, including Robert Owen's Grand National Consolidated Trade Union which gathered 500,000 members, failed due to short-term aims which set groups of workers against each other. The Tolpuddle Martyrs were transported when they sought to unionise. Employers organised themselves into mutual assistance societies to root out unions in their workplaces. Taxes continued to place a higher burden on the poor than on the rich. The Corn Laws kept food prices artificially high, but Parliamentary attempts to repeal them failed. And, crucially, the economic slump combined with a series of poor harvests meant that for most workers strike action was not a realistic option.

That slump was born out of the Whig administration's economic incompetence. Between 1836 and 1868, 63 banks crashed in England. The subsequent drop in investment caused high unemployment at a time of high food prices. Financial panic in America, when President Andrew

Jackson refused to re-charter the Bank of the United States, sparked a further crisis in British industry because much bullion had been invested across the Atlantic. The result was even higher unemployment.

The cradle of Chartism was the London Working Men's Association, set up in 1836, which appealed to respectable skilled craftsmen. Its secretary was William Lovett, a mild-mannered Cornish cabinet-maker who believed that political and social equality could be achieved by legal redress, self-help and education. Aged 36, his fisherman father drowned before he was born and his mother ensured a strict Methodist upbringing. He had come to national prominence five years earlier when he refused to be drawn for service in the London Militia, adopting the slogan 'No Vote, No Musket.' Robert Gammage, an active member of the Association, wrote of him: 'Possessed of a clear and masterly intellect and great powers of application, everything that he attempted was certain of accomplishment, and, though not by any means an orator, he was in matters of business more useful to the movement than those who were gifted with finer powers of speech.'[1]

Lovett was heavily influenced by Robert Owen. Together with William Place, a master tailor, he drew up the People's Charter. It had six key aims: annual general elections, universal suffrage for men, secret ballots at elections, the abolition of the property qualification for MPs, the payment of MPs to allow working men to stand, and equally sized constituencies in terms of electorate. Educated and politically mature working men flocked to the Charter. Meetings in support of it were held at Kersal Moor, Manchester and Hartshead Moor, Leeds, in 1838. The Birmingham Political Union was revived and helped to launch it nationwide in 1839 when the first Chartist Convention was held with the declared aim of organising a national petition and forcing it through Parliament. It met in London on 4 February with 53 delegates, although the number meeting at any one time never exceeded 50 in order to stay within the draconian laws still in force. Half were from London, eight were from Birmingham and 20 were from the industrial North. The meeting, which opened with prayers from a clergyman-delegate, was judged a 'sober, dignified' affair.

One visitor wrote:

We left the National Assembly Hall impressed with a very high admiration of the business-like, quiet and respectable manner in which all their proceedings were carried on, and the spirit which pervaded the assembly. It was evident that a class of elderly, bald-headed men, of whom one of the delegates from Lancashire may be mentioned as a good specimen, are the brains of the Convention, and direct everything except its tongue. The tongue, however, was always an unruly member, and they have provided against this as well as they can by resolving that they will not collectively be held answerable for what any member may say.[2]

The Convention quickly became bogged down in endless arguments about aims and tactics. Some, such as George Julian Harney, advocated a general strike if Parliament rejected the petition. Others called for patience. The age-old dilemma of when violence is justified to combat injustice was aired ad nauseam. In the militant North patience wore thin. There had already been reports of Newcastle-upon-Tyne ironworkers manufacturing weapons, of arming meetings in Leeds, of murdering the 'tyrants'. The *Northern Star,* a radical publication taken over by the demagogue Feargus O'Connor, preached near-revolution if the Chartist aims were not met. He was the self-appointed leader of the Physical Force Chartists who spoke in lurid terms of being ready to 'die for the cause'[3] and scorned the peaceful tactics of Lovett and his compatriots. In a speech at Manchester O'Connor proposed a date, 29 September, for violent action if Parliament refused to grant every point in the Charter. Sir Charles Napier, despite having some sympathy for the Chartists, was put in charge of 6,000 troops in the Northern district and charged with maintaining law and order.[4]

On 7 May 1839 the great petition was ready. It was said to be three miles long with 1.2 million signatures, although some were undoubtedly bogus. More mass meetings followed and the authorities were alarmed at reports that a million men had gathered at Kersal Moor on 25 May.

That was the calm period. On 14 June the Birmingham MP Thomas Attwood, a banker and founder of the Political Union, introduced the Charter to Parliament where it languished without debate. There were disturbances in Birmingham's Bull Ring as the Convention conducted its own heated debate. On 12 July Attwood and John Fielden, MP for Oldham, proposed that the Commons should consider the petition. Disraeli backed their appeal. The motion was duly defeated by 235 votes to 46.[5] The result was pandemonium.

The Convention itself collapsed when a motion for a general strike was defeated. Its leadership were divided and indecisive, its membership shared feelings of hurt, betrayal and anger. William Lovett was arrested and imprisoned for twelve months for seditious libel, it being alleged that he had described the Metropolitan Police as a 'bloodthirsty and unconstitutional force'. Later he wrote of his ordeal:

> I was locked up in a dark cell, about nine feet square, the only air admitted into it being through a small grating over the floor, and in one corner there was a pailful of filth left by the last occupants, the smell of which was overpowering. There was a bench fixed against the wall on which to sit down, but the walls were literally covered with water, and the place so damp and cold, that I was obliged to keep walking round and round, like a horse in an apple-mill, to keep anything like life within me.[6]

Chartism itself was on the verge of disintegration. Its leaders had managed to exercise control while there seemed some hope in the political processes, but the Commons vote killed that hope. Local demands for direct action were now reaching fever pitch. Violent insurrection seemed inevitable. In Monmouthshire, it proved to be so.

* * *

The Chartist Movement gained strong support in the Welsh industrial valleys, especially amongst Irish immigrant miners and ironworkers. One of their firebrand leaders, Henry Vincent, issued a call to arms in April 1839: 'I could not help thinking of the defensible nature of the country in the case of foreign invasion. A few thousand armed men on the hills could successfully defend them. Wales would make an excellent republic.'[7]

Such fiery talk found ready ears amongst working men who toiled underground while their well-fed masters enjoyed the fruits of their labour. William Jones wrote of Merthyr, 'where black beings dwell, amidst fire and smoke, who dive into deep caverns, where opportunities are afforded them to concoct their treasonable designs against the inhabitants of the upper world'.[8]

Later in April Chartists armed with pistols, pikes and bludgeons forced their way into the Trewythen Arms at Llanidloes to rescue comrades previously arrested for rioting. They turned out the landlord and his family, ransacked the inn, attacked police officers and 'ran a spike through the hat of the resident magistrate'. The *Cambrian* reported that the Montgomeryshire Militia were ordered to stand to arms and, if necessary, the South Salopian Yeomanry 'will be instantly marched to the neighbourhood'.[9] The Lord Lieutenant of Monmouthshire called for a division of the 'gallant 29th' from Bristol. In May large numbers of Tredegar miners had given strike notice ahead of a Chartist demonstration to be held at Duke's Town, five miles away. They urged the unemployed to join them. The newspaper predicted serious disturbances and acting magistrate Samuel Homfray banned the sale of alcohol on the day of the demonstration. Any riotous intentions were dispelled by the arrival of troopers.[10]

Meanwhile the pit owners and ironmasters were organising their own fight-back. Crawshay Bailey, the ironmaster of Dowlais in the Merthyr district, fortified his mansion against attack from his own workforce. He chaired an anti-Chartist meeting where speakers contrasted 'the happy, well-fed, well-housed working classes of Britain' with those of such countries as Canada or France where 'revolution or Roman Catholicism or laziness or dishonesty had caused butchery and inhumanity'. Such a rosy picture directly contradicted that painted in a Government Commission report into life in the Valleys. One Commissioner said: 'I regard the degraded condition of the people of Monmouthshire as entirely the fault of their employers, who give them far less tendance and care than they bestow on their cattle ...'

The working people of South Wales put their trust in a number of Chartist zealots who, like Henry Vincent, were now openly advocating armed revolution. Vincent was by now languishing in prison, but others of like mind included John Frost, Hugh Williams, Charles Jones, Zephaniah Williams and John Rees. Several rioters from Llanidloes were sentenced to a lifetime's transportation and there were sporadic protests across the Valleys. The Chartist leadership, possibly hoping to foment more widespread agitation, called a monster rally at Newport, on the edge of the South Wales coalfields on 4 November 1839. The outcome was bloody.

An estimated 5,000 men, many armed, approached Newport from different directions in three columns led by John Frost, a 55-year-old local draper and former mayor of Newport who had attended the National Convention, Zephaniah Williams and William Jones. Frost, fanatical and brave, was certainly the overall leader. His motives for such drastic, doomed actions, are unclear. It is said that he was under the impression that if he could start a revolt in South Wales, a similar uprising would spread across the North of England under the leadership of Feargus O'Connor. He was mistaken. O'Connor had already left to visit Ireland.

The winter weather was against the adventure from the start. Jones's column got lost in a heavy rainstorm and never arrived. Williams's column was largely dispersed as the men tramped through the pitch-black night. Only Frost's column made the journey intact, many hours late, and headed for the Westgate Hotel. The authorities knew the route in advance and a small detachment of troopers were waiting for the marchers.[11]

What happened next will always be a matter for controversy, but it was claimed that someone within the drenched and footsore ranks of the Chartists fired a pistol at the soldiers. The troops fired one disciplined, well-aimed volley into the crowd. Within seconds 24 men were lying dead and many more wounded. Some Chartists hid in the yards and outbuildings and the soldiers fired at random. 'Soon there was a scene,' said a witness, 'dreadful beyond expression – the groans of the dying – the shrieks of the wounded, the pallid, ghostly countenances and the bloodshot eyes of the dead, in addition to the shattered windows and the passages deep in blood.' Shocked and bewildered, the crowd dispersed in all directions, heading for the relative safety of the hills they knew so well. Another 125, including many injured, never made it and were arrested in a sweep by soldiers, police officers and the henchmen of the vengeful bosses.

A law report suggested that the marchers intended to arrive in Newport in the early hours but were delayed by the appalling weather:

> They were armed with guns, pistols, pikes, swords and heavy clubs. When they entered the town, their first enquiry was for the military, and where they were stationed; and being informed that a small detachment of them were stationed at the Westgate Hotel, the mob forced in front of it, and immediately commenced an attack by firing through the windows into the house. The military (about 30 soldiers of the 45th Regiment) under the direction of the Mayor, Mr Thomas Phillips, promptly returned the fire; and in a very short time several of the rioters were deprived of life, and lay weltering in blood to the dismay of the survivors, who very soon retreated in great disorder.[12]

The Mayor was wounded by a gunshot in the left arm and a cut to the right side, while a sergeant, a private and two shopkeepers were also

4   The attack on Westgate Hotel, Newport
Illustrated London News

injured and several Special Constables received scratches. The *Annual Register* recorded: 'The Mayor, who acted with much coolness and intrepidity, read the riot act, amongst showers of bullets, before he ordered the military to fire.' Witnesses from within the crowd either claimed no shots were fired before the soldiers' volley, or there were one or two aimed at windows. The *Register* continued: 'The bodies of many rioters were found in the streets and in the fields. Their dress and appearance indicated them to be working men in full employ; as, indeed, the Welsh miners are generally.'[13]

A £100 reward for the capture of John Frost was issued but within hours he was found at the home of his friend and printer, Partridge, supping on bread and cheese. Both were arrested and, the authorities claimed, they both possessed pistols, percussion caps and bullets. Zephaniah Williams was caught on a Portuguese vessel off Cardiff. William Jones also failed to escape capture and, together with many more dispirited prisoners, they were committed to Monmouth gaol on charges of high treason and sedition. A special commission was set up for their trial.

The authorities were in no mood for mercy. One contemporary report, out of many, expressed the terror of a better-organised insurrection: 'The people among the hills remained for some time in a very disturbed state, and great alarm was felt lest further attempts at insurrection should be made.'[14] On 7 November a public meeting organised by Newport tradesmen and masters thanked the soldiers for their defence of the town, 'thus saving it and the whole of England from rebellion.' Lieutenant Gray, the young officer in charge of the troops at the Westgate Hotel, was promoted to Captain. The *Cambrian* claimed that the Chartists had planned similar attacks on Cardiff and Pontypool to spark a general uprising throughout South Wales and, ultimately, across Britain. On 9 November Lord Normanby sent a letter to the Mayor of Newport expressing Her Majesty's 'high approval of the conduct of the magistrates'.[15] A few days later Major Phillips was informed of Queen Victoria's bestowment of a knighthood which, when he recovered from his wounds, was conferred on him at Windsor Castle.

In December inquests were held on ten of the dead rioters and in every case the verdict was 'that the deceased came by his death by an act of justifiable homicide by some persons unknown'. A constable told the Newport coroner:

As soon as the firing ceased I came into the Westgate and saw five persons, three dead and five not dead, but they died soon afterwards. Two were by the back door, two in the passage, and one in the pantry. I was then informed that the soldiers were short of ammunition, and I went to the body of the one in the pantry and found 25 rounds of ball-cartridge in his trouser pocket, which I handed to Lt. Gray, and he immediately divided it amongst the soldiers.[16]

At the subsequent trial of 23 alleged insurrectionists the defence counsel, Mr Rickard, argued eloquently that a rebellion could hardly have been started by a famished and hungry mob freezing in the winter cold and poorly armed. The jury disagreed when it came to the ringleaders. Frost, Jones and Williams were found guilty and sentenced to death. Petitions from towns across Britain implored the Queen for clemency. A massive strike crippled the Monmouth collieries and no one would work alongside the prosecution witnesses. The sentences were commuted to life transportation to Australia.[17]

Chartists continued to campaign for Frost's release and in 1854 the Chartist MP Thomas Duncombe finally persuaded premier Lord Aberdeen to grant a pardon. Aberdeen stipulated that he must not re-enter British territory. Frost and his daughter emigrated to America but two years later the Government relented and he came home. Frost retired to Stapleton, writing newspaper articles on universal suffrage and prison reform. He died, aged 93, in July 1877.[18]

*   *   *

In the aftermath of the Newport Rising the Government concentrated on arresting or simply detaining the Chartist leaders across Britain, and by June 1840 at least 543 had been held for varying periods. The tactics proved successful and a putative uprising in Sheffield was a fiasco.

In July 1840 William Lovett was released, but his health had been broken by prison conditions and he was forced to spend time recuperating in Cornwall. When he returned to London he opened a bookshop in Tottenham Court Road. Although many still regarded him as the leader of the Chartists, he was constantly under attack from Feargus O'Connor and others who advocated violent action rather than Lovett's brand of moral force. Lovett retired from politics in 1842 and set up a national association to provide circulating libraries to educate the workers. He wrote school textbooks and taught evening classes. None of his projects made him money and he died, impoverished, in August 1877.

In his book *Life and Struggles* he wrote:

As regards the best means of obtaining our Charter, we are of those who are opposed to everything in the shape of physical or violent revolutions, believing that a victory would be a defeat to the just principles of democracy. The political despots ... calling up the passions in the worst forms, must necessarily throw back for centuries our intellectual and moral progress.[19]

But Chartism was not dead, nor the violent passions which continuing injustice aroused.

9
The Chartists and the Plug Plot Riots

'If you can't fight, you can torch'

Historian Robert Gammage said that no one should ever doubt Feargus O'Connor's desire to better the lives of the common people. But his 'excessive hankering after popularity purchased at any price' was both the secret of his success and a cause of Chartism's ultimate failure. 'It led him to lend his influence, whenever the time arrived, to knockdown every man who promised to rival him in the people's estimation.'[1]

O'Connor was born in 1796, the son of a United Irishman. At the age of 24 he inherited an estate in County Cork, but became a reforming landlord opposed to tithes and the power of the clerics. In 1832 he was elected MP for County Cork on a platform of universal suffrage. His mentor was Daniel O'Connell, the leader of the Irish Radicals. On being elected O'Connor immediately tried to usurp him and the two men became bitter foes. He lost his seat in 1835 and tried to stand for Oldham following the death of William Cobbett. O'Connor's intervention split the Radicals and the Tories were let in. O'Connor teamed up with William Lovett in the London Working Men's Association but, as we have seen, could not stomach being overshadowed and opposed Lovett's brand of Moral Force Chartism. His advocacy of violent action led to his being expelled from the Chartist Convention platform. He responded by setting up a rival Chartist movement. O'Connor also became an implacable enemy of the Anti-Corn Law League. He developed a Land Plan based on the belief that smallholdings could grow more than large farms, better combat famine and end Britain's reliance on imported food.

Four months after the Newport Rising, for which the authorities heaped partial blame on his head, O'Connor was tried at York for publishing seditious libel in the *Northern Star*. He spent 18 months editing his periodical from a prison cell. He outraged other Chartist stalwarts without his flair for publicity and self-promotion by telling his readers that for several years 'I led you single-handed and alone.'

On his release in August 1841 he took control of the National Charter Association. His ferocious and unfair attacks drove out Lovett and other former leaders and again split the movement. But his fiery style struck many chords among working people who felt betrayed by the moderates and who seethed after the debacle of Newport.

Their anger was fuelled when, on 4 May 1842, Thomas Duncombe presented to Parliament a Chartist petition signed, it was claimed, by 3,250,000 people. It again demanded the six main points of the original Charter and complained about factory conditions, church taxes, the Poor Law, the 'cruel wars against liberty' and the 'unconstitutional police force'. Even more radically, to early Victorian ears, it contrasted the Queen's income of '£164 17s 10d a day' with that of the 'producing millions'. The House of Commons rejected it by 287 to 47. All the work done to rebuild the Chartist Movement had, it appeared, come to nothing, and a wave of unrest swept Britain's manufacturing heartlands where support for Chartism had always been strongest and where the employers had begun to impose arbitrary pay cuts.

It began in July among Staffordshire coalminers. It quickly spread to the factories of Lancashire, then the textile areas of Cheshire and Yorkshire. Eventually it would hit 14 English counties, plus eight in Scotland and one in Wales. On 3 August 10,000 colliers and ironminers around Airdrie, Lanarkshire, downed tools and began to rip up the potato fields for food. Similar disturbances erupted elsewhere. The cotton masters of Lancashire responded with another wage reduction. By the 11th of that month over 100 cotton factories plus dyeworks and machine shops were idle as 50,000 workers went on strike. The actions were known as 'Plug Plots' because strikers removed boiler plugs to halt the works.

Ironically, Feargus O'Connor, who had done so much to agitate for action, initially condemned the strikes which he saw as playing into the hands of the Anti-Corn Law League. His critics said it was because he was not seen to be leading the strikers. But the authorities had little

5   The Plug Plot Riots
Illustrated London News

doubt that he and his Physical Force Chartists were involved. One official account said: 'Disturbances of a most serious nature, originating in a strike for wages, and inflamed by political excitement through the Chartists and other agitators, broke out ...'

The full extent of Chartist involvement has long been debated. It seems most likely that the outbreaks were due to a combination of circumstances in which both Chartists and the bosses played a part. The strikes in Lancashire were led by power-loom workers who since 1840 had been at the forefront, alongside the cotton spinners, of the war of attrition over wages and prices. Their union had in 1840 been savagely defeated in a strike against wage cuts imposed by Stockport bosses. The employers again justified further wage cuts on a collapse in profits in the winter of 1841–42, but it seems certain they were out to crush both the unions and support for Chartism. Those trade union leaders who had earlier been defeated concluded that their cause could only be won through political power. At a meeting called in Manchester of all trade societies in the region, 58 trades representatives voted for an immediate strike for the Charter, 19 had no mandate backed the majority, and only seven were instructed to strike solely for wages. The strikes in Lancashire and across the Pennines erupted first in areas with a history of Radical and Chartist activity. Richard Otley said at his later trial that in the manufacturing districts four out of five of the working classes were either actual Chartists or held Chartist principles.[2]

The leadership the Chartists provided was often uncoordinated but driven by the same spirit as their eager audience. F.C. Mather wrote:

> The ordinary coalminer or cotton operative who struck work and endeavoured to persuade others to do likewise, did so out of a sense of exasperation induced by a long series of wage reductions. Without this impetus no amount of oratory would have produced an outbreak as widespread as the Plug Plot. However, the importance of leaders, who suggested when the time was ripe to strike, which factories should be turned out by force, and what should be demanded as the price of returning to work, can scarcely be denied. There is evidence that, in Stalybridge and in the Staffordshire Potteries, the workpeople had local trade committees to formulate their demands, but enthusiasm was principally sustained at large open-air meetings, where directions were also issued as to where the mob should proceed, what should be their terms and how they should behave.[3]

The good behaviour of the crowds at such meetings in support of the strikes was noticeable. On 15 August, at a mass meeting of strikers at Ashton, where the bosses had imposed a wage cut of 25 per cent, the secretary of the local Chartists warned against committing any breach of the peace. The meeting agreed to reconvene every morning and evening at 5 o'clock and the crowd then set off for Rochdale to turn out any mills which might still be working. Banners were held aloft and loaves on sticks as the crowd was swelled to 12,000 by contingents from Oldham and Shaw. The women led the singing as they marched. They called to onlookers 'Come along with us and you will have something to eat.'[4] A few days later at the regular Ashton meeting a pensioner, Benjamin Dunkerley, told the crowd: 'You can't have a fair day's wage for a fair day's labour without the Charter.' A speaker who dared to suggest that the strikes should concentrate on pay rather than the Charter was howled down to cries of 'Put him out of the cart for a fool as he is.' At a meeting in Oldham on 19 August, a speaker was arrested for sedition despite being a Special Constable. He told the crowd: 'It is not a question of wages now, it is for the Charter ... if we can only obtain that, we will fix the price of labour and when and how it is to be paid.'[5]

The Chartist leadership, aware that the strikes and turnouts could lead to a general rising, continually stressed the need for discipline and organisation, and condemned any moves towards looting or the destruction of property beyond the pulling of the boiler plugs. In his later trial Christopher Doyle said: 'If there be any party who more than another ought to be thanked for preserving the peace, it is the Chartist body. Their constant motto has been peace, law and order.' That may have been true, but the organisational skills of the Chartists spread the strikes to connect up each area of silent mills and factories. That meant moving into areas with large numbers of troops, and violent clashes were inevitable.

Halifax, a hotbed of Chartism, saw one of the worse. Strikers crossed from Rochdale to Todmorden on 12 August, and moved to Hebden Bridge the following day, closing mills and letting off mill-dams on the way. On the outskirts of Halifax they were joined by large numbers of local men, mainly factory hands and navvies. At dawn on the 15th an excited local crowd gathered at Skircoat Moor to greet the strikers. Magistrates ordered the meeting to disperse. The crowd formed into a procession and marched towards Luddenden Foot to join the men from Todmorden and Hebden Bridge. Hand-loom workers who joined them placed their shuttles in a communal bag and left it at a public house for safe keeping. One marcher recalled:

> It was a remarkably fine day, the sun shone in its full splendour. The broad white road with its green hedges was filled with a long black straggling line of people, who cheerfully went along, evidently possessed of an idea that they were doing something towards a betterment.

The various contingents joined up to hear speaker Ben Ruston condemn the masters who had, he claimed, provoked the strikes as part of their campaign against the Corn Laws. Refreshment was treacle beer from a milk can and food offered freely by local people.

The procession, by now 5,000 strong, entered Halifax singing the 100th Psalm and led by the women marching four abreast. In the town they prepared to close those mills still operating. Before they could do so another procession of about 5,000 approached from Bradford. An onlooker recalled:

> The sight was just one of those which it is impossible to forget. They came pouring down the wide road in thousands, taking up the whole breadth – a gaunt, famished-looking, desperate multitude armed with huge bludgeons, flails, pitchforks and pikes, many without coats and hats, and hundreds upon hundreds with their clothes in rags and tatters. Many of the older men looked footsore and weary, but the great bulk were men in the prime of life, full of wild excitement. As they marched they thundered out a stirring melody.[6]

Soldiers were unable to prevent the two large processions joining together and the Riot Act was read. The military commander later complained in his report that when any portion of the crowd was confronted by his troopers they would simply melt away to re-form in another part of the town or in adjoining fields. An observer wrote: 'Perhaps the women were at this time the more valiant. Approaching to the very necks of the horses they declared they would rather die than starve, and if the soldiers were determined to charge, they might kill them.' During this first day a number of arrests were nevertheless made and 18 considered the most serious offenders were to be held overnight in lock-ups before being sent to Wakefield for charging. The crowds split largely into local people who retired to their homes and the strikers who camped on the moor above the town. There some of the women taunted the men for cowardice when facing the troopers.[7]

Early the following day the 18 arrested men were taken by soldiers to the railway station at Elland and put on the Wakefield train. The crowd, realising it was too late to rescue their comrades, decided to ambush the returning soldiers. F.H. Grundy, a civil engineer working on the Halifax railway link, found the route to Elland 'like a road to a fair or to the races ... all busy, women as well as men, rushing along the various lanes over my head with arms and aprons full of stones.' A high wooded bank overlooked the road and Grundy realised the danger to the troops. On the pretext of inspecting a partially built railway bridge he set off to warn the soldiers but was turned back by two of his own workers. One said, kindly, 'Thou'll nobbut be murdered, and then cannot do any guid.' Grundy described the scene when the soldiers trotted down the road with the empty cart used to transport the prisoners:

> They slow into a walk as they breast Salterhebble Hill. Then a loud voice shouts 'Now, lads, give it 'em!' From every wall rises a crowd of infuriated men, and down comes a shower of stones, bricks, boulders, like a close fall of hail. 'Gallop! Gallop!' comes the order, as their leader spurs his horse up the steep hill. But the men, jammed together, cannot gallop. They come down pell-mell, horses and riders. Those who can get through ride off at speed after their officer. Then the command came 'Cease throwing.' Eight horsemen, bleeding and helpless, crawled about the road seeking shelter. Down come the hosts now, and tearing the belts and accoutrements from the prostrate hussars, the saddles and the bridles from the horses, they give three cheers and depart.[8]

The comrades of the fallen soldiers took swift revenge. They stormed out of their billets in strength and rode down crowds wherever they gathered. The crowds panicked and ran, but Grundy recalled that the troopers 'followed the flying people for miles. Many a tale of wounded men lying out in barns and under hedges was told ...' It was reported to the Home Office that at least two of the rioters and one soldier died. Thirty-six prisoners were sent for trial. Several received severe sentences, including one of transportation for life.

A meeting of Chartists in Manchester was called on 17 August to install a memorial to Henry Hunt in the Every Street chapel. Delegates set out from across the Midlands and the North. One of them was Thomas Cooper, a 37-year-old Leicester man with little formal education who had taught himself to become a schoolteacher before becoming a full-time reporter for the *Lincoln Mercury*. In 1840 that paper sent him to report a Chartist meeting in his home town. While taking notes he was convinced of the cause, he joined the Chartists and became its leading figure in Leicester, starting and ending all meetings with prayers. He produced a book of Chartist songs and hymns and opened a shop for the movement's publications alongside a coffee-house. In 1841 he was elected Chartist MP for Nottingham at a by-election, but failed to hold it at the general election three months later. Growing increasingly militant, Cooper joined Feargus O'Connor in advocating Physical Force Chartism. Gammage wrote:

> Cooper warmly denounced the wrongs to which the working class were subjected. Possessed of a dashing style of oratory, restless energy, and indomitable will, he placed himself at their head. The unemployed working class followed him by thousands through the streets, cheering in spite of their distress... Cooper was the man to whose voice the people always listened, and whose dictates they always obeyed.

On his journey Cooper stopped and addressed enormous meetings across Staffordshire. At one such, at Hanley, a resolution was passed that 'all labour cease until the People's Charter becomes law of the land'. Cooper later admitted that he had 'struck a spark which kindled all into combustion'. Dorothy Thompson wrote:

> The combustion did not end in the district until police stations had been destroyed, prisoners released, poorhouses torn down, and the homes of unpopular magistrates and coal-owners sacked and burned. This was the crowd of the middle-class nightmare ...

Cooper dodged the police and arrived on foot at Crewe station and entered Manchester convinced that the spread of the strike would and must be followed by a general outbreak. A Chartist colleague recalled looking at Manchester from his railway carriage and saw the City of Long Chimneys with every stack smokeless. He swore and said: 'Not a single mill at work! Something must come of this, and something serious too!'

The strikes spread rapidly. Strikers marched from factory to factory to ensure a full turn out. Those marches were often considerable; North Staffordshire miners reached Poynton colliery near Stockport, around 25 miles, before being repelled by troops. A young worker, Ben Brierly, vividly recalled the month which turned into a general strike, and more, in the North: 'I entered into the movement with all the zest of youth, and rushed into danger heedless of consequences. I was present at plug-drawings everywhere, disguised by appearing in my shirt sleeves, my paper cap, and the leather apron I wore at my velvet loom ...'

Dorothy Thompson wrote:

> 1842 was the year in which more energy was hurled against the authorities than in any other of the nineteenth century. More people were arrested and sentenced for offences concerned with speaking, agitating, rioting and demonstrating than in any other year, and more people were out on the streets during August 1842 than at any other time. It was the nearest thing to a general strike that this century saw.[9]

Other historians have agreed, describing it as the first general strike in any capitalist country. F.C. Mather wrote: 'The stoppage was never completely general in the sense of nationwide, but in many towns and districts there was, indeed, an almost complete suspension of labour in factories, coal mines and other large establishments, while domestic handworkers often turned out to demonstrate and to compel others to join them.'[10] The propertied classes saw it as much more than a strike. An Accrington postmaster wrote: 'It is more like a revolution than anything else in this neighbourhood, and we fear that the plunder and mischief is not at an end.' His boss, the Secretary of the Post Office, described it as 'a commotion such as we have not seen for half a century'.[11]

The forces of law and order gathered. Magistrates called up pensioners into local militias and swore in special constables. A steady stream of police reports were despatched to the Home Office. A police spy at Huddersfield reported: 'The native operators are quiet, but evidently wish success to what may be called an insurrection.' At Dewesbury the magistrate reported that on one day the strikers had stopped 38 mills. After a mass meeting in the same town the magistrate reported: 'The rioters have not yet proceeded to outrage, but we cannot help perceiving that this state of things cannot last much longer. The rioters seem almost famished for want of food.' At Leeds and Cleckheaton troops and Special Constables prevented crowds of strikers entering either town.

There were violent incidents across much of the country: the destruction of Birley's mill near Oldham and a police station at Newton;

6   The attack on Preston, 1842
Illustrated London News

rioting in Stockport where the mob broke into the Union workhouse and took away 672 7 lb loaves; a bloody clash between rioters and troops in Preston where soldiers, angered by being stoned, fired into the crowd leaving 'several persons wounded, three or four mortally'; an attack on the Adelphi Works at Salford in which troops again fired on rioters, wounding five; skirmishes at Bradford; more rioting at Dunfermline and Glasgow; another conflict at the village of Walton where the police were nearly overpowered; a volley by soldiers at Blackburn in which a young girl died; attempts at Rochdale, Bury, Macclesfield, Bolton and Huddersfield to wreck railway lines, all unsuccessful.

The *Register* reported the spread of the disturbances:

> The Staffordshire and Warwickshire mining districts were placed in a like state of commotion from the turn-out of the colliers, aggravated by the exertions of the Chartists, who are there numerous. At Stoke-upon-Trent, on the 15th, they sacked and destroyed the contents of the Court of Requests, the Police Office, and the houses of some private gentlemen. The men employed at Lord Ward's collieries at Dudley were attacked by a mob, and many of them seriously wounded. At Burslem the house of Mr Parker, a magistrate, was burnt to the ground, the Town Hall, Police Offices, and several private houses ransacked; a conflict ensued with the military, who shot three of the ringleaders dead on the spot, and seriously wounded 12 or 14 others.[12]

And so it went on for two violent weeks.

The authorities reacted, as they had done so many times before, with mass arrests. Cooper, just before his own capture, told the Manchester conference: 'We must get the people out to fight; and they must be irresistible, if they were united.'[13] But half-starved strikers and their families could not hope to take on troops, and the mass population, although sympathetic, were not prepared to join a general outbreak. The strikes themselves began to falter and then peter out, although some districts held out longer than others. Some bosses restored wage reductions, but mainly the strikers were starved back to work. Their leaders were divided and O'Connor maintained his opposition in the *Northern Star*. The trade delegations voted for an end to the action. And then the trials began.

In some areas the treatment meted out to the strikers and demonstrators was harsh; in others it was almost fair. Scores came up at

York Assizes where individual cases generally came down to questions of identity. A man called Mitchell was convicted of looting from an injured soldier and was given ten years' transportation. Another, Wilkinson, was sentenced to 18 months' imprisonment for stabbing a constable. Others received gaol terms of between two and six months, while some were discharged and simply bound over to keep the peace. At Salford Sessions six Lancashire rioters were convicted but many more defendants were acquitted by a jury considering disturbances at Clifton on 20 August. However, in the same court most of the 78 charged with rioting at Heywood on the 17th were convicted by another jury and their sentences ranged from two months' to two years' imprisonment.

In the Stafford Special Commission Court the elderly blacksmith Joseph Cappur was tried on a charge of sedition. The main witness against him, a grinder called William Smallwood, reported the colourful language the defendant had used, including a threat to put all the bishops and clergy into a ship and send them 'to be assassinated by the Hindoos'. Smallwood reported that on one occasion Cappur had told a group of women whose husbands were on strike: 'If you can't fight you can torch.' Smallwood admitted under cross-examination that Cappur had sued him for a debt and that there was bad blood between them. Another witness testified that the blacksmith's calls to arms had been greeted with laughter and cries of 'It's only old Cappur.'[14] Buffoon or not, Cappur was convicted and given two years in Stafford gaol.

The alleged Plug Plot leaders also faced retribution. Thomas Cooper faced the same Special Commission Court charged with sedition. Asked how he was pleading, Cooper replied: 'If I am charged with inciting persons to cease from labour until they obtain the Charter – if that is illegal, and if that be a breach of the peace – then I am bound in honour to admit that I did urge them to do, and that I am guilty.' The Solicitor-General called for a lawyer to advice Cooper. When that gentleman whispered into Cooper's ear, the Chartist roared: 'No; I shall not tell a falsehood.'[15] He, too, was given two years. The Home Secretary, Sir James Graham, decided that Feargus O'Connor should be charged as a general conspirator. He regarded the Irishman, and other delegates to the Chartist Convention, as the same as 'the worst of the defendants who headed mobs, made seditious speeches, and stopped mills and factories'. He told Sir Robert Peel: 'I shall blend in one association the head and the hands – the bludgeon and the pen, and let the jury and the public see in one case the whole crime.'[16] Graham also proposed a general persecution of the Radical press. But O'Connor was correctly acquitted of inciting or organising the strikes – he had railed against them in his publication.

The Special Commission was not so lenient with working-class men caught in their net. A total of 274 prisoners came before them. Many of the cases were almost identical and the first, of nine young men and boys charged with riotous and tumultuous assembly at Longton, near Stoke-on-Trent, is typical. The case centred on the destruction of a house belonging to the Reverend Benjamin Vale on 15 August. His wife, Mary Ann, testified that a mob stormed the property and she tried to close the shutters. 'The mob, however, reached the house before she could do so', said a contemporaneous report.

> She was greatly alarmed, her husband not being at home. They demanded money and drink; which at first she refused; but she afterwards gave them her purse, containing about 5s or 6s, and desired the servant to give them some drink. They then proceeded to the study and commenced destroying and burning books and furniture. Some went up the stairs and set fire to several of the rooms; others followed the servant to the cellar with a sheet, which they set on fire; and they then commenced drinking whiskey. Witnesses fled as soon as they saw the whole house in flames, and took refuge in an adjoining cottage; when Jabez Phillips, one of the prisoners, came up and said they were 'going to London to burn, and bring all things to their proper level.' Dr Vale returned while the house was burning; but a friend prevented his entering it.

The crowd had swelled to several hundred as the Reverend gentleman's possessions, including a piano, were put on a bonfire. Dragoons arrived, drawn by the flames, and arrested the accused. There was no evidence against two boys arrested, another was acquitted, and the remainder were found guilty despite pleas from their counsels that they were 'persons who were on the verge of starvation which must have driven them into a state of temporary madness'.[17]

In total the Stafford Special Commission Court sentenced no fewer than 54 to transportation – eleven for life, 13 for 21 years, and the remainder for ten or seven years. One of those sent away for 21 years, William Ellis, was described as 'the most dangerous man in the Potteries'. A further 146 received imprisonment with hard labour for two years or less. Fifty-five prisoners were acquitted and the remainder were discharged or saw their cases postponed. Other special courts were set up. The Lancashire one, held in Liverpool, considered 117 cases, almost all charged with riot, conspiracy, incitement to turn out workmen, and plug-pulling.[18]

* * *

When Thomas Cooper emerged from Stafford gaol he had changed his mind about the morality of using physical force to achieve Chartist aims. He attacked Feargus O'Connor over his Land Plan and accused him of using money raised for the cause to prop up the *Northern Star*. O'Connor promptly had him ejected from the National Charter Association. Cooper continued to write for newspapers but spent most of his time as a travelling preacher after he joined the Baptists in 1856. He died in 1892.

O'Connor launched his Chartist Land Plan in 1845 and two years later had persuaded 70,000 to pay £100,000 into a fund to buy Heronsgate, a large estate in Gloucestershire which he promptly renamed O'Connorville. The idea was that the land would be divided into plots, subscribers would draw lots and the winners would obtain a cottage with three or four acres of land. It was a disaster. By 1850 the company was teetering on bankruptcy and 'winners' were being evicted.

He was characteristically undeterred by such failures and remained the dominant figure in the Chartist Movement, combining bravura with outrageous claims after he was again elected to Parliament representing Nottingham. In one speech at Kennington Common, called to present a redrawn Charter to the Commons, he claimed to have received 100 letters warning him he would be killed if he spoke that day. He said:

> My children ... My answer was that I would rather be stabbed in the heart than abstain from being in my place. My breath is nearly gone, and I will only say, when I desert you may desert me ... I will go on conquering until you have the land and the People's Charter becomes the law of the land.[19]

They had much longer to wait, not least because O'Connor's leadership became increasingly erratic. He claimed that the Charter had by now gained 5,706,000 signatures. When examined by a committee of MPs the total was found to be 1,975,496, and some of those were clearly forgeries. O'Connor was accused of destroying the credibility of the Chartists by exaggeration, bluster and personal vendettas.

The decline of the Chartist Movement had begun after the failure of the 1842 strikes. For the working man conditions improved markedly during the administration of Sir Robert Peel, taking some of the teeth out of Chartism. The repeal of the Corn Laws in 1846 and the introduction of free trade undercut some of their key economic arguments.[20] The 1847 Factory Act introduced shorter working hours for all employees, while a Public Health Act the following year resulted in some improved sanitation in the terraced homes thrown up around the factories. The price of food fell. The moderate founders of Chartism became disillusioned and left or were ousted by the Physical Force militants. Unity disappeared, as did proper organisation and a sense of shared purpose. People began to mock empty promises. Chartism was hugely important to the development of the working-class movements which followed it, but in the short term it failed.[21] In 1858, the year of the final National Chartist Convention, an Act was passed declaring that ownership of property was no longer necessary for Parliamentary candidates. That, and further strides towards universal suffrage, killed the Chartist Movement.

Feargus O'Connor did not witness the end. He was committed to a mental asylum in Chiswick after assaulting several fellow MPs. He was found to be in the later stages of syphilis. He died at the end of August 1855.[22]

10
Cunninghame Graham and Bloody Sunday

'Full tilt at the police'

Robert Bontine Cunninghame Graham, one of Britain's most colourful politicians, confronted hostile Indians in Texas, fought with peasant revolutionaries in South America, and rode with gauchos in Argentina. He witnessed slave trading and gun-running, drove mustangs and mules, suffered blistering heat and famine and endured poverty and fortune alike. He emerged largely unscathed – until he clashed with police batons in Trafalgar Square.

He was born in London on 24 May 1852, the son of a Scots laird and long-time Whig who could trace a direct ancestral line to Robert the Bruce, and his infancy was largely spent with his Spanish grandmother. After an unhappy schooling in Harrow, which was not suited to his wild nature, he decided to seek adventure in South America, the place of his grandmother's birth. He spent 16 turbulent years in the Americas, interspersed with frequent trips home to the family's Scottish estate at Gartmore, and earned the nickname 'Don Roberto'.

While the adventurer was away riding with revolutionaries and driving cattle, Britain was undergoing more political turbulence. Britain's soldiers, sailors, merchants and diplomats were painting the globe imperial pink in the name of Queen Victoria, its engineers and scientists were transforming the nature of everyday life, and riches poured into its thriving ports. The middle classes were settling into mundane prosperity and the working classes were slowly obtaining the vote and better wages and conditions. But such outward harmony only disguised ongoing divisions.

7   Tom Merry's cartoon of Robert Cunninghame Graham
St Stephen's Review, January 1888

The 1862 Lancashire cotton famine, caused by the blockade of raw material from the Confederate states during the American civil war, saw a major riot in Stalybridge and smaller ones across the county. But it was the dignified suffering of hundreds of thousands who did not resort to violence which pricked the nation's conscience. A massive charity effort was established which proved a precursor to the welfare state. A huge programme of public works designed to improve health and communications was started. And the general behaviour of the multitude – a Relief Commission report found that crime went down during the long months of destitution and desperation – led to the Second Reform Law becoming law in 1867. William Gladstone said:

> What are the questions which fit a man for the exercise of a privelege such as the franchise? Self-command, self-control, respect to order, patience under suffering, confidence in the law, regard for superiors: and when were all these great qualities exhibited in a manner more signal, even more illustrious, than in the conduct of the general body of operatives in Lancashire under the profound affliction of the winter of 1862?

The Act gave the vote to ordinary householders in towns, including almost all male adult cotton workers.

But the Act had not healed social divisions. Workers were demanding trade union representation, socialist tracts were devoured as the working class became more literate, the demands for Irish Home Rule undermined administrations, and religious strife was encouraged by Christian fundamentalists. Reformists battled with the police in Trafalgar Square, in 1867 a Protestant zealot fomented anti-Catholic violence in Birmingham, there were food riots in Devon and election riots in Blackburn, and in 1869 in Mold, Flintshire, two miners and two women were shot dead by soldiers as a mob tried to rescue prisoners. Drunken riots by navvies building England's rail network resulted in many deaths. In Exeter a riot was sparked by the cancellation of a municipal fireworks display.

Early in 1883 Cunninghame Graham's father died after a fall from a horse, leaving debts of over £100,000. Cunninghame Graham and his young wife returned and decided to honour them in full. They struggled for over a decade to save the estate but Cunninghame Graham's restless spirit needed some release from the intricacies of large-scale farming.

In Scotland and London he began attending socialist meetings to listen to William Morris, George Bernard Shaw, H.M. Hyndman, Keir

Hardie, John Burns and others. He proved to be a born speaker himself, precise, elegant, theatrical, humorous, passionate and scornful by turns. Asked for his views on the army, he replied: 'I have a hereditary regard for the ancient and honourable profession of arms; but I would like to see a time when no soldier would be seen, except, perhaps, a stuffed specimen or two in a museum.' His politics were driven not so much by structured idealism as by sympathy for the underdog. He contested North West Lanarkshire as a Liberal in 1882 and won the seat on his second attempt in 1886. To the suprise of the party which had adopted him as their candidate, he entered Parliament as its first socialist MP.[1]

He quickly became Westminster's *enfant terrible,* a 34-year-old employing irony and sarcasm against his elders. He cut a striking figure with wild hair, a Spanish-style beard and moustache and the styles of the Scottish Highlands and the Argentine pampas competing in his clothing. In his maiden speech he attacked the Government's legislative programme for ignoring the 'awful chasm' between rich and poor, the over-taxation of the lowest paid, and the depression in commerce and agriculture. The Queen's Speech, he said, comprised 'nothing but platitudes, nothing but views of society through a little bit of pink glass'. He concluded with a wide-ranging onslaught:

> The society in which one man works and another enjoys the fruit – the society in which capital and luxury makes Heaven for 20 thousand and a Hell for 30 million, that society whose crowning achievement is this dreary waste of mud and stucco (the Houses of Parliament) – with its misery, its want and destitution, its degradation, its prostitution, and its glaring social inequalities – the society we call London – that society which, by a refinement of irony, has placed the mainspring of human action, almost the power of life and death, and the absolute power to pay labour and to reward honour, behind the grey tweed veil which enshrouds the greasy pocket of the capitalist.

In a later speech he declared: 'We look confidently for the time when the Government will take possession of the mines and machinery of this country, and work them for the benefit of the country and not in the selfish interests of the capitalists.'[2] He became an Establishment hate-figure and in 1887 he was suspended for being the first MP on record for saying 'damn' in the Commons Chamber.

In May 1887 several Socialist meetings were broken up by the police and Cunninghame Graham protested that England was 'a free country for a man to starve in – that is a boon you can never take away from him – but it appears that in the future it is not going to be a free country to hold meetings in'. His words swiftly came true.

Gladstone's Government had fallen largely because of opposition to his Irish Home Rule legislation and Lord Salisbury had resumed office. An outstanding sore was the imprisonment of the MP William O'Brien and other Irish patriots.[3] A meeting was planned for Trafalgar Square by the Metropolitan Radical Association to demand O'Brien's release and to give a voice to the 80,000 unemployed in London. On 8 November 1887 the head of the London police, Sir Charles Warren, prohibited all meetings in the Square, on the grounds that it was a hereditary possession of the Crown and the public had no legal right to assemble there. Warren also urged the Home Office to recruit 20,000 Special Constables to deal with Socialist meetings in London. He wrote:

> We have in the last month been in greater danger from disorganised attacks on property by the rough and criminal elements than we have been in London for many years past. The language used by speakers at the various meetings has been more frank and open in recommending the poorer classes to help themselves from the wealth of the affluent.[4]

The following Sunday, the 13th, 1,600 constables held the Square, with many more patrolling the Strand, Whitehall and Northumberland Avenue, but by the afternoon a large crowd had gathered in neighbouring areas. The weather was cold and drizzly, but the crowd was good humoured and dressed in their Sunday best. William Morris and Annie Besant made speeches expressing support for O'Brien and the right to free speech. Both led an abortive raid to penetrate the police lines, but were dispersed. George Bernard Shaw and his mother were there but stayed well clear of the action. The crowds ringed the Square and thronged Charing Cross. Mounted police and 300 Grenadier Guards repeatedly broke up processions before they reached the outskirts of the Square, capturing ornate banners and tearing them apart. But some demonstrators got through to the Square's perimeter.

The Times gave the following account:

Soon after four o'clock things were at their height in the vicinity of
Trafalgar Square, and a desperate and concerted attempt was made to
break through the police into the centre. About 200 men, headed, it is said,
by Mr Cunninghame Graham MP, rushed from the corner of the Strand
near Morley's Hotel and went full tilt at the police, who were drawn up
four deep at the corner of the square. It was a very determined onslaught
and evidently made by men acting together according to a preconcerted
plan. For a few moments there was a hand-to-hand tussle and fists were
seen to be uplifted high and being freely used. Some of the attacking party
had sticks, but it was mainly a battle of fists. The police momentarily lost
ground owing to the rush of their opponents, and it seemed as if the line
would be broken and an entrance effected. Other constables, however, were
soon to the rescue and the attackers were beaten back. A moment later they
were in full retreat.[5]

Another eye-witness account, by Charles Finger, contradicts the claim
that it was a pre-planned attack on the police line:

Cunninghame Graham, fired by a sudden flame of resentful anger, turned
and said something that I, being too far off, could not hear, and those
nearest him set up a shout. So there came a surging forward, with Graham
and John Burns in the forefront, and then a confused running. Once I saw
Graham, saw his hatless head and bushy hair as he assailed the police.
Someone struck at him with a sword. But the Londoners had neither the
heart nor the courage to follow him, so the end of the attack came with the
same rough mauling of the two leaders, who were seized by a dozen hands
and then taken captive into the middle of the hollow square.[6]

Planned or impulsive, Cunninghame Graham did lead the charge and
actually penetrated the lines of mounted police by gently catching the
horses' bridles and slipping, initially unnoticed, through with his friend,
the socialist engineer John Burns. He was immediately cut down by a
policeman's baton which left a deep gash in his head. The police kept
battering him as he lay, clearly badly injured, on the ground. Burns
tried bravely to shield him with his own body and the two men were
arrested and charged with riot and assault on the police.[7]

The violence inflicted on Cunnighame Graham frightened his wife,
watching from a hotel window, who thought he was dying, and inflamed
the crowd.[8] Another surge hit the police ranks but was easily repulsed.
At 4.30 p.m. two squadrons of Life Guards rode up from Whitehall
and charged with drawn sabres to disperse the crowd. The cavalry
rode at increasing speeds round and round the perimeter of the Square,
scattering demonstrators wherever they gathered. Screams of pain and

panic competed with the drumbeat of hooves on cobbles. There were many severe injuries from sword slashes, batons and flailing hooves. George Barnes, a 32-year-old Scottish textile mechanic, was ridden down and badly hurt. Monsieur Andreux, an ex-ambassador of France, was bowled over and hit on the head in the charge as he walked out of the Hotel Metropole. Alfred Linnell, an innocent bystander, was ridden down and died from his injuries.[9]

A witness, Walter Crane, reported:

> I never saw anything more like real warfare in my life – only the attack was all on one side. The police, in spite of their numbers, apparently thought they could not cope with the crowd. They had certainly exasperated them, and could not disperse them, as after every charge – and some of these drove the people right against the shutters of the shops in the Strand – they returned again.

Another, Edward Carpenter, recalled:

> A regiment of mounted police came cantering up. The order had gone forth that we were to be kept moving. To keep a crowd moving is, I believe, a technical term for the process of riding roughshod in all directions, scattering, frightening and batoning the people. I saw my friend Robert Muirhead seized by the collar by a mounted man and dragged along, apparently towards a police station, while a bobby on foot aided in the arrest. I jumped to the rescue and slanged the two constables, for which I got a whack on the cheekbone with a baton, but Muirhead was released.[10]

When the one-sided battle ended, Cunninghame Graham was allowed to wash his head with a bowler hat full of water scooped from a fountain by Burns. They were taken up the steps towards the National Gallery through ranks of Grenadier Guards with bayonets fixed. A sergeant prodded Cunninghame Graham with the butt of his rifle.[11]

Fifty prisoners, most bleeding, were taken into custody in that phase of the 'battle' (the total arrested that day topped 300) and kept in King Street and Bow Street police stations. Cunninghame Graham, his face a mask of blood, was held in the latter but refused bail offered by his relative, Colonel William Hope VC. He was kept at Bow Street for three days, the first 24 hours without food or drink or medical attention. When his mother brought him food she found him sitting on his bunk with his head covered in congealed blood. He greeted her with a self-deprecating joke. Don Roberto and Burns shared a cell next to another which held two drunken prostitutes. Burns passed the first few nights singing snatches of *The Mikado*.[12]

The Establishment press and law-abiding citizens deplored the riot. An editorial in *The Times* suggested that Cunninghame Graham should no longer continue to sit as a magistrate in three counties of Scotland or as an MP.[13] The Radical press took a different view. *Reynolds News* editorialised:

> Peaceable citizens, men, women and even urchins barely entering their teens, were in many hundreds of cases, ruthlessly ridden down by mounted blackguards and bludgeoned by police infantry. To crown it all the shameless order was given to bring in the military, to shoot down the unarmed bread earners of London in cold blood.[14]

Such exaggeration did little for the cause. Across the Channel, the independent *La Liberté* put it better: 'Force alone upholds the law when it has lost its moral prestige.'

At the subsequent trial the police claimed that Cunninghame Graham had hurled his hat away with the cry of 'Now for the Square!'[15] Cunninghame Graham and Burns were sentenced to two months' imprisonment in Pentonville.

As he began his sentence the forces of law and order increased their grip. Meetings of the unemployed were banned and those of political movements suppressed. Processions were bludgeoned by police batons and staves. Permission for Linnell's funeral cortege to pass through Trafalgar Square was refused. The funeral was held on 20 November and there was a huge turnout. Charles Finger recalled: 'We marched in our thousands from Soho to Bow, hedged and surrounded by police mounted and afoot.'[16] William Morris addressed the mourners:

> Our friend who lies here has had a hard life, and met with a hard death; and if society had been differently constituted, his life might have been a delightful, a beautiful, a happy one. It is our business to organise for the purpose of seeing that such things do not happen; to try and make this earth a beautiful and happy place.[17]

On leaving the cemetery the crowd came up hard against police ranks but another riot was narrowly avoided.

When he was released, after six weeks picking oakum with time off for good behaviour, Cunninghame Graham was asked by friends how he found Pentonville. He replied: 'All right, but I wouldn't send my friends to it.'[18] Back at Westminster he tried to raise the question of police tactics which turned a legitimate demonstration into a bloody riot. His Parliamentary colleagues were not interested. The Prime Minister, Lord Salisbury, greeted him: 'Well, Mr Graham, are you thinking where to put your guillotine?' He replied: 'In Trafalgar Square, of course.'[19]

*   *   *

John Burns, who had tried to shield his friend from bludgeoning and shared a filthy cell with him as prostitutes bawled obscenities through the bars, rose to the Cabinet. After what became known as 'Bloody Sunday' he was convinced that socialism would be achieved through trade union activism rather than Parliamentary processes.[20] He helped to organise the 1889 London dock strike in which 10,000 men demanded better pay and conditions (see following chapter).

Robert Cunninghame Graham continued to champion free speech, the rights of workers and relief for the unemployed. He was again suspended from the Commons in September 1888 for protesting about the working conditions of chain-makers. He repeatedly tried to introduce a bill for the eight-hour working day but, not suprisingly, Lord Salisbury refused to allocate Parliamentary time for it to be debated. Two girls named Macdonald were sentenced to a month's hard labour for sleeping on a doorstep in Westminster. Cunningham Graham got them off hard labour.[21] But generally the Government regarded him as a nuisance rather than a real threat. George Bernard Shaw used him as the basis for Saranoff, the Bulgarian braggadocio, in *Arms and the Man* and in *Captain Brassbound's Conversion*.

Cunninghame Graham was a co-founder, with Keir Hardie, of the Scottish Home Rule Association and grew increasingly radical. He was actively involved in the Matchgirls Strike led by Annie Besant and in the Dockers' Strike. He opposed injustice both at home and abroad. He condemned the murder while a captive of Sitting Bull, saying in a letter to the *Daily Graphic*: 'Whether in Patagonia, on the Pampas, or on the prairies of the North West, the treatment that the whole Indian race has received, whether at the hands of the Spanish or English Americans, is a disgrace and a scandal.' In July 1889 he attended the Marxist Congress of the Second International in Paris. A year later he made a speech in Calais which was considered so inflammatory that he was arrested and expelled from France. He stood as the Scottish Labour Party candidate for Glasgow Camlachie in the 1892 general election, but was defeated. His Westminster career was over.

By the end of the decade his efforts to save the Gartmore estate were finally frustrated. His main income came from his massive output as a writer, covering politics, history, travel biography, autobiography and 17 collections of short stories. He continued to be politically active, largely in the cause of Scottish Home Rule. During the First World War he bought horses for the British Army in the Argentine markets, and cattle in Colombia to feed the troops. He was the first President of the National Party of Scotland, founded in 1928. That same year, in the election for the Lord Rectorship of Glasgow University, he lost to Stanley Baldwin, then Prime Minister, by only 66 votes.

Towards the end of his life he said that his political career had amounted to 'ploughing sand' and that the only thing he had achieved as an MP was improving the working conditions of the chain-makers. In January 1936 he set off for one last journey to the South American pampas. He was seen off at Paddington station by his old comrade A.F. Tschiffely, who had completed the famous horseback ride from the southern tip of South America to the snowfields of North America. Tschiffely later wrote:

> Somehow I sensed that this would be the last time that I would see his flowing shock of silvery-white hair, and that I would never again shake his strong and friendly hand; the hand which was equally dextrous with the reins, the *lazo*, the revolver and the sword as it had been with the pen, the hand that had helped the fallen to rise and had done many noble deeds.[22]

When he reached Rio de Janeiro he was losing weight at an alarming rate. He died in his hotel on 20 March 1936, aged 83.[23]

When the news reached England Ramsay Macdonald wrote:

> His Socialism was based on romantic ideas of freedom and his profound feeling for the bottom dog. He was a very typical Scot. His temperament was that of a soldier of fortune. That was Graham. I always think of him as a finely Caparisoned medieval charger, fighting towards some great ideal ...

11
The Featherstone Riot

'This imprudence cost him his life.'

The annual Doncaster races, in 1893, began on 5 September. Sticking to tradition, the Chief Constable of Yorkshire's West Riding sent a detachment of 259 constables, a quarter of his entire force, to keep order in the town during a boisterous week. It was a bad misjudgement.

Since the end of July a miners' strike had closed 253 pits employing 80,000 people, and the owners had responded by forcing a lockout. August had progressed reasonably quietly, but there was an angry mood about, a premonition of violent confrontation.

*   *   *

By the later part of Victoria's reign the fight for better conditions for the working class had shifted towards the trade unions and industrial battlefields. The old leaders, wedded to the tactics of compromise and conciliation rather than confrontation, were being challenged by young firebrands such as Keir Hardie, the Scottish miners' leader, before he entered Parliament. The cause of militancy was helped by a series of spectacular and unexpected victories.

In 1888 the prominent Fabian Annie Besant wrote a furious editorial in the small weekly journal the *Link* highlighting the poor pay and conditions suffered by London matchgirls employed by Bryant and May. It caught the public's imagination and sympathy but also aroused the ire of the girls themselves, 672 of whom came out on strike. Public funds poured in, bigger newspapers championed the girls, and the company gave in. Militants in other industries took note.[1]

Will Thorne, a gasworker employed by the South Metropolitan Gas Company, set up a union at East Ham with the secretarial help of Eleanor Marx. Within four months its membership was 20,000 strong. By August 1889 Thorne threatened strike action unless working hours were reduced from twelve to eight a day. His case was well-argued and clearly just, and the company capitulated immediately.

Within days of that victory Ben Tillett, secretary of a small dockyards union, called for help to settle a relatively minor dispute over bonus payments. Three days later 10,000 men were out and after a few weeks the London Docks, the biggest in the world, were paralysed. The strikers' leaders, most notably John Burns, retained public sympathy by ruling there should be no violence during mass meetings. They were aided by Police Superintendent Foster who ensured that his constables exercised restraint while policing the daily march on Tower Hill to hear speeches from Burns and Tom Mann.[2] This time, however, the bosses did not cave in. After two weeks the Great Dock Strike was on the brink of collapse, and could only keep going after Australian dock hands and other sympathisers on the other side of the world contributed £30,000 to the strike fund. Public support waned after violent clashes at the dock gates provoked by company attempts to bus in scab labour. After five weeks Cardinal Manning used his influence to bring the bosses to the negotiating table and the dockers won their demand for an increase from sixpence to eightpence in overtime payments.

As trade fell and Britain moved into a periodical slump, the unions became embroiled in increasingly bitter battles, most of which they failed to win. The Lancashire cotton workers went on strike for five months in 1893 but were forced back to work with most of their demands unmet. In the same year William Collison set up the National Free Labour Association to provide non-union workers for strike-hit industries. That saw an escalation of violence on picket lines, although there is no evidence that it featured in the bloody climax to the 1893 coal strike.

That nationwide stoppage was provoked by coal masters who insisted in wage cuts due to fluctuating markets. The strike was effective. Industries dependent on coal went on short-time working. In London the price of coal went sky-high. Railway companies reduced their train services. The mayors of manufacturing towns urged the coal masters to settle, but both sides were intransigent. After two months tempers were running high.

The confrontation came at Featherstone, a village six miles from Wakefield where the Ackton Hall colliery employed 800 miners, half of them below ground. The company's production had stopped when the underground men walked out, but most of the surface workers continued to be employed cleaning up the various premises. And each day a gang loaded up coal slack which had accumulated around the yards and which was then either sold or used to raise steam for the surface engines and brickworks. At first a blind eye was turned to work which could be construed as strikebreaking. That changed on the first day of the races.

At noon a large crowd entered the Ackton Hall yard and stopped any more slack loading. The following day a delegation approached colliery general manager Alfred Holiday and demanded that the slack-gathering must stop until the strike and lockouts were over. Holiday indignantly refused but, aware that feelings were running high, agreed to suspend the loading for a few days. The delegation appeared satisfied and there was no trouble at Featherstone that day. But elsewhere tempers were erupting. Just four miles away at Nostell colliery there were disturbances, and in the Burnley area 188 police were drafted in to halt two hours of rioting.

When Holiday went to work on 7 September he found 200 men and youths carrying sticks waiting outside his office. He insisted later that he had recognised none of his own employees, and that they were all outside troublemakers. They accused him of breaking his promise of the previous day that no more slack would be loaded. They did not believe his denials and overturned six loaded wagons parked in the yard. Satisfied, the crowd walked away. Worried that they might return, Holiday drove his trap to Pontefract to call for more police to reinforce the sergeant and two constables stationed at Featherstone. He was met sympathetically but told that all available officers were out responding to other calls for protection.

On his return to Ackton Hall, Holiday found a larger crowd busy emptying coal onto the railway lines from seven 10-ton wagons which had remained in a siding since the start of the strike. The manager took a train past them to seek help from the military authorities in Wakefield. He was promised that infantry would be sent by rail later that afternoon from York barracks. When Holiday returned to the colliery for the third time that day he found that a mob had smashed most of his office windows.

Meanwhile, the promised military train, holding 53 men and two officers of the 1st battalion, South Staffordshires, was delayed. Their commander, Captain Barker, told that an attack was being planned at the nearby Sharleston colliery, reluctantly agreed to split his force. He sent his lieutenant and 25 men to Sharleston, and took the remaining 28 men plus three constables to Featherstone where, he was told, a magistrate would be waiting for him.[3]

There was no such greeting at the station and Barker formed his men up before a jeering crowd. He then marched them through packed and noisy streets to the colliery yard. Holiday welcomed them gratefully, but Barker told him that his troops could not be used without the presence of a magistrate. In the meantime his men were put out of sight on the third floor of a large engine shed.

At six that evening the crowd returned to the colliery yard. Again there was an angry face-off between Holiday and their leaders. He was repeating his promise that no more slack would be loaded for a couple of days when a more menacing group approached from across the railway tracks. He later testified: 'I should think there were 500 or 600 of them, and all carried sticks, mostly heavy bludgeons, and looked a very bad mob altogether.' Holiday, who was no coward, walked up to them and asked their business. They demanded the withdrawal of the police and military, and surrounded the manager in a threatening manner. A police inspector and sergeant joined him and urged him to return to the colliery building for his own safety. All three were pelted with stones but managed to scramble back across the railway lines and take refuge in a house by the station.[4]

From within they heard the sounds of rioting as dusk gathered: 'a tremendous crashing of glass, which kept on continuously with shouts and yells – a tremendous din'. Colliery windows were shattered and their frames ripped out. Men were seen piling timber and wood shavings against the office walls and around the colliery workshops. Captain Barker, still inside the engine shed with his men, reported: 'I went to the window and looked out and here I saw the yard suddenly filled and swarming with men and boys, nearly all of them with sticks and bludgeons and throwing immense stones...' When the soldiers were discovered a section of the crowd surrounded the engine shed and hurled missiles through the windows, injuring several. A delegation pushed their way in and Barker was told that unless he and his men left, the building would be burnt down with them in it. Barker looked at their grim and determined faces and agreed to leave provided they promised to halt the indiscriminate vandalism. He marched his troops back to the railway station where they stood on the platform to await orders from the missing magistrate, Mr Clay from Wakefield.

Clay, however, had misunderstood the Chief Constable's instructions and had gone to the wrong colliery. When the military had not arrived he had gone home. Holiday, Barker and Police Inspector Corden, huddled together at Featherstone station. They saw the rioters break the promise to stop the destruction and fires blazed around the colliery joiners' shops and timber stacks. They decided they must find another magistrate, Bernard Hartley at Pontefract. Holiday's groom and a constable were sent by pony trap to Hartley's home, where they found him eating dinner. Hartley leapt into their trap, collected a copy of the Riot Act from the local police, and was driven to Featherstone station.[5]

Hartley agreed that the troops and a handful of police officers should return to the colliery to restore order. They recrossed the railway track to the yard in the coal-black night and confronted around 2,000 rioters lit by the glow from burning buildings. Barker and Hartley stepped forward.[6] The latter recalled: 'I took off my hat and then commanded silence, and I told them I was a magistrate, and I called upon them in the name of the Queen to disperse peaceably and quietly ... My appeal to them was received with jeers and shouts of derision.'

When the two men rejoined the troops they were showered by bricks and stones. A soldier was hit in the face, while another received a crippling blow to the leg. Barker, Hartley and Inspector Corden were also struck, but not so seriously. The soldiers and police held their position for almost 30 minutes as several more men dropped. Just before 9.00 p.m. Hartley read the Riot Act and later justified his action by telling an inquiry: 'I found it was a highly dangerous crowd; they were turbulent in a surging mass. They were waving their sticks and hats and shouting.' For a few moments both sides held back, but then the mob recommenced their howling and 'the stones were thrown in larger numbers than before'.

The troops fixed bayonets and advanced in line across the yard. The crowd retreated before them, through the main colliery gate and into the street outside. Barker was reluctant to risk his men in the darkness beyond the light cast by the burning buildings. As he paused the crowd surged back and attacked the Pontefract fire brigade as they arrived on the scene in two horse-drawn wagons. Three firemen were badly cut or bruised as they wrestled their apparatus into the yard. Hartley told the subsequent inquiry:

> I saw the critical state of things. The mob was surrounding us, and I felt that any further delay or appeal to the mob would be useless, and I saw that I must either withdraw the troops from the premises and leave the colliery to the mercy of the mob, or I must give the order to fire. I felt I had no other alternative, and I gave the order.

He wrote the order on a sheet of paper and handed it to Barker, along with a verbal request that the first volley must fire blank cartridges. Barker's men each had 80 rounds of ball cartridge, but no blanks as army regulations forbade their use on riot duty on the grounds that they would encourage any mob to believe that troops were bluffing. When Barker explained that to him, Hartley asked that the troops fire as few rounds as possible. Barker ordered two men to assume firing positions, one kneeling, the other standing behind. The pair fired directly into the crowd, again complying with army rules to minimise the risk of bullets hitting distant bystanders. Amazingly, neither shot inflicted casualties despite the almost point-blank range. The crowd roared that blanks were being fired and resumed their brick and stone bombardment.[7]

Barker waited five minutes before ordering an eight-man section to fire one round each. This time there were immediate cries of pain. Several in the crowd were injured. James Gibbs, 'a respectable young man and a Sunday school teacher', was watching the riot with his brother from a vantage point outside the main entrance. He was shot fatally in the chest. A miner, Thomas Clark, was also killed by a soldier's musket ball as he stood close by Gibbs. Neither man was taking part in the riot. The following inquiry concluded that Gibbs was an 'innocent spectator' who had concluded from the first ineffectual volley that the troops were firing blanks. On Clark, the inquiry stated, 'the fair inference from the evidence was that he was not taking part in the riot. On the other hand he was standing close to where the thick of the riot was, and he had not moved away. This imprudence cost him his life.'[8]

One of the injured waved a white hankerchief, the troops held their fire, and the crowd drifted away. Several set fire to a wooden bridge leading from the colliery across an adjoining road, but it was merely a final act of defiance. The fire brigade doused the flames while Barker and his men stood by in the yard until 11. p.m., when they were relieved by large reinforcements from Pontefract.

The inquiry which followed concluded that Hartley was right to order the troops to fire and Barker had no alternative but to obey. Their report said:

> The troops were in a position of great embarrassment. The withdrawal of half their original force had reduced them to so small a number as to render it difficult for them to defend the colliery at night time. The crowd had been for some time familiarised with their presence and had grown defiant. All efforts at conciliation had failed. Darkness had meanwhile supervened, and it was difficult for Captain Barker to estimate the exact number of his assailants, or to what extent he was being surrounded and outflanked. A charge had been made without avail, much valuable colliery property was already blazing, and the troops were with difficulty keeping at bay a mob armed with sticks and bludgeons, which was refusing to disperse, pressing where it could into the colliery premises, stoning the fire engine on its arrival, and keeping up volleys of missiles.[9]

The committee nevertheless also concluded that 'the modern rifle and cartridge with its full charge of powder' was so lethal that the army should consider using less dangerous armaments in suppressing riots in densely populated districts. Two years later a follow-up Home Office inquiry tried to codify the use of military might in civil disturbance. Troops should only be used 'as a last expedient'. Their proposals were formally adopted and incorporated into the Queen's Regulations.[10]

Within days of the Featherstone Riot 200 more soldiers and 300 extra policemen were sent to the West Riding from London, Cheshire and the East Riding. There were serious skirmishes in Sheffield and Barnsley, where miners attacked scab labour, and the trouble spread to Nottinghamshire and Derbyshire. Miners from Yorkshire and the Midlands travelled to Llanelly to dissuade Welsh miners from returning to work. They were 'severely maltreated' by the locals while the Inniskilling Dragoons looked on.

The Welsh miners were the first to return to work, but elsewhere the strike remained solid. In mid November, after 15 weeks of crippling stoppage, the Prime Minister, William Gladstone, decided to intervene. In a dramatic midnight Commons statement he said:

> The attention of Her Majesty's Government has been seriously called to the widespread and disastrous effects produced by the long continuance of the unfortunate dispute in the coal trade. It is clear from information that has reached the Board of Trade that much misery and suffering are caused not only to the families of the men directly involved, but also to many thousands of others, not engaged in mining, whose employment has been adversely affected by the stoppage. The further prolongation of the dispute cannot fail to aggravate this suffering, especially in view of the approach of winter, when the greatly increased price of fuel is likely to cause distress among the poorer classes throughout the country.[11]

He appointed Lord Rosebury to chair a forum bringing together the coal masters and the miners' unions.

The peace conference was held at the Foreign Office on 17 November with 14 delegates from each side. After six hours of tough talking behind closed doors, a deal was agreed. The miners were to return immediately to work at their old wage rates. The question of future pay changes would be considered by a Board of Conciliation. For the miners it was a victory, bought at a high price. Peace returned to the coalfields but few predicted it would last long.

12
The Suffragettes and Black Friday

'What a sordid day!'

The testimony of a young woman shocked Edwardian sensibilities:

> Several times constables and plain-clothes men who were in the crowd
> passed their arms around me from the back and clutched hold of my breasts
> in as public a manner as was possible, and men in the crowd followed their
> example. I was also pummelled on the chest, and my breast was clutched
> by one constable from the front. My skirt was lifted up as high as possible,
> and the constable attempted to lift me off the ground by raising his knee.
> This he could not do, so he threw me into the crowd and incited the men
> to treat me as they wished.

Her offence was to march on Parliament as a Suffragette. Many had
suffered much worse during the struggle for female emancipation. But
it was the sexual nature of the savagery demonstrated by the police
on 18 November 1910 which resulted in that day becoming known
as 'Black Friday'.

Concurrent with industrial unrest, female suffrage was a cause which
both men and women with radical views could easily identify with as the
nineteenth century came to a close. They argued that advances in wages
for working men could not alone tackle the inequalities which hit the
poorest hardest, but also affected the more prosperous. The emerging
women's movement grappled, as men had done before them, with the
issue of when violent action could be justified. As their forefathers
had discovered, the moral issue became easier when confronted with
state violence.

* * *

Emmeline Pankhurst was born in Manchester in 1858 and had a conventional, privileged education, attending finishing school in Paris when she was 15. Her father, however, the successful businessman Robert Goulden, was a veteran campaigner against slavery and the Corn Laws, while her mother Sophie was a radical feminist who took her daughter to women's suffrage meetings. When she was 20 Emmeline married Richard Pankhurst, a socialist who drafted the 1869 Municipal Franchises Act which allowed unmarried women householders to vote in council elections. Their radicalism was passed on to their four children, Christabel, Sylvia, Frank and Adela.

The family grew frustrated with the moderate, middle-class activism of the National Union of Women's Suffrage Societies led by the law-abiding Mrs Millicent Garrett Fawcett. Emmeline made many visits to local workhouses in her role as a Poor Law Guardian and was deeply shocked by the condition of the inmates, particularly women and girls. What horrified her most was the exploitation of females driven to prostitution and the vices of the flesh. She became convinced that the genteel ways of Mrs Fawcett and her supporters were no match for the state's opposition to female suffrage, and that a new organisation was needed to recruit working-class women to the struggle. They found eager recruits among the factory women of Manchester. In 1903 the Pankhursts founded the Women's Social and Political Union (WSPU) with the motto 'Deeds Not Words'.

The initial response was apathy. No Government or party was prepared to risk the impact on their own fortunes of giving 6 million people with indeterminate affiliations the power of the vote. Newspapers were weary of the issue and few meetings went reported. By 1905 the Pankhursts, and Christabel in particular, decided that more attention-grabbing tactics were needed rather than reasoned argument. The result was a violent revolution to attain the holy grail of equal citizenship.[1]

Emmeline was recognised as the driving force, vital and resourceful. A Manchester teacher, Teresa Billington-Greig, described both sides of a remarkable woman:

> She had beauty and graciousness, moving and speaking with dignity, but with no uncertainty of mind or movement. Later I was to see her captivating the mob, turning commonplace men and women into heroes, enslaving the young rebel women by the exploitation of emotion. She was ruthless in using the followers she gathered around her, as she was ruthless to herself. She

was a most astute statesman, a skilled politician, a self-dedicated reshaper of the world – and a dictator without mercy.[2]

As the movement grew, she imposed iron discipline. Annie Kennedy would recall:

> Nuns in a convent were not watched over more and supervised more strictly than were the organisers and members of the Militant Movement. It was an unwritten rule that there must be no concerts, no theatre, no smoking; work and sleep to prepare for more work was the order of the day.[3]

On 13 October 1905 Christabel Pankhurst and Annie Kearney heckled minister Sir Edward Grey at a meeting in London, demanding to know when the Liberal Government would give 'votes to women'. They refused to shut up and the police were called to evict them. During the ensuing struggle a constable claimed that both women kicked him. They were arrested, charged with assault and subsequently fined 5 shillings each. When they refused to pay they were thrown in gaol. Edwardian Britain was shocked by women using noisy and violent tactics to win the vote, and subsequently choosing a common cell when they were thwarted. It was a spectacle which quickly became all too frequent.

Emmeline moved to London to join her daughters and over the next seven years she was imprisoned frequently for acts of civil disobedience. During one six-week sentence for street-brawling she became ill while held in a freezing solitary cell. Over one 18-month period, although now in her fifties, she endured ten hunger strikes. Women of all classes were inspired by her example. Hundreds went to prison and suffered the pain and indignity of force-feeding. The well-known actress Kitty Marion was force-fed more than 200 times in one year. The Suffragettes – so named by the *Daily Mail* – took each decision individually, rather than on the instruction of their leaders. The WSPU developed a sophisticated media operation, holding breakfast press conferences as women were released, highlighting the agonies suffered in prison, and striking medals for their heroines. The more roughly such women were handled, by police and gaolers, the more militant they became.

No Liberal minister was spared heckling at public meetings, windows were smashed, Parliament was besieged by protesters, and petitions were presented. But ministers urged patience, and the Suffragettes did not receive the full support they expected and demanded from the

8   A poster for the January 1910 general election campaign, drawn by Alfred
Pearse
Museum of London, Suffragette Fellowship Collection

Labour Movement. In 1908 two women, Miss Nell and nurse Olivia Smith, chained themselves to the railings outside 10 Downing Street, a tactic which became popular as it allowed time for speeches before the police could cut them free and remove them. But it was the tactic of hunger strikes which aroused the greatest sympathy and support.

Marion Wallace Dunlop went on hunger strike after being sentenced to one month's imprisonment for wilful damage – rubber-stamping a Bill of Rights message on the wall of St Stephen's Hall. She was freed after 91 hours of fasting, but few other women got off so lightly. Force-feeding had been introduced after a violent demonstration at Bingley Hall, Birmingham, when a number of women refused to take the food in Winston Green gaol. One of them, Mrs Mary Leigh, described the invasion of her cell by two doctors and four wardresses. 'Held by the wardresses, the two-foot long tube was forced up my nostril by a doctor', she later attested.

> The sensations of the tube's progress up my nose and down my throat was very painful. The drums of my ears seemed to be at bursting point and there was a terrible pain in my throat and chest. They pushed nearly two feet of the tube into me. The doctor then stood on a chair holding the funnel end of the tube above my head. He then started to pour a liquid mixture of milk and eggs into the funnel. After a few moments, he decided that the liquid was not going down fast enough, so he pinched my nostril with the tube in it and squeezed my throat, causing me even more pain.[4]

Such stories leaked out to prison and there was press uproar, but MPs and ministers were apparently unmoved.

Sylvia Pankhurst, a well-known artist who is too often overlooked in histories of the family, established the East London Federation of Suffragettes and the weekly newspaper the *Women's Dreadnought*. She created many of the images forever associated with the cause, most notably an angel carrying the trumpet of freedom and the recurrent motif of Joan of Arc. She too suffered imprisonment, but began to move away from her family because of her belief that the cause was not just for women, but for Socialism. She was increasingly fearful that too many Suffragettes, including her family, were motivated by hatred towards men rather than by a desire for equal treatment under the law. She wrote bitterly that Christabel was 'preaching the sex war deprecated and denied by the older Suffragettes'. She had a point. Christabel, in her writings, appeared obsessed with prostitution and the male vices. Men, through sexual diseases, were 'the exterminators of the species'.[5] Women, on the other hand, were inherently moral, chaste and clean-living. She rejoiced, however, in the failure to cure VD because the strivings to do so by the medical profession were an attempt to enable men to 'go and sin in safety'. Such extremism was not shared by most followers who braved force-feeding and beatings in the name of equality and simple justice.

The Suffragettes next targeted Lloyd George during a visit to Newcastle. The police erected barricades and searched buildings, seeking for a mass of women demonstrators. In fact only a dozen women were deployed to shower Lloyd George's arrival party with stones. Mrs Jane Brailsford attacked a police barricade with an axe. She and the other volunteers were arrested and sentenced to a month apiece. In the gaol they answered every question with the call 'Votes for women', went on hunger strike and were force-fed. They were roughly handled by the wardresses and some Suffragettes tried to barricade themselves in their cells or set fire to the meagre furnishings. Each attempt was met with hosings of freezing water.

Such brutality hardened hearts. During the summer of 1908, rallies in Hyde Park passed off relatively peacefully, but the viciousness of the punishments doled out to protesters turned 1909 into the most violent year of protest so far. Various women's suffrage bills had failed to clear Parliamentary hurdles and across the nation frustration was expressed at meetings which at their peak were running at a rate of 1,000 a month. On the night of 29 June groups were sent from Caxton Hall with bags of stones to smash the windows of Government building in Whitehall. By the following morning 108 had been arrested, while Asquith was besieged in his own Kentish home by stone-throwers despite personal Special Branch protection. Christabel Pankhurst declared: 'This is war.'

At the end of 1909 Winston Churchill was attacked with a dog whip at Bristol station by Theresa Garnett. He later told a female delegation: 'I am bound to say I think your cause has marched backwards.'[6] At the Lord Mayor's banquet, attended by Churchill and premier Asquith, the event was infiltrated by two Suffragettes posing as kitchen staff. Amelia Brown and Alice Paul hid under a bench and, as the guests stood to toast the King, Brown threw her shoe through a window. Both were given a month's hard labour. Such demonstrations grew more common in 1910, an election year which saw the Liberal administration in deep trouble. The Suffragettes were determined to exploit the political turmoil at Westminster to achieve their own ends.

Parliament was to reassemble on 22 November and the Suffragettes organised a deputation to the House before then. On the 18th, women from across the country assembled at Caxton Hall as the Cabinet met. Those picked for the deputation wore small white-satin badges. Emmeline Pankhurst addressed them:

> In quietness and assurance shall be your strength. You are acting legally in persistently endeavouring to see Mr Asquith. All your other kinds of effort having failed, you will now press forward in quietness and peaceableness, offending none and blaming none, ready to sacrifice yourselves even unto death if need be, in the cause of freedom.

Despite her stirring words, the women gathered there did not expect to become martyrs. They had received assurances from Westminster Police that they would not be molested and it was rumoured that Churchill had ordered no arrests. Furthermore, the deputation which Mrs Pankhurst personally led was headed by stately dowagers in their seventies and such distinguished figures as the scientist Hertha Ayrton, Princess Sophia Duleep Singh and Dr Louisa Garrett Anderson.

The deputation and their supporters set off down Victoria Street to the cheers of people on passing buses. But as they reached Parliament Square their escort of uniformed Westminster Police faded away and the women were confronted by hundreds of grim-faced police officers they did not recognise and other tough-looking men. Hertha Ayrton wrote:

> We were not long in finding out what it meant. Before any of us could get into the House, we had to run the gauntlet of organised gangs of policemen in plain clothes, dressed like roughs, who nearly squeezed the breath out of our bodies, the policemen in official clothes helping them. When Mrs Pankhurst and Mrs Garrett Anderson had got through, it was still worse for the rest of us. I nearly fainted and Louise Garrett Anderson succeeded in making them let me through. Mrs Saul Soloman was seized by the breasts and thrown down. Women were thrown from policemen in uniform to policemen in plain clothes literally till they fainted.[7]

The twelve-strong deputation all got through to the steps of Strangers' Entrance and were surrounded by a strong cordon of police. There they stood for six hours as more violence was inflicted on the women outside.

When May Billinghurst trundled her wheelchair up to the railings of Parliament she was arrested and roughly thrown to the ground. Ada Wright recalled:

> When we reached Parliament Square, plain-clothes men mingling with the crowd kicked us, and added to the horror and anguish of the day by dragging some of our women down side streets. There were many attempts at indecent assault. The police rode at us with shire horses, so I caught hold of the reins of one of the horses and would not let go. A policeman grabbed my arm and twisted it round and round until I found the bone almost breaking and I sank to the pavement, helpless. A contingent of the United States Navy was in London at the time, and they lined up outside Westminster Abbey and watched the proceedings. I was continually tripped up by the police and thrown to the ground in the sight of the American sailors. Each time I got up, and once more made a show of advancing on the House of Commons, only to be thrown to the ground once again. As I leaned against the railings after one of these episodes, a sense of the humiliation I was undergoing came over me. I wondered what my relations would think of me if they were to see me. When night came, I was mercifully arrested. After a long proceeding in the police station, we were bailed out and I returned to where I was staying at one o'clock in the morning. I said to myself with a shudder: 'What a sordid day!'[8]

During that long afternoon and evening a constant stream of casualties were brought back to Caxton Hall, where an anteroom was converted into a makeshift hospital. Christabel Pankhurst, working in her office at Clement's Inn was told by a member of the Men's Political Union: 'They've brought up a lot of the police from the City, and they're bashing the women.'

Another protester wrote:

> For hours I was beaten about the body, thrown backwards and forwards from one to another, until I felt dazed by the horror of it. Often seized by the coat collar, dragged out of the crowd, only to be pushed helplessly along in front of one's tormentor into a side street ... while he beat one up and down one's spine until cramp seized one's legs, when he would then release one with a vicious shove, and with insulting speeches, such as 'I will teach you a lesson. I will teach you not to come back any more. I will punish you, you ——, you ——.' Once I was thrown with my jaw against a lamp-post with such force that two of my front teeth were loosened. What I complain of on behalf of us all is the long-drawn-out agony of the delayed arrest, and the continuous beating and pinching.[9]

Despite Churchill's alleged orders, over 100 women were arrested, although most were immediately bailed. The following morning a photograph of Ada Wright laying barely conscious on the pavement was splashed across the front page of the *Daily Mirror* with the headline 'BLACK FRIDAY'. The Government tried without success to suppress the photograph. That, and the need to deploy police to Wales to tackle coal strike disturbances, had an immediate effect. When the charged women went to court, the prosecutor announced: 'The position has been considered by the Home Secretary who has come to the conclusion that no public advantage would be obtained by proceeding with the prosecution.' They were discharged singly and in batches. Antonia Raeburn commented: 'In court, instead of being treated like political prisoners, the women were dealt with like naughty children.'[10] No policemen, in uniform or plain clothes, were charged with any acts of violence and indecency.

Asquith was severely criticised in *The Times* for letting the women go and for promising the deputation that he would make a statement on women's suffrage the following Tuesday. On the eve of his statement Suffragettes held vigil in the bitter cold outside the Commons, having been denied access while the House was sitting. When Asquith rose the following day he dismissed the suffrage question with non-committal posturing.

Three hundred Suffragettes gathered again at Caxton Hall were told the news and once again marched down Victoria Street, this time heading for the Prime Minister's residence. Mrs Bowerman Chibnall told a policeman who barred her way: 'It is my intention to go to 10 Downing Street or die in the attempt.' The response was 'Die then!' followed by a heavy truncheon blow to the head. She recalled: 'I found afterwards that so much force had been used that my hairpins were bent double in my hair and my sealskin coat was torn to ribbons.'[11]

For a time, however, the women outnumbered the police and some wielded splintered banner poles which inflicted painful scratches rather than broken bones. Cabinet ministers returning to their grace and favour homes were jostled and Asquith himself was bundled into a motor car to escape. Windows were shattered before the police regained control, arresting Mrs Pankhurst and 175 others.[12]

Churchill ordered that all the prisoners, including Mrs Pankhurst, be discharged, save for those who admitted violent assault. The handful who were convicted were fined but elected to go to prison instead. All were out by Christmas.

According to Suffragette propaganda, Black Friday made martyrs of two women. On Christmas Day Emmeline's sister Mary, who had been badly manhandled, took ill at the family's festive party. Some hours later Emmeline found her dead in bed. The following week Henria Williams, another who had been in the thick of the fray, died of a heart attack.

*   *   *

Black Friday forced the Suffragettes to rethink their tactics. Large deputations were now considered too dangerous. Instead, the most militant went underground and waged guerrilla warfare, a term they used themselves, against the Liberal Government which so steadfastly refused them the vote. Women armed with hammers attacked store windows in Oxford Street and teashops in the Strand. Window-smashing erupted across the country. The perpetrators made no attempt to flee, were quickly arrested and rarely put up a struggle. The direct onslaught against property enraged the forces of the Establishment. *The Times* editorial said:

> No-one can surely have imagined destruction on this scale in London as the work of a few unbalanced women whose only grievance lies in an insignificant point of Parliamentary procedure affecting a measure they have at heart. There is only one explanation for this crowning folly, which is not merely folly but crime, that the obvious movement of public opinion from indifference to hostility has reduced them to despair.[13]

Letterboxes became the next targets. A hatchet was thrown at Asquith's carriage during his official visit to Dublin. There were reports of Suffragettes practising with revolvers. A group of militants, including three men, hatched a plot to kidnap Lloyd George. They leased a cottage near New Forest heathland on which he regularly strolled, equipped a pantry with window bars and locks, and bought straps to secure their prey. They almost caught him on a golf course, but their car was locked up and the opportunity was missed.

Even more militant women turned to arson, encouraged by Christabel while she was shopping in Paris, having fled from the prospect of another gaol sentence. The burning of the Regent's Park refreshment kiosk was the first in a continuous campaign aimed at empty property. St Catherine's Church in Hatcham, London, was one of many more substantial buildings burned down. Others reduced to ruins in 1913 included Lady White's mansion near Staines and the St Leonards house of Arthur du Cros MP. Railway stations were also gutted, explosives were found in St Paul's Cathedral, and there was an attempt to fire the Theatre Royal in Dublin. The first week in April, following another term of imprisonment imposed on Mrs Pankhurst, saw an orgy of criminal damage: four houses were set ablaze at Hampstead Garden Suburb; a bomb wrecked an empty railway carriage at Stockport; another bomb exploded at Oxted station; a mansion near Chorley Wood was destroyed by fire; arson at Ayr racecourse caused £3,000 worth of damage; a house in Potters Bar, a mansion at Norwich and a hayrick near Nottingham were fired; suffragettes charged an ancient cannon in the ruins of Dudley Castle and caused a massive explosion; attempts were made to fire the stands at Cardiff racecourse, but these were foiled – all within seven days. A Leeds tailoress, Leonora Cohen, was arrested by Beefeaters in the Tower of London as she tried to attack the Crown Jewels with a filed-down iron bar. Not even works of art were safe. Mary Richardson slashed Velásquez's Rokeby Venus at the National Gallery, prompting the closure of the Royal Academy and the Tate Gallery. Such outrages caused massive indignation. But sympathies shifted when the Suffragettes got their first public martyr.

Emily Wilding Davidson, an Oxford graduate, had always been a firebrand. She was involved in the Newcastle attack on police barricades and was badly injured when she threw herself over a prison staircase in a failed attempt to avoid force-feeding. On 4 June 1913 she wound a Suffragette flag beneath her coat, bought a third-class return ticket to Epsom, and went to the races. As the King's horse thundered around the bend, Emily stepped out from the dense throng and tried to grab the bridle. The jockey and horse were unharmed but Emily was badly trampled. She never recovered consciousness and died four days later. Solemn crowds lined her funeral procession, and men were seen crying alongside women.[14]

Later some feminists took a fresh look at the tactics employed by the Pankhursts, Sylvia excepted, and which encouraged martyrdom. Almost a century later Melanie Phillips wrote:

Harsh though the word may seem, such manipulative cynicism is the hallmark of terrorism. Worse still, the Suffragette leaders washed their hands of any responsibility for the followers they lured into violence. It was an act of monstrous cowardice that made victims of the very women they were purporting to lead to liberation.[15]

But it was the Great War, not individual deaths, which finally gave the Suffragettes victory. Several days after war was declared on Germany, those Suffragettes in prison were released. Emmeline responded by suspending militant action and told her followers to help with the war effort. As millions of men volunteered or were called up, the Suffragettes campaigned to be allowed to do 'men's work' in the munitions factories, transport and other key services. With a £2,000 grant they organised a London demonstration. Women now carried banners with such slogans as 'For Men Must Fight and Women Must Work'. The WSPU newspaper changed its name from the *Suffragette* to *Britannia*. It attacked anti-war activists such as Ramsay MacDonald and lambasted 'Bolshevik women trade union leaders'. Sylvia Pankhurst and her mother were deeply alienated. The daughter accused her of neglecting the needs of working class women and of using her considerable clout to encourage young men to sign up for the killing fields of France. Christabel disagreed, and in July 1915 she led 30,000 women down Whitehall behind the banner 'We Demand the Right to Serve'.

With the carnage on the Front, the right was quickly granted. At least 1.6 million women went to work, including 200,000 in Government departments, 500,000 in private clerical offices, 250,000 on the land and a massive 800,000 in engineering works and production lines, mostly in the twelve months after Christabel's demonstration. There was one exception – women in domestic service dropped by 400,000.

By 1916 Herbert Asquith fully realised that, with so many women doing war work, they would have to be given the vote. The women's suffrage bill was debated in June 1917 and the following January 6 million women over 30 were finally able to cast their votes. Over 1,000 women had been jailed during the campaign, with hundreds suffering force-feeding, assault and hard labour. But it was the death of men in their hundreds of thousands which ultimately gave women the vote. Mrs Pankhurst said: 'Is it not wonderful that the war has finally brought us victory?'

British society was changed for ever. The influx of women workers did, however, add to industrial unrest. Few were in trade unions, they cared little about established trade practices, they were not eager to stand aside when men returned to claim their old jobs. They clashed with socialist shop stewards who had opposed the war, and with conservative trade unionists who could not stomach equal pay for women. Such concerns would add to post-war industrial turmoil.

Mrs Pankhurst spent several years in the US and Canada lecturing on venereal diseases. When she returned in 1925 she joined the Conservative Party. Her daughter Sylvia was appalled, but Emmeline was also furious with her for having an illegitimate baby. The family feud continued until 1928 when, while standing as a Tory Parliamentary candidate, Emmeline died from a recurring stomach ailment she had suffered since being force-fed and having her stomach pumped during her frequent hunger strikes.

Equal voting rights for men and women over the age of 21 were finally achieved in the same year.

13
Churchill and the Troops

'more like a revolution than strike'

In the first decade of the twentieth century Winston Spencer Churchill was a genuine popular hero. He was a veteran of exciting campaigns, a world-famous war correspondent, a bestselling author, and a dashing aristocrat who switched from Tory to Liberal and espoused causes designed to improve the lot of the working man and ordinary families.

Within a few years that image was tarnished by his apparent eagerness to send troops into working communities. Fairly, or unfairly, the stain of Tonypandy would stay with him to his grave.

*   *   *

Churchill was indeed a key player in the great reforming Liberal Government after the Tories were ousted in 1906 with the help of the newly renamed Labour Party. As President of the Board of Trade Churchill was pivotal in the introduction of major reforms. He established Labour Exchanges, helped steer through the National Insurance bill and was further involved in laying the foundations of the welfare state. Successive Acts strengthened safety precautions in the mines and provided meal breaks for shop assistants. But the administration became bogged down in disputes with their Labour allies over trade union recognition. A commission recommended that the unions be given legal entity without legal immunity. In addition, the 54 Labour or Lib-Lab MPs appeared more concerned with arguing the merits of ideological socialism than in the pragmatic schemes offered by Churchill and Lloyd George. There was conflict within both Parliamentary chambers and the administration, especially after the 1910 election left the Government with no overall majority.

Britain hit an economic slump in 1908 and for two years unemployment stuck at around 4 per cent. Most workers had seen few concrete benefits from the Government's social reforms, and militancy increased within the trade union and labour movements. When Churchill was moved to the Home Office he was immediately confronted with the Suffragettes and with a series of major strikes and public disorder after several years of relative industrial peace. Whereas before the Cabinet reshuffle Churchill's role would have been one of conciliation, now his role was to maintain law and order.

The first crisis began as a loading dispute between unionised dock workers at Newport and the shippers Empire Transport and Holder Brothers. The bosses tried to employ labourers supplied by the Shipping Federation. The dockers went on strike and forced the scab workers from the town. Less than 300 strikers were involved, but the docks were brought to a halt and there were reports of looting and criminal damage. Local magistrates complained that the 'free' labourers had been assaulted and intimidated. They requested police reinforcements and troops.

Churchill was initially unsympathetic to the employers. He telegraphed his Permanent Under-Secretary Sir Edward Trump, saying: 'The Empire Transport Company should be made to realise that employing large droves of men from London to break the strike is a very strong order. Do not on any account give them or the public the impression that we approve their action.'[1]

He was also extremely wary against deploying soldiers against British citizens. Churchill had always had an ambivalent attitude to the armed forces. Early in his career he had been a glory-hunter who lobbied his influential family to get him a campaign medal for the North West Frontier, even though he was far from the action. His courage at the Battle of Omdurman was unquestioned, if impetuous. And his escape from the Boers provided him with the story of a lifetime, and one he milked ruthlessly. However, throughout, it was clear that his martial ardour was intended to give himself a stepping stone to a life in politics. He had a distaste for soldiering and a disgust for butchery.

On 21 May 1910 the Mayor of Newport telegraphed the Home Office: 'Serious riots anticipated here in consequence of dock strikes. At a meeting of borough magistrates here this morning it was unanimously resolved that the War Office be requested to hold in readiness 200 infantrymen and 100 mounted men to assist the local police and 500 imported police.'[2] Newport's Chief Constable requested another 250 police officers. Churchill authorised the despatch of the requested police reinforcements from Bristol, Merthyr, Glamorgan and Monmouth, but held back the troops. He regarded the strike as so little threat to public order that he took off for a short holiday in Lucerne.

The telegraph wires burned hot between Wales and London, and the frustrated magistrates wired a request for troops directly to the War Office. Troup wrote to Sir Edward Ward, Permanent Under-Secretary for War:

> The state of things at Newport is serious, and Mr Churchill, before he left, had considered the possibility of ... troops. He is most anxious to avoid their being used, and is doing all he can by offering to supply Metropolitan Police and otherwise to avoid the necessity; but of course if the Mayor or Magistrates requisition them, they must be ready to go. Mr Churchill asked me specially to impress on the War Office that *mounted troops* should be sent. They are far more effective than infantry in dealing with a riot, and the risk of their employment leading to loss of life is much less.[3]

The troops were not needed. Within 24 hours of the last telegram the strikers met the employers using the Board of Trade as an arbitrator. The dispute was settled. The exchange of messages had shown that Churchill may have had a reluctance to deploy troops, but it was an emotion he could overcome.

*   *   *

Since Featherstone there had been a serious overhaul of the system by which troops could be deployed to counter civil disturbances, and the degree of force which could be employed. Local magistrates who called in the military were required to remain at the scene and advise officers. That inevitably led to tricky questions of who was in charge and who should ultimately take legal responsibility for fatal blunders. The system was rough and ready but seemed to be effective. Official records show that in the 30 years prior to 1908 the military was called in to help civil authorities 24 times across England and Wales, but the only time firearms were used was at Featherstone. A Select Committee review that year recommended a clearer chain of command between Chief Constables, magistrates and military officers, and urged more effective warnings before troops opened fire. But the use of blank ammunition as warning shots was definitely ruled out. The Secretary of State for War, Richard Haldane, said:

> I think it is most undesirable because the mob get it into their head that you have nothing but blank cartridges and they come on and get killed. The military authorities say: 'We are here, and if we use our firearms, it is to kill.' That is why we demur to being called out except in the last and most perilous necessity. If the mob get the impression we are there with only blank cartridges the result will be bloodshed galore.

An opportunity to test the revised procedures came in November 1910 in the Rhondda Valley. A small-scale dispute over pay differentials in the working of hard and soft coal seams escalated until almost 30,000 miners were on strike in the region. The owners, who operated the Cambrian Combine, were intransigent and demanded full protection from the civil authorities. And they collectively agreed to underwrite any owners whose pits were shut down. Even before the strike was called the Chief Constable of Glamorgan, Captain Lionel Lindsay, anticipated serious trouble. He called in police reinforcements from Swansea, Cardiff and Bristol and concentrated them in Aberdare and the Rhondda. His forces were still spread thinly and he was unable to guarantee protection for all the Combine pits. He put his heaviest concentrations at the Glamorgan colliery at Llwynypia, to protect the power house there. The miners recognised that they had a hard fight on their hands and at a mass meeting at the Empire Theatre, Tonypandy, they decided to embark on mass picketing. There aim was to deny access to any workmen or managers who would be unable to maintain the ventilation and pumping machines on the surface which kept the underground workings viable. Shortly after dawn on 7 November a bugle call summoned thousands of strikers to march on their neighbourhood pits. At Tonypandy a crowd of strikers attacked the pit head and put out the boiler fires which operated the ventilation system. Large-scale pickets were mounted on those pits which remained open, preventing access by scab labour. One by one they were forced to close. Angry clashes turned into three days of more indiscriminate vandalism, violence and some looting.

The only colliery left open was the Glamorgan at Tonypandy, which had been turned into a fortress by the presence of at least 100 policemen. In it Lindsay established his operational HQ. It was of critical importance as the power house contained a massive pumping plant capable of extracting up to 5,000 gallons of water per minute. Electrical power was supplied from a large generator in the colliery yard. Both bosses and strikers knew that if the plant was shut down, Number 2 pit would have to close permanently. If there was to be any confrontation, it would be there.

Throughout the 7th, crowds gathered outside the entrance, jostling blacklegs as they left the morning shift. Generally the strikers were good-humoured and some waved Union Jacks. Around 9.00 p.m. the crowd grew more determined to halt officials due to relieve the day shift. A group of youths charged police officers guarding the entrance but were beaten back. The miners' leader, Will John, called for calm and peaceful persuasion. Most obeyed, but a little while later more youths took positions on a nearby embankment and began stoning the police, some of whom were injured. Lindsay ordered a baton charge on the crowd. That resulted in hand-to-hand fighting which continued sporadically until midnight. Wooden palings were ripped down, exposing the power house, and the pay office was wrecked. But the police kept charging until the crowd broke and ran towards Tonypandy town square a quarter of a mile away.

Earlier in the day local magistrates had asked Captain Lindsay for military assistance. Lindsay, applying set procedures, passed on the request to the officers commanding garrisons in Shrewsbury, Chester and Salisbury. Lindsay also called in police reinforcements from Cardiff, Swansea and Bristol, plus another 100 men from the Glamorgan county force. Two hundred cavalry troopers and two companies of infantry were to be immediately sent from Salisbury. The scene was set for the clash of bayonet against pit prop, sabre against mining helmet. That was halted by an extraordinary, and unexpected, intervention.

Early on 8 November Winston Churchill held a conference with Richard Haldane, and both agreed that the disorder must be suppressed by police action alone, if that was at all possible.[4] The soldiers would only be sent in if the police were swamped by rioters. It was a brave decision which runs counter to the myth of Tonypandy. Lindsay was told that 300 more Metropolitan Police officers, 100 of them mounted, were to be sent by train to Tonypandy forthwith. The cavalry were sent to Glamorgan and put on standby. But the two companies of foot soldiers would remain at Swindon to await further orders. Strike leaders were told that the troops would be held back while the police maintained the peace. Churchill appointed 38-year-old Maj.-Gen. Nevil Macready to command all the troops in the region. Macready was experienced in civil disorder, having served six years as a staff officer with the military police in the Middle East and having been in charge of military aid to civil authorities within the Foreign Office. Macready embarked by train to Glamorgan with a message from Churchill to 'act as you think best for the preservation of order and the prevention of bloodshed ... vigorous baton charges may be the best means of preventing recourse to firearms'.[5]

While the Metropolitan Police were delayed for an hour on trains, the rioting in Tonypandy and surrounding pit villages worsened. During the afternoon of the 8th, a mass meeting of miners at Tonypandy's athletics ground welcomed Churchill's telegraphed assurances that the troops would be held back and the meeting broke up in an orderly manner. But at 5 p.m. a group of youths began throwing stones at the Glamorgan colliery, shattering every pane in the power house and making work inside impossible. Lindsay ordered his mounted police to clear the roadway. They succeeded, but when they returned so did their assailants, and several officers were injured. Large wooden palings were torn down and strewn on the road to hamper further mounted charges. The battle raged for two hours, with numerous baton charges, and there were many casualties on both sides. The South Wales *Daily News* reported: 'Repulsed by the police after a sanguinary baton charge, the strikers, reinforced, returned again to the attack, and were once again charged by mounted police, dozens being rendered prostrate by blows from police batons.'[6] Lurid stories began circulating of fatalities. In fact, just one miner died from a blow on the head, most probably from a police baton. But that death, and false rumours of many more, fuelled the fury of the strikers and pickets. Lindsay telegraphed: 'Position grave.' However, the police on the scene successfully repulsed all attacks on the colliery before the Metropolitan reinforcements arrived.

The angry and battered strikers retreated to Tonypandy and vented their fury there. A correspondent for the London *Standard* reported:

> They spent some three hours looting and rioting in the town. For a quarter of a mile practically every shop had its front smashed in. The street was littered with goods of all descriptions – drapery, millinery, groceries, provisions, and chemicals. The rioters ran around unmolested with armfuls of loot. Some carried rolls of cloth, hats, umbrellas and bundles of clothing.[7]

Fifty-eight shops in the town were attacked and only two were untouched. One was a jeweller's protected by heavy roller shutters. The other was a chemist owned by former Welsh rugby international Willie Llewellyn.

There was similar uproar at Aberaman where an attack was launched on the Powell Duffryn washery. Two thousand men and a large number of women were in the onslaught and several policemen were seriously injured. The *Daily News* reported:

> The rioters climbed over the fencing and set fire to a quantity of straw stored in a railway wagon. Immediately there was a huge conflagration and expensive property was in imminent peril. Prompt rescue measures were taken and the fire was extinguished ere much damage had been done. The mob only yielded to a series of baton charges, and the crowd rushed pell mell along the canal bank, many being jostled into the canal.[8]

Churchill then took the unprecedented step of putting all the forces, around Tonypandy, 1,400 policemen and 500 troops, under the sole command of General Macready. The infantry at Swindon and the cavalry waiting at Cardiff were sent forward to Pontypridd and 500 more embarked on trains.[9] At lunchtime on the 9th a squadron of the 18th Hussars, dressed in khaki and carrying carbine swords, trotted into Tonypandy as shopkeepers were boarding up their shattered premises with wood and corrugated shutters, which earned the town the nickname 'Zinc City'. They took up positions overlooking the Glamorgan colliery as hundreds of local people either watched in silent disbelief or hooted their derision. Sir Wyndham Childs, the officer commanding the squadron, wrote later in life that the damage he saw to Tonypandy town centre was worse than anything he saw in France during the Great War after a German withdrawal. The shopkeepers were relieved, but other townsfolk saw it as an army of occupation. Later that day as the Hussars were heading back to Pontypridd they were met by a hostile crowd at Porth. They held back until 50 Metropolitan Police arrived to open up the road. Several regiments of infantry were sent into the Valleys, including the Lancashire Fusiliers, the Somerset Light Infantry and the West Ridings.

The military deployment was constitutionally questionable in the absence of martial law. On the other hand, Churchill's reluctance to put troops in the front line against the strikers infuriated the Establishment. *The Times* led the criticism:

> Mr Churchill hardly seems to understand that an acute crisis has arisen, which needs decisive handling. The rose water of conciliation is all very well in its place, but its place is not in face of a wild mob drunk with the desire of destruction. Men's lives are in danger, not to mention the poor horses ...[10]

Churchill had taken a big gamble, but his choice of Macready helped him win. Macready was a tough man who displayed even-handedness and tact. He ignored the local magistrates, whom he suspected of bias against the miners, or worse, and refused to be dictated to by the mine owners. It was a strict rule that no officers or men were billeted with the employers, or enjoyed any hospitality from them. A staff officer acted as liaison with the workmen's strike committee. The soldiers were kept in the background, and during the whole of the disturbances not a single shot was fired. Although their very presence was intimidating, the soldiers kept on amicable terms with the miners and several football matches were arranged between them. The bosses protested that this was not what they expected, but Macready was equally firm with the miners. Any picket-line violence was swiftly suppressed by large bodies of baton-wielding police. Through his liaison officer he repeatedly warned the strike committee of the legal restrictions on picketing.

Such tactics swiftly paid off, picket-line violence and rioting stopped almost at once, and the strike began to fade. By the end of the week Churchill was able to reassure King George V: 'Reports from the whole of the Rhondda are satisfactory. Absolute order has been maintained around all the threatened collieries. A few trifling incidents of window-breaking have occurred in two of the villages.' He explained his decision to hold back the troops:

> The force of picked constables experienced in the handling of crowds was for every purpose better suited to the needs of the situation than an equivalent body of military. Infantry soldiers can if attacked or stoned only reply by

fire from long-range rifles which often kill foolish sightseers unconnected with the riot, or innocent people at some distance from it.

He continued:

> The insensate action of the rioters in wrecking shops in the town of Tonypandy, against which they had not the slightest cause for animosity, when they had been foiled in their attacks upon the colliery, was not foreseen by anyone on the spot, and would not have been prevented by the presence of soldiers at the colliery itself. The whole district is now in the efficient control of the police, and there appears to be no reason at present why the policy of keeping the military out of direct contact with the rioters should be departed from.[11]

The King agreed, and Churchill also received strong support from the Manchester *Guardian*, which said in an editorial:

> One can imagine what would have happened if the soldiers instead of the policemen had come upon the rioters while they were pillaging. Bayonets would have been used instead of truncheons; the clumsier methods of the soldiers would have exasperated the crowds, and instead of a score of cases for the hospital there might have been as many for the mortuary.[12]

Despite such liberal verdicts in the immediate aftermath of Tonypandy, a legend was born in the Valleys and continues to circulate today. Churchill's son Randolph wrote over 50 years later:

> Socialist propagandists have sought to make martyrs of the miners of Tonypandy comparable to those of Tolpuddle in 1834. Tonypandy in reality is only distinguished from the other Welsh villages involved because of the high degree of looting in which the miners indulged; but a lie once started can seldom be overtaken.[13]

The strike dragged on, and with it the military occupation. Macready arranged daily meetings with the strike leaders to defuse possible confrontations. In his autobiography Macready said that when the strike committee gave their word 'it was scrupulously adhered to, a line of conduct which the employers might well have imitated'. The strike committee, for their part, never once complained about the military presence, not even when troops were deployed to guard the court house at Prontypridd while their comrades faced trial under the Conspiracy and Property Act.

In December 1910, 13 miners from Gilfach Goch were summoned to attend the magistrate's court to answer charges of intimidating a colliery official. At dawn on the 14th the bugles called and 10,000 men flocked from across the district to accompany the 13 miners to court. They sang as they walked the six miles from Rhondda to Pontypridd, and were encouraged by their womenfolk. The procession was two miles long and led by a banner proclaiming 'Hungry as Lions'. The defendants wore their summonses pinned to their hats as badges of honour. A ring of police and troops prevented all but the defendants entering the town, so the demonstrators congregated at the Rocking Stone, a historic meeting place on the common overlooking Pontypridd. Again the younger element called for a violent attack, but this time they were shouted down.

The trial lasted six days and each morning the procession was repeated. On 20 December the magistrate, D. Lieufer Thomas, delivered his judgment. The town was barricaded and shuttered by shopkeepers fearful of a repeat of Tonypandy. A hundred Cardiff officers brought the police strength around the court house to 400, plus two troops of infantry and a squadron of the 18th Hussars. They were not needed. Only 600 demonstrators arrived that morning. The rest wanted to avoid bloodshed, or were intimidated by the overwhelming forces of law and order. Two of the strikers were sentenced to six weeks' imprisonment. The pair were smuggled under heavy escort out the back entrance and through a churchyard to a railway goods yard where they were put on a special train waiting to take them to Cardiff gaol. The other defendants were either fined or discharged. The sentences were read out to miners' representatives and passed on to their comrades waiting by the Rocking Stone. The strikers listened in silence and their leaders led a glum procession back to the Rhondda.[14]

After more than nine months out, in August 1911, a settlement was finally reached in what had become one of the most bitter industrial conflicts witnessed anywhere in the British coalfields. They were largely starved back to work, with no increase in the cutting prices which had sparked the dispute. Over £1 million in wages was lost and after the strike the employers were unable to find work for 3,000 men.[15]

The army of occupation was withdrawn but, bizarrely, the bosses were less than thankful for their role. The Glamorgan Coal Company sued the county council for the cost of feeding and billeting several hundred policemen in the Rhondda. The case dragged through the courts until, in 1916, the company settled for £10,000.

Churchill's role, as we have seen, remained controversial. The employers condemned him for holding back the troops, while Keir Hardie condemned him for sending them in. Tonypandy became a symbol of class struggle in Britain.

*   *   *

In June 1911 Britain's docks were hit by further strikes after seamen called for stoppages to support their claims for better wages and overtime pay. They spread from Southampton to other ports across the country. At the end of the month dockers rioted in Cardiff and began burning warehouses. A detachment of infantry was sent in to restore order. On 1 August the Port of London was halted by a dock strike and when troops began to unload a ship they were physically threatened, although there was no serious violence. Railway workers and other transport unions gave the strikers their support, officially and unofficially. Goods porters working for the Lancashire and Yorkshire railway struck over their own grievances. Porters working for other railway companies joined them. In Manchester engineering workers walked out in sympathy. After another week of clashes and paralysed ports, food supplies in the South of England began to run low. The London fruit and meat markets ran out of produce. Tempers snapped in the blistering heat of an unusually hot summer. The Government was seriously alarmed and Churchill shared the concern that Britain was heading into a period of unprecedented industrial unrest. He wrote:

> A new force has arisen in trades unionism, whereby the power of the old leaders has proved quite ineffective, and the sympathetic strike on a wide scale is prominent. Shipping, coal, railways, dockers, etc etc all united and breaking out at once. The general strike policy is a factor which must be dealt with.[16]

Churchill prepared to order a force of over 20,000 troops into the London docks to unload the cargoes from strikebound vessels. Units in Woolwich, Aldershot and Shorncliffe were issued with ammunition and rations and were put on readiness to confront the strikers at a moment's notice. The order was not given because the London employers, the Port Authority, gave in to the strikers' demands and the Port was reopened.

The Port Authority was forced to pay the men 7d rather than 6d an hour, plus increased overtime rates. Those working elsewhere for the shipping companies, which already paid 7d, demanded a penny increase as a differential. The dockers of Liverpool and Manchester struck on 1 August. Over 20 ocean liners were held up and more than 20,000 men were on strike. The dispute was settled within eleven days when the arbitrator, Sir Albert Rollit, judged the men's demands to be fair. They got their 8d. In the meantime, however, the carters had come out in a separate dispute. The supply of provisions were threatened, although pickets allowed ice through for hospitals and coal for waterworks. Newsprint failed to get through to newspapers, taxi-drivers ran short of petrol, pickets were set up outside Smithfield Market and there were some disturbances. The carters too settled, for a 72-hour week for 27 shillings pay. But by then the ship owners, exasperated by weeks of disruption and sympathy stoppages, called a lockout for 14 August. The Home Secretary sent a letter to all Chief Constables reminding them that under the 1906 Trades Disputes Act, peaceful picketing was permitted. But he pointed out that pickets should be limited in number, be clearly identified by badges, and they had no right to enter private premises.

Most trouble was expected in Liverpool where Tom Mann was organising the dockers. Two hundred troops of the Yorkshire Regiment were already stationed in the city. Two naval gunboats were ominously anchored in the Mersey. Such a display of state power did not intimidate the strikers and on 13 August a meeting of transport workers in front of St George's Hall turned into a riot. Police lines were showered with missiles, several baton charges were made on the crowd and the troops fired several volleys over their heads. Around 200 people were injured on both sides. The following day the lockout began and affected 25,000 workers. The strike committee retaliated by calling out 75,000 more. There was some rioting that evening, but it involved local rough-house elements rather than strikers.

The next day brought more serious violence. Prison vans transporting convicted rioters from the courthouse to Walton gaol were attacked in Vauxhall Road by a large crowd. Desperate attempts were made to free the prisoners and the Riot Act was read. When that had no effect in dispersing the crowd, the prison convoy's cavalry escort opened fire. Vauxhall Road became a bloody battlefield. Two rioters were killed

– one by a shot from a trooper of the 18th Hussars, the other by a shot from the crowd – and a constable was kicked to death. Violence spread throughout the city and the infantry made several bayonet charges to clear the streets. Street lamps were extinguished and barbed wire entanglements set up. Food was brought into the city under a convoy of troops. Liverpool's head constable wired the Home Office:

> The rioting took place in an area where disorder is a chronic feature, ready to break out when any abnormal excitement is in force. The object was purely and simply to attack the police, whom they tempted into side streets in which barricades of sanitary dustbins and wire entanglements were placed. The mob pursued the same tactics, stoned troops and police from the windows and house tops, but troops and police worked admirably together, and reduced the neighbourhood to peace. The troops fired a few shots (officers' revolver shots I think) at the house tops, whence the stones came. Six privates and two constables received minor injuries. A great deal of damage to houses and shops, especially public houses and provision shops, but food does not seem to have been the object, as the bread was thrown about the street.[17]

As the dead and injured were taken away, and night fell, the rioting gradually subsided. The Royal Navy cruiser HMS *Antrim* was sent to the Mersey to back up the gunboats following a joint appeal from the Lord Mayor of Liverpool and the Mayor of Birkenhead. Blue-jackets (Royal Marines) were deployed to man the Mersey ferries. Another cruiser, HMS *Warrior*, was held in readiness off the Isle of Man. The Lord Mayor telephoned Lord Derby at Harrogate and complained that London did not realise that these were no ordinary riots but 'a revolution in progress'. Derby passed on the complaint to Churchill and added: 'The city is in a state of siege – the hospitals have but two days supply – and in 48 hours all poor people will be face to face with starvation and God alone knows what happens when that moment arrives.' The King telegraphed Churchill:

> Accounts from Liverpool show that the situation there more like revolution than a strike. Trust that Govt while inducing strike leaders and masters to come to terms will take steps to ensure protection of life and property ... Strongly deprecate half-hearted employment of troops: they should not be called on except as a last resource but if called on they should be given a free hand and the mob should be made to fear them.

Once again Churchill was reluctant to see the widespread deployment of the military, despite further rioting in Glasgow and Cardiff, and encouraged Chief Constables in the troubled areas to recruit extra Special Constables. But on 18 August his attitude changed when the four railway unions called the first national rail strike. Their militancy had increased during the sympathy action in support of the dockers, but their own grievance was the stubborn refusal of the rail companies to recognise their existence and their right to negotiate on behalf of their members. The Prime Minister, Asquith, offered the railwaymen a Royal Commission but they turned it down, saying it would take too long to report. Asquith replied: 'Then your blood be on your own head.' Churchill decided that troop deployments were now needed to protect the rail network from sabotage. Soldiers were encamped in the London parks and others sent to Birmingham and Sheffield. Six thousand men in London answered appeals for Special Constables. On the 19th new orders were issued to all mayors and Chief Constables in the disturbed areas: 'Officers commanding the various Military areas to use their own discretion as to whether troops are or are not to be sent to any particular point.'[18] The army regulation requiring a requisition for troops was suspended.

The strike quickly took hold, 200,000 men were involved within hours and much of the country's industrial production was virtually halted overnight. The worst stoppages where within the rough geographical square marked by Newcastle, Liverpool, Coventry and Hull, and in South Wales. There were disturbances at Derby and Llanelly. At Blackpool thousands of factory operatives and their families were stranded without cash at the end of their annual summer break. Some went by steamer to Preston and then walked home. Others tried to walk the whole way and a convoy of carriages and motor cars were sent out to help them. At Fleetwood churches and theatres were opened to shelter hundreds more returning from excursions on the Isle of Man. In London the Great Western, Great Central and Brighton lines were halted, and St Paul's and Cannon Street stations closed. Strikers stoned some trains, attacked level crossings and signal boxes and clashed with the troops defending them. Astonishingly, there were no serious injuries and no direct fatalities. Both sides exercised caution. Soldiers did fire on some occasions, but over the heads of threatening crowds. In one incident the capture of a train was only averted by a military officer travelling as a passenger who formed a company of soldiers on leave. On the evening of the 19th the Mayor of Birkenhead telegraphed:

> Fifty infantry have been withdrawn from the town. There have been several collisions between strikers and police. I do not think I have sufficient forces at my disposal. If you cannot send me more military or naval support, I cannot answer for the safety of life or property.[19]

He need not have panicked. By midnight the railway strike was called off.

The settlement was brokered by Lloyd George, the Chancellor of the Exchequer, who ensured that the employers met union representatives in negotiations, thereby recognising the unions. He warned both sides that if Britain was paralysed, Germany was poised to take advantage of the crisis and invade. Churchill himself maintained that the Government's show of force had made the strikers think again. The union leaders described the agreement as 'a magnificent victory'. All strikers were to be reinstated, Conciliation Boards were to meet immediately to settle outstanding grievances, and a special commission was to be set up. But the settlement was initially rejected by strikers in Manchester and other parts of the North, and in South Wales.

Two days after the settlement there was the most serious incident when a train was held up by rioters at Llanelly, the engine driver was knocked unconscious and the carriages were looted. Troops fired on the crowd, killing two men and wounding several others. The rioters looted shops and the freight yard until a boiler blew up, killing five more. In the memories of many, this incident became forever muddled up with Tonypandy.

There were further disturbances in Darlington and Hull, and in Ebbw Vale and Tredegar attacks were made on the property of Jewish shopkeepers. Gradually, however, the trouble died down and the men went back to work.

Churchill faced down the muted criticism voiced at the time over his use of troops. In a Commons speech he said that in the industrial heartlands – from Liverpool and Manchester in the West to Hull and Grimsby in the East, the continuation of the railway strike

> would have produced a swift and certain degeneration of all the means, of all the structure, social and economic, on which the life of the people depend. If it had not been interrupted it would have hurled the whole of that community – between 15 and 20 million people – into an abyss of horror

which no man can dare to contemplate. No blockade by a foreign enemy could have been anything like so effective in producing terrible pressure on these vast populations as the effective closing of those great ports, together with the paralysis of the railway service.

The debate has continued ever since. At that stage in his career Churchill regarded himself as a friend of the working class, an instigator of social welfare, a champion of union recognition and a protector of civil rights. He was indeed reluctant to use troops, with all that entails for the rights and freedoms of British citizens.[20] But the record shows that when he believed state power to be threatened, he was swift in the deployment of military might. Some contemporary commentators believed he was too ready to believe his own lurid rhetoric, seeing revolutionary dangers where they did not exist. Lloyd George and other Cabinet colleagues were not so keen on confrontation, preferring to negotiate settlements or sit out turbulent events. That was not in Churchill's character. So the myth of Tonypandy may have had some substance after all.

14
The Police Strike

'a definite act of mutiny'

In August 1919, gunboats returned to the River Mersey. Lines of troops advanced with bayonets fixed down the streets of Liverpool. A man waving a claw hammer was shot dead. The Riot Act was read for the last time on mainland Britain. Working-class women paraded the streets swathed in looted furs. Dockside pubs barred their doors. All this mayhem was sparked by an event which now seems almost impossible – the police went on strike.

*   *   *

The National Union of Police and Prison Workers was formed, despite the hostility of the authorities, in 1913. At first confined to London, it spread nationwide in subsequent years, and for obvious reasons. The outbreak of the Great War brought greater responsibilities for the police forces of Britain. Their duties ranged from seeking fifth columnists and black marketeers to patrolling vastly inflated garrison towns and curbing disorder when food shortages began to be felt. One of the most unpopular tasks was checking on the wives of men serving in the armed forces to see if they were squandering their separation allowance on drink. The London police protected the capital's German population when Zeppelin raids led to the anti-Hun riots which saw shops, barbers and butchers targeted by mobs. As the war progressed they were employed to confront industrial agitation, particularly in the munitions factories. But their own militancy also increased as the war dragged on.[1]

The main complaint was over pay and hours of work. The weekly rest day, established in 1910, was scrapped during the war. Officers worked seven days a week, their hours were lengthened, as were their beats. Wartime inflation meant that they were paid less for doing more, dissatisfaction spread through the ranks and the police union's membership swelled. Police pay was outstripped as industry faced acute labour shortages when more men were sucked into the trenches. By 1917 the average pay of a London labourer was £2 8s 9d, and a skilled fitter could expect £3 7s 4d, but a top rate police constable received just £2 8s including wartime cost-of-living bonuses. The Home Office refused repeated petitions for modest increases in police pay. Early in 1917 the Government decided that policemen were no longer exempt from the military service and it soon became clear that some police authorities were deliberately choosing union members for police service overseas.[2]

In August 1918 a Boer War veteran and ex-Guardsman, PC Thomas Thiel, was sacked from the Metropolitan Police for his union activities. The dismissal provoked the first police strike. Six thousand union members in both the Met and the City of London force walked out in a display of solidarity which shook the authorities. They marched through London, four abreast, behind a solitary piper. Crowds cheered them as they converged on Whitehall. Guardsmen armed with rifles were discreetly deployed outside Government offices in Whitehall, even though the only reported outbreak was the looting of a shop during the first night of the strike. The strike lasted less than a week but was almost total. So was the victory.[3]

British troops were that month engaged in the last, desperate, bloody battles on the Western Front, and the last thing the Government needed was such a threat to law and order on the Home Front. Ministers, after years of war paranoia, were terrified of anarchy. It was clear the strikers had public opinion on their side. Lloyd George met the strike leaders at 10 Downing Street and the Prime Minister promised a pay rise, a war bonus and the introduction of police widows' pensions. Thiel was reinstated. A further trawl of provincial police for military service was dropped. But one aspect of the deliberations was ambiguous, perhaps deliberately so. Lloyd George said that he could not recognise a police union in wartime. The strike leaders went away believing that his statement meant that the union would be recognised when peace came, especially as it had been agreed that a representative board would meet regularly at Scotland Yard to discuss pay and conditions. Lloyd George, wily if not downright slippery, intended never to recognise a police union.

As soon as the strike was settled, the Prime Minister sacked Sir Edward Henry as Metropolitan Police Commissioner, and replaced him with General Sir Nevil Macready, the man who had proved his toughness and fairness at Tonypandy.[4] Macready resolved pettier operational problems and on the key questions of pay and conditions left ordinary coppers with the impression that he was on their side. But on the question of recognising a police union he was implacable. Discussing the possibility of another police strike, he said in a letter to the Home Office: 'I do not think the main body of the force will be led away a second time, but it is just possible that a few hot heads may attempt a strike and, if so, it must be smashed once and for all time; otherwise, I do not think you will ever have any peace with the police in this country.'

His judgement, though accurate in its broad sweep, did not recognise the strength of discontent amongst the police in the big, industrial cities. In Liverpool officers flocked to the union because of the excesses of the Watch Committee, which was possibly corrupt, a Chief Constable who clearly showed contempt for his men, poor police accommodation, and the traditional antagonism of the local populace. The union was strong in Birmingham, and that prompted scares amongst the authorities when the Great War ended and the Russian Revolution produced a new enemy. The Chief Constable of Birmingham, Sir Charles Rafter, wrote to the Home Office that police union recruiters were linked to the trades council, which was linked to the Independent Labour Party which was linked to the anti-conscription movement. 'The ultimate object of this,' he wrote, 'is to organise a strike of all trades, in which the police would take part, so that it may assume the form of a revolution.'[5] Other Chief Constables took note and refused to allow any policemen in their forces to attend union meetings.

Their fears were exacerbated when union members began to dominate the representative board established, by Government consent, within the Metropolitan Police. The board was critical of Macready's leadership, especially when he appointed Brig. Gen. Horwood as his assistant. That encouraged the growing suspicion that the police were becoming militarised, a force to suppress the discontent felt as hundreds of thousands of servicemen discovered that they were not returning from the trenches to a land fit for heroes. Such concerns came to a head in May 1919 after a clash in Hyde Park between police and members of the National Federation of Discharged Soldiers. A line of mounted police in Parliament Square was swept away by demonstrators heading for Buckingham Palace and the House of Commons. The police union blamed militarisation for the violence, and in a statement urged closer co-operation between the police and organised labour.[6] The Establishment was, rightly, shocked.

The committee, headed by Lord Desborough, appointed after the previous year's police strike, presented its finding. The Home Secretary, Edward Shortt, accepted immediate, significant pay rises. But there was a price. The police would forever be banned from union membership. On 8 July Shortt presented a bill to establish a police federation, as a relatively toothless alternative to a union, with a police council also set up as a consultation body. Shortt told the Commons that police union officials were in close touch with the extremists of the *Daily Herald* whose sole aim was social revolution.[7] The proposed legislation threw down the gauntlet to the union. At various meetings union members, some of whom had fought in France, declared that this was now a question of fundamental rights. A motion passed in Birmingham said: 'This is not solely the policemen's fight but an effort to safeguard the elementary rights of citizenship and freedom.' The Labour Party agreed. The MP Jack Jones of the General Workers Union, said: 'The Government is mistaken if they imagine that we are going to stand idly by while they make it known that workmen, because the police are workmen, may not belong to a certain trade union, and if they do belong to it the Government are going to bring the whole power of the state against them.'[8]

The union called a ballot of all members. The results were clear cut: 44,359 voted in favour of strike action, with only 4,324 against. The union executive hesitated before taking the logical next step as they were aware of plans for the military to take over police functions. They also wanted an opportunity to meet the Prime Minister, who was away in Paris. The delay gave Macready time to appeal directly to his men's sense of personal loyalty. He also warmly backed the option of a federation with powers to negotiate for police officers across

Britain. Individual police officers began to count their newly enhanced wage packets, which were stuffed with back pay, and militancy waned. Eventually the strike was called for 31 July.

It was a fiasco. At 10.00 p.m. on the first day the Station Sergeant reported that only one officer had not shown up for work. The sole striker, PC James Marston, was telling a strike rally in central London that victory was certain. By midnight only 240 men in 17 divisions had joined the strike. Macready issued a Special Order a few hours later warning that every officer who did not turn up for duty would be sacked immediately with the loss of all pension entitlement. In London only 1,056 Metropolitan Police and 57 City officers out of a total strength of over 19,000 came out. Almost 120 struck in Birmingham, holding peaceful meetings in the Bull Ring, but in most provincial forces, men satisfied at the recent pay rise and fearful for their pensions burned their union cards. The exception was Merseyside – 954 came out in Liverpool, 114 in Birkenhead, 63 in Bootle and one in Wallasey.[9] And the result there was just what the authorities had feared – anarchy.

In tough areas of the city over the August Bank Holiday weekend people took full advantage of the lack of bobbies on the beat. On Friday the 1st the pub landlords put their shutters up at closing time and waited behind the flimsy defences for the mob. The following morning the Lord Mayor appealed to the Home Office for troops and a warship, and took action himself by calling up all Special Constables and non-striking policemen. He appealed to law-abiding citizens to join them in defending life and property. Several infantry units were hurriedly assembled from the soldiers and sailors at hand who were not visiting family elsewhere during the holiday. A battleship, HMS *Valiant*, and two escorting destroyers set off from Scapa Flow, two days' sailing away. By Saturday night there were around 900 soldiers in the city, mainly kept out of sight, and around 1,200 non-striking policemen and more Specials.

The violence kicked off when a youth threw a brick through the plate-glass window of Latarche the jeweller's shop in London Road. Widespread looting and destruction fanned out within minutes. Drunken men, in parties of up to 30, crashed out of pubs and hammered down the defences of the shops closest. Food, clothing, drink and jewellery were the main quarry and by midnight London Road was strewn with broken glass and discarded plunder. A correspondent wrote:

Gangs of youths and young men proceeded along the thoroughfare, stopping at first one shop and then another. The air resounded with the crash of huge plate glass windows. The looters carried pieces of iron, heavy stones and other missiles, which they used to demolish the panes, while, in some cases, the doors were prised open with the ease and ingenuity of the cracksman. Huge gaps in the windows having been made, the youths, fearless of pieces of glass, jumped in and made lightening sweep of the articles. The roadway was littered with goods from watches to costumiers' dummies.[10]

In London Road 'rough-looking women' pointed out the shops with the greatest opportunities for plunder. Ever afterwards the riot was known as 'The Loot'. The depleted police force, even stiffened by Special Constables, were too few to even try to control the mob. They awaited the troops.

Shortly after midnight on the Sunday morning a magistrate arrived in an armoured car, escorted by infantry with bayonets fixed. He read the Riot Act through a megaphone, but his words were largely unheard in that noisy bedlam. The troops were lined up across the road and advanced on the crowd with bayonets at the ready. The rioters appeared to flee, but merely dodged down sidestreets, swerved behind the troops, and resumed the looting. Moreover, the orgy of destruction began to spread across the city. Royal Marines disembarked at the pier head and joined the police and troops in house-to-house searches of the slums of Liverpool and Birkenhead, looking for stolen goods.

There were savage, hand-to-hand battles in streets, alleys and yards, some involving a handful of people, others hundreds. There were frequent baton charges, the soldiers used their rifle butts, and the rioters used stones and improvised cudgels. A contingent of CID men were in the thick of some of the heaviest fighting, using their heavy batons. In one mêlée Detective Sergeant Levitt was severely injured in the face by a rifle butt aimed at a rioter. A correspondent wrote: 'Bayonet charges were the order of the night, for while events were going forward in London Road, the Scotland Road and Great Homer Street areas were centres of similar trouble ... So serious did the state of affairs become here that a volley of rifle fire was tried as an expedient.'[11] The fight only ended when dawn broke.

The rioters returned to their homes, the wounded were tended in makeshift hospitals, and the shopkeepers swept the debris from their premises and counted the cost of lost stock. There was an uneasy lull, but no one expected it to last throughout Sunday. The Government, realising that the forces of law were stretched to breaking point, diverted an infantry battalion which had been due to embark for India, sent several more detachments from nearby camps, and even supplied a troop of tanks, some of which were drawn up outside St George's Hall.

The Times correspondent wrote:

> Central Liverpool tonight represents a war zone, and as I write this evening the report comes that there has been firing and wounds. Soldiers with steel helmets and fixed bayonets patrol the streets. Vast crowds gather and gaze on the scenes of last night's orgy of destruction, and St George's Hall presents an impressive background to a laager containing hundreds of soldiers. There are military lorries containing complements of armed men, awaiting any call that may be made, and, grimmest and most significant of all, several tanks. Hundreds of yards of shop frontages in London Road, Byrom Street, Scotland Road, and elsewhere are boarded up or in the process of being so protected, but, in most cases, the precaution has been taken too late, for last night boot stores, jewellers' shops, furniture houses, and big stores were smashed, looted and wrecked. London Road is the Ypres of Liverpool.[12]

During the Sunday afternoon several soldiers tried to arrest a gang of drunks led by the well-known petty criminal Cuthbert Howlett as they broke into the dockside liquor stores of J.P. O'Brien and Co., and carried off crates of beer and whisky in handcarts. Later children were seen selling bottles of beer and stout in the street at a penny a time. A crowd whistled and shouted encouragement to the looters as Howlett, wielding a claw hammer, called on his compatriots to resist the troops. A short but fierce struggle ensued and the heavily outnumbered soldiers were ordered to fire above the heads of the menacing crowd. One rifle went off prematurely and struck Howlett as he clambered onto the running board of a troop lorry. He stumbled across the street and collapsed unconscious with blood pouring from a thigh wound. The crowd found a stretcher and took him to the Northern Hospital where he died several hours later.

His death, and a weekend of heavy drinking, ensured that the mayhem which followed Sunday night's pub closing time was even worse than the night before. The mob was now interested less in looting and wanton destruction, more in attacking the troops and police – anyone in uniform – with stones, bottles, bricks and sticks. Again the police responded with baton charges, the soldiers with another bayonet charge. One looter was hit in the neck by a rebounding bullet when soldiers fired into the air. A musical instrument shop in Scotland Road was smashed open and looters dragged pianos into the street where they 'thumped them in a frenzied endeavour to demonstrate their defiance of law and order'. Shortly after 1.00 a.m. a police baton charge broke up the al fresco concert. *The Times* man reported:

> The tactics of the mob were similar. Men and women, and even children, dashed tumultuously into the broad, well-lighted thoroughfares, armed with bricks and stones, to demolish the few remaining windows and take aim if the chance offered at either police or soldiers. Upon the crowd in London Road soldiers turned out, firing warning shots; then, clubbing their rifles, they advanced and the crowd fled. Half an hour later the rioters returned. This time they were met by a large body of police – real police – who came along from their headquarters four abreast, and, deploying across a good length of the road, advanced at the run with their batons drawn. This was more than the crowd could stand, and they scattered. The police passed on, clearing a good length of the road, and at an interval behind came a force of soldiers. Some of the more daring of the rioters had already returned, and when the police faced round, they found themselves between the two forces. The struggle was sharp but short, and the rioters did their best to make a speedy escape.[13]

The battles in darkened streets and pit-black alleys continued throughout the night, with no side able to claim victory.

Meanwhile, Birkenhead across the Mersey was also in turmoil, with 96 police on strike out of a strength of 225. Forty shops were wrecked and looted, with damage estimated at £30,000. Over 700 soldiers, some with machine-guns, poured into the town. A double cordon of troops was put around the town hall. The Riot Act was read and 50 arrests were made. *The Times* reported:

> Public houses, grocers' shops, boot shops, and general stores and pawnbrokers' premises were ransacked and prisoners captured had all kinds of loot in their pockets. A novel means was adopted to catch them. A motor lorry was run right up to the door of the premises being wrecked and the looters were thrown into the van before they were aware of what was happening. Women are included in the prisoners. The military with fixed bayonets are guarding the wrecked shops and special constables have been ordered to report for duty.

At daybreak on Monday morning there was a steady downpour and the rioters, drenched by rain and spattered by blood, drifted home. The men in uniform were left in control of the urban battlefield.

Liverpool remained quiet for the rest of the day. The hospital wards and police cells were both crammed full. All commercial property in the docklands districts was either damaged, looted or destroyed. Armed sentries stood outside official buildings, while more guarded crossroads. Patrols clattered up and down, while lorry-loads of fresh troops arrived in convoys. The battleship *Valiant* and her two escorting destroyers steamed into harbour. The city was fast becoming a place of military occupation. Any inhabitants tempted to repeat the disorder took note and stayed at home. Over 350 people were locked up, charged with looting. Those who ventured out on what was a bank holiday were thoughtful rather than festive, observers noted. A limited strike by tram workers added to the welcome calm.

An analysis of the damaged area suggested that the destruction was not indiscriminate. Pubs were largely left alone, although a few tills were rifled. The premises targeted contained boots, male and female clothing, pawned goods, food, sweets, jewellery and tobacco. A chewing-gum store was also completely cleared out. The total cost of the damage was reckoned to be over £200,000.

The local courts were kept busy. Around 50 of those charged were juveniles. Most of the rest were adults charged with looting or being in possession of stolen goods. In one case six men and two women were charged with stealing whisky worth £1,200 from O'Brien's warehouse. Bizarrely, a Special Constable was fined for drunkenness after he kicked a constable on the shin while signing on. A young Birkenhead man was charged with stealing 63 watches and 41 rings. Another man, who had won a Distinguished Conduct Medal during the war, was sentenced to two months' imprisonment. His past conduct must have been taken into consideration because the average sentence for looting was three months.[14]

*   *   *

The police strike fizzled out. Support promised by other unions never materialised, although it was considered by the executives of the dockers and railwaymen. On 4 August Home Secretary Shortt told the Commons that the police strike was 'a definite act of mutiny by men who had broken their oaths, set aside their duty to their fellow citizens, and were attempting to defy the authority of Parliament'.[15] Three days later the City of London police passed resolutions condemning the actions of the strikers.[16] By then the strike was effectively over and dispirited policemen tried to return to duty. Even that was denied them.

The police union was never recognised by any Government and every policeman who struck, more than 2,000, was sacked with the loss of all pension entitlement. Not one was ever reinstated despite representations on behalf of individuals which continued until as late as 1950. PC Marston and other police union leaders in London were put on employers' blacklists. They could only find work with the All Russia Co-Operative Society which imported Soviet goods into Britain. During the anti-Soviet hysteria of the 1920s, the Society was shut down and they were out of work for a second time. The police federation was created in lieu of a union with industrial teeth. The military stayed in Liverpool for the rest of August, until the police replacements were sufficiently trained. Dismissed police officers held demonstrations, but few came to listen to their grievances.

Any hopes of the police becoming allies of the Labour Movement were crushed along with the police union. Successive governments deployed the police against strikers, using, as in the General Strike of 1926, civil emergency as the excuse. And they were rewarded for their diligence. When the General Strike crumbled after nine days, *The Times* launched a police fund to express the nation's gratitude for 'the large measure of peace and safety' they had enjoyed during the stoppages.

15
Mosley and the Battle of Cable Street

'Thuggery, buggery, hunger and war!'

Oswald Ernest Mosley was born in Mayfair in 1896, the eldest son of a baronet. After his parents' marriage failed he was brought up by his mother and educated at West Down private school and Winchester. He spent six months at Sandhurst before being commissioned into the 16th Lancers in October 1914. He swiftly switched to the Royal Flying Corps and served as an observer. While trying to obtain his pilot's licence he broke his ankle and, after a short spell in the trenches, was invalided home. He spent the rest of the war pushing paper at the Ministry of Munitions and the Foreign Office. During that period in Whitehall he made powerful political contacts and became Conservative MP for Harrow at the 1918 general election. Two years later he married Lady Cynthia, daughter of Lord Curzon. He seemed set for a conventional Establishment career but was caught up in the post-war spirit of free thinking. He attacked excessive military spending and the deployment of the Black and Tans in Ireland, and became first an Independent and then a Labour supporter shortly after Ramsay MacDonald formed its first Government in 1924. MacDonald described him as 'one of the greatest and most hopeful figures' on the political scene. Regarding Harrow as a hopeless seat, he came within 77 votes of defeating Neville Chamberlain at Birmingham Ladywood. He remained out of Westminster for 18 months before taking Smethwick in a 1926 by election.[1]

Mosley spent his time away from Westminster evolving his economic theories and wooing the Labour left. His charisma and forceful oration saw him tipped as a future Labour leader. He succeeded to his father's baronetcy, his wife was elected MP for Stoke-on-Trent, and he took ministerial office in the second Labour Government of 1929 as Chancellor of the Duchy of Lancaster, serving on the Cabinet unemployment committee. In 1930 he wrote a memorandum calling for radical measures to tackle the Depression, including extensive state intervention and a public works programme. When it was rejected he flew into a rage and resigned from the Government.

The following March, bolstered by his own self-belief, he launched his New Party with his wife. At the 1931 general election Mosley and all 23 other New Party candidates were defeated. Early the following year Mosley visited Italy and met 'Il Duce'. Observing Benito Mussolini at first hand, he concluded that there was no future in Parliamentary democracy. Dictatorship was the answer. On his return he formed the British Union of Fascists (BUF). He targeted, with some success, respectable figures on the Conservative right, aided by Lady Cynthia until she died in 1933. He adopted the black shirt, Roman salute and pageantry of Mussolini. Mosley was in his element. Fanfares greeted him as he marched into meetings surrounded by uniformed bodyguards and illuminated by spotlights. Blackshirt stewards violently ejected hecklers. Mussolini secretly sent funds, while Lord Rothermere's newspapers gave slavish support. The *Daily Mail*, reporting a packed Albert Hall meeting, described Mosley as 'the paramount political personality in Britain'. Its reporter, Ward Price, declared that 'the Blackshirt Movement was caught up on such a wave of deep-seated popular enthusiasm as must sweep it to victory'.[2] Rothermere himself wrote:

> Timid alarmists have been whimpering that the rapid growth in numbers of the British Blackshirts is preparing the way for a system of rulership by means of steel whips and concentration camps. Very few of these panic-mongers have any personal knowledge of the countries that are already under Blackshirt government. The notion that a permanent reign of terror exists there has been evolved entirely from their own morbid imaginations, fed by sensational propaganda ...[3]

At its peak in 1934 the BUF had 50,000 members. Initially inspired by Italian fascism, Mosley moved steadily towards the Nazi philosophy of totalitarianism embodied by Adolf Hitler.

Mosley's firebrand speeches attracted both disillusioned workers and dilettantes. For a while fascism, although repugnant to most voters and the middle classes, was fashionably chic among the aristocracy.

Mosley played up to that, attending the most fashionable parties and night clubs, chasing women and proposing amusingly bizarre solutions to unemployment, such as building a mid-city airport on the roof of Victoria station. Churchill saw him as a 'gilded butterfly', Trotsky as an 'aristocratic coxcomb', and F.E. Smith as a 'perfumed popinjay of scented boudoirs'.[4] James Lees-Milne, who observed him at a meeting, wrote:

> His eyes flashed fire, dilated and contracted like a mesmerist's. His voice rose and fell with hypnotic cadence. He was madly in love with his own words. The posturing, the grimacing, the switching on and off of those gleaming teeth, and the overall swashbuckling so purposeful and calculated, were more likely to appeal to Mayfair flappers than to sway indigent workers in the Potteries.[5]

On the streets and in the meeting halls, however, Mosley was seen as a much more sinister threat. He quite blatantly sought to promote the BUF by violent means, advocating at the same time the rule of law and 'the good old English fist'. His bodyguards and followers carried knuckledusters and rubber coshes, and used them frequently. David Low, who attended a BUF meeting, wrote:

> Mosley spoke effectively and at great length. Delivery excellent, manner reckless. Interruptions began, but no dissenting voice got beyond half a dozen sentences before three or four bullies jumped on him, bashed him and lugged him out. Two such incidents happened near me. An honest looking blue-eyed student type rose and shouted indignantly 'Hitler means war!' whereupon he was given the complete treatment.[6]

Mosley ran his Blackshirts on harsh military lines. A private barracks in Chelsea had punishment cells in the basement. Mosley insisted that fascism was the only solution because 'when the crash came the man who could control the streets would win'. His open tactic was to provoke violent retaliation, especially from the communists.

One of his most successful, and violent, events was the June 1934 rally at the huge Olympia exhibition centre in Kensington. Peers, MPs and aristocrats arrived in Rolls-Royces and attired in evening dress to join 12,000 people in one of the largest indoor meetings ever held in Britain. They were stopped outside the hall by hostile demonstrators from the East End. A police report claimed that the group was led by communists anxious to bring off a 'spectacular coup' against the fascists. A strong police cordon prevented a head-on clash and the demonstrators were forced to use words rather than fists. They shouted:

> Hitler and Mosley, what are they for?
> Thuggery, buggery, hunger and war![7]

Mosley, after some delay, entered the hall behind a phalanx of Blackshirts and strutted the length of the arena before mounting the rostrum. Opponents had infiltrated the audience and his speech was constantly interrupted. Mosley, who wanted to show his men could match Hitler's Stormtroopers, was well prepared. Every time a heckler shouted he halted his speech and spotlights were trained on the dissenter. Teams of jackbooted Blackshirts then descended on him and threw him out, making free use of coshes and knuckledusters. Soon there were heaps of bloodied and barely conscious protesters outside the exits, including some women. The police expressed horror at the violence, but they were under orders not to intervene within the hall. One constable complained that his superiors prosecuted communists with 'enthusiastic zeal' while treating the fascists with 'indifference to approval'.[8] It was regarded as a miracle that no lives were lost.

The violence shown, and the anti-Semitism and extremism expressed by Mosley, shocked Middle England. Conservative MP W.J. Anstruther-Gray wrote in the *Daily Telegraph*:

> If anyone could have told me before I went to the meeting last night that I would ever be in sympathy with Communist interrupters, I would have called him a liar. But I had not been at the meeting for more than a few minutes before all my sympathies were with the men that were being handled with such gross brutality. Something must be done to prevent last night's disgusting behaviour.[9]

By 1936 the high point of the BUF was past. The Conservative Government still, in its higher echelons at least, treated the fascists with either amused contempt or equated them with hunger marchers. Increasingly the public regarded them as dangerous bully boys. The revulsion grew when the BUF applauded Hitler's murderous 'Night of the Long Knives'. Mosley was now solidly linked to Hitler, just as the communists were in bed with Stalin. Even Lord Rothermere withdrew his support and membership of the BUF fell by four-fifths within a year. Mosley, instead of rowing back from his vicious anti-Jewish rhetoric, intensified it to appeal to racists in East London where there was a large and relatively prosperous Jewish community.

Mosley needed a grand gesture to pull together his increasingly feeble and fragmenting organisation. He planned the biggest demonstration so far, a march into the East End on 4 October 1936. It would start outside the Royal Mint and head eastwards along Cable Street into Shoreditch, Limehouse, Bow and Bethnal Green. Mosley planned to make several speeches along the route. His open aim was to provoke violent opposition.

The Police Commissioner, Sir Philip Game, deployed 6,000 men to keep order. Anti-fascists, including their street leader, Jack Spot, built a number of massive barricades across the route using household furniture, torn up flagstones and four trams left standing idle at key points by their anti-fascist drivers. A lorry full of bricks was overturned. Communists, Jewish organisations, local housekeepers, shopworkers, sympathetic professionals, tradesmen, builders and dockers gathered for war. Young activist Bill Fishman wrote:

> From out of the narrow streets, alleyways and main thoroughfares came the steady tramp of marching feet, growing in intensity as the columns were swelled by reinforcement. A forest of banners arose, borne aloft, with the watchwords THEY SHALL NOT PASS emblazoned in a multi-variety of colours. Loud speaker vans patrolled the streets booming out the message for all to rally to the defence lines at Cable Street and Gardiner's Corner. Mass battalions mobilising spontaneously from the ranks of mainly local folk.

The Battle of Cable Street was about to begin.

Around 3,000 fascists were met at the assembly point opposite the Tower of London by Mosley and his Blackshirt bodyguard, formed into military lines and standing to attention. Their opponents, more in number, jostled around the silent fascist lines and the police were forced to create a cordon around the Blackshirts. Mosley stood to attention in his open Bentley, jackboots gleaming, and raised his arm in the fascist salute. He slowly stepped out of the car and walked along his lines in a tour of inspection. Enraged, the crowd surged forward in attack and the police cordon drew truncheons and hit back, arresting some demonstrators and bloodying others. Game told Mosley that the march could not proceed until the barricades were cleared. Mosley appeared satisfied. Most of his Blackshirts, under strict orders, had not moved a muscle.[10]

Mounted police charged the barricades and were met by bricks, bottles and stones. Each time the police broke through the anti-fascists retreated to the next line of defence. The Blackshirts remained standing to attention, watching impassively as police and demonstrators waged increasingly vicious warfare. Jan Dalley, Diana Mosley's biographer, wrote:

> Sir Philip Game wanted to impose his authority on both sides, and was not about to surrender rule of the streets to the East Enders any more than to Mosley's men, but he was outmanoeuvred by Mosley's tactics. It was an extension of his rule for stewards at meetings – if the police arrived, they were to stop fighting instantly and just stand still – and it was a brilliantly effective way of getting the police and protesters to fight each other.

Time and again the police launched mounted charges which pushed people through the plate glass windows of shops lining the routes, but they could make little impression on the larger barricades or the sheer mass of the crowd. Joyce Goodman recalled:

> There were horses coming straight into the crowd, and the police were hitting out indiscriminately. We never saw a fascist that day. We were fighting the police. They were just hitting everyone, there were women going down under the horses' hooves. Absolute terror ... People were knocked to the ground and the horses didn't care who they trod on ... But Mosley never got past. It was a heavy atmosphere. Many people were afraid, they stayed in their houses and wouldn't come out. But a lot of us did.

Two hours of bitter fighting left more than 100 people injured and 83 anti-fascists arrested.[11] Game telephoned the Home Secretary, Sir John Simon, who gave his authority to call the march off. Mosley instantly turned his troops around and marched them in impeccable order to Charing Cross pier, dismissing them after a vainglorious speech. The communists said it was a 'humiliating defeat'. Mosley felt he had won a battle of wits.

That night the BUF put out a statement:

> The decision to ban the Blackshirt march was immediately obeyed, because the British Union obeys the law and does not fight the police. On this occasion Socialists, Communists, and Jews openly organised, not only to attack the meetings but to close the streets of London by violence to members of the public proceeding to these legitimate meetings. The Government has taken no action against the organisers of this violence and illegality.[12]

A few days later Mosley flew to Berlin and married the glamorous Diana Mitford in the drawing room of the Goebbels family home, in the presence of Adolf Hitler.

The day after the 'battle' Herbert Morrison condemned the Government's initial unwillingness to ban the BUF march. On 7 October Sir John Simon responded that he was not a dictator with power to prohibit demonstrations as he saw fit, and any moves towards such powers would need further legislation.

As he spoke, tensions were again growing in the East End and the Jewish community sent urgent requests for protection. On the 12th gangs of young BUF members, taking advantage of the withdrawal of police to keep order at a communist gathering, burst into Mile End Road and smashed up Jewish shops. The Government finally bowed to Labour demands for more effective action against the fascists. The next month ministers unveiled a Public Order Bill which outlawed the wearing of black shirts or any other political uniforms. It was also an offence to take part in 'organising, training or equipping any persons for the purpose of forming a private bodyguard or for using or displaying physical force in promoting any political object'. The police were given powers to change the route of processions, while local authorities could close off any district if there was a threat of violence. Furthermore, it was made an offence for anyone to carry offensive weapons at any public meeting, or to use abusive or threatening language or behaviour with intent to cause a breach of the peace.[13]

Despite his bravado, Mosley and the BUF were a busted flush in Britain. After Cable Street he found it impossible to book venues for large events. Marches were impromptu walkabouts, although Mosley tirelessly toured poor areas shouting his 'Britain First' message from his loudspeaker lorry. The BUF dwindled, although it did make some inroads into the East End in the March 1937 election, polling 23 per cent in Bethnal Green, 10.3 per cent in Limehouse and 14.8 per cent in Shoreditch.

Shortly before the Second World War broke out Mosley organised a vast peace rally in Earl's Court and during the early stages of the 'Phoney War' he marched in Bethnall Green and spoke in Victoria Park. In May 1940 Mosley and his wife were interned along with other suspected traitors under the Defence of the Realm regulations. Altogether 1,769 British subjects were interned, of whom 763 had been

BUF members, he protested that he would never betray Britain and was released by Home Secretary Herbert Morrison on health grounds in 1943, but his influence was largely gone. During the post-war years he lived mainly in France and wrote a series of self-justifying books. His name was invoked by fascist thugs during racial troubles in the 1950s, but he rarely addressed them directly. As leader of the Union Movement between 1948 and 1966 he advocated European unity on racial lines. He tried to return to Parliament twice, but lost his deposit in North Kensington in 1959 and in Shoreditch in 1966. He died in Orsay, France, in December 1980. His widow Diana died in August 2003, worshipping to the end her fascist husband and treasuring the memory of Adolf Hitler.

Jennie Lee, who knew Mosley in the 1920s, wrote:

> He had a fatal flaw in his character, an overwhelming arrogance. An unshakeable conviction that he was born to rule drove him on to the criminal folly of donning a black shirt and surrounding himself with a band of bullyboys, and so became a pathetic imitation Hitler, doomed to political impotence for the rest of his life.[14]

16

The Notting Hill Race Riots

'We were not prepared to go down like dying dogs'

Notting Hill was the setting for a series of running battles in which a generation of immigrants, proud to be British but aggrieved at being confronted with blatant bigotry, fought back against the sons of the Blackshirts. In doing so the mainly Afro-Caribbean minority regained some of their pride but faced a backlash, both in the streets and in the legislature, which would have profound effects on future generations.

In the context of this book, the riots were also an example of politically motivated hooliganism failing in the short term but succeeding in its wider aim of inciting racial hatred and imposing immigration controls.

*   *   *

Britain's major ports have had ethnic populations for centuries. The trades in slaves and other commodities linked the nation to the Caribbean, West Africa and India, while the nineteenth century saw an influx of Africans, Arabs, Chinese and other diverse peoples who worked the great trade ships and, later, the liners. Inevitably there were violent clashes – in 1910 Cardiff's Chinese community was attacked – but they were relatively rare. Britain's first major modern race riots erupted in the immediate aftermath of the First World War. During that global conflict lascars increasingly found work ashore due to manpower shortages. The return of servicemen at the war's end, the competition for jobs, housing and women, and a decline in the merchant shipping industry all contributed to heightened tensions. Shipping companies increased them by recruiting firemen and stokers in colonial ports at cheap rates.

In South Shields the town's black population increased fourfold during the war as West Indian and West African seamen joined an established community of Somali and Arab seafarers. Violence erupted in January 1919 when a number of Arabs, who had just paid their £2 stamp to clear their union book, were refused work. J.B. Fye, an official of the stewards and cooks union, incited a gang of foreign white seamen against the Arabs. Fye punched one of the Arabs, who hit him back. An infuriated white crowd then chased the Arabs to Holborn, the town district where most of them lived. Friends and relatives of the Arabs fired warning shots over the heads of the mob, which then turned and fled back to the docks. The Arabs followed them to the Shipping Office, which was wrecked in the ensuing fight. Army and navy shore patrols were called in to restore order and twelve Arabs were arrested. At Durham assizes three were acquitted and the rest were sentenced to between one and three months' hard labour. Fye was convicted of using language likely to cause a breach of the peace.[1]

That same spring demobilisation swelled the former slave port of Liverpool's black population to around 5,000 and tensions mounted as black and white competed for work. Those tensions reached boiling point when 120 black workers employed in the port's sugar refineries and oilcake mills were sacked because white workers refused to work alongside them. Most of the sacked men were at the end of their credit limit and faced eviction from their lodgings. They joined several hundred black ex-servicemen, many of whom had lost limbs, who were destitute. In May the secretary of the Liverpool Ethiopian Association urged the Colonial Office to repatriate the men with a £5 per head bursary for food. At the same time a deputation representing 5,000 jobless white ex-servicemen complained that black workers were undercutting them in the employment market. The port was a racial tinderbox and on 4 June 1919 it exploded.

Two Scandinavian sailors stabbed the West Indian John Johnson in the face because he refused to give them a cigarette in a pub. The next evening eight of his mates returned to the pub, found the assailants, drenched them with beer and attacked them with iron bars, knives and razors. In the bar brawl a policeman was knocked unconscious. The two Scandinavians and three of their friends were taken to hospital, but only one was seriously hurt. The police responded by raiding boarding houses used by the black seamen. A more serious fight ensued in which one police officer was shot in the mouth and another in the neck. A third was slashed across the face and a fourth suffered a broken wrist. As the news spread a lynch mob formed outside the lodgings. Charles Wooten, a 24-year-old black ship's fireman, ran out of one of the houses and was pursued by two policeman and an enraged crowd up to 300 strong. The policemen caught him at the brink of the dock but he was snatched from their grasp by the mob. Wooten was hurled into the dock and pelted with bricks and rocks as he tried to swim. Eventually his corpse was dragged out. No one was arrested for the murder.[2]

Over the next three days white mobs ruled Liverpool's rough streets attacking any black faces they found. Three West Indians were stabbed on the 8th. Up to 10,000 young men, apparently well organised, sought out Negroes and savagely beat them up. The victims included a black ex-serviceman who wore three medals for wartime exploits. On the 10th houses believed to have black occupants in Toxteth were systematically looted and set on fire. Black people sought refuge in police stations and the offices of the Ethiopian Association.[3] *The Times* reported:

> White men appear determined to clear out the blacks, who have been advised to stay indoors. This counsel many of them disregard, and late on Sunday a large body of police had to be requisitioned to prevent serious consequences. Whenever a negro was seen he was chased and, if caught, severely beaten ... The district was in uproar and every coloured man seen was followed by large hostile crowds. In two instances the negroes, on being attacked, pulled out knives and razors and attempted to stab some of the crowd. One was heard to shout, 'Come on, you English dogs, I will do for you.'[4]

The violence gradually abated, but many scars were left behind.

That turbulent year saw similar race riots in dockland areas of Glasgow, London, Barry, Newport and Cardiff. The Newport outbreak was sparked when a returning white soldier knocked a black man to the ground for walking with a white girl. In a two-hour battle a Chinese laundry and several lodging houses were wrecked and furniture burnt on street bonfires. The immigrants defended themselves with revolvers, pokers and sticks. A police baton charge was made against the white mob. The *Morning Post* reported: 'Stones and iron bolts were thrown, and towards midnight the crowd had increased to several thousands. No blacks were to be seen on the streets.'[5]

In Cardiff, after a blisteringly hot day, a carriage 'containing coloured men and white women, apparently returning from an excursion' – according to the Head Constable's report – attracted a 'mixed crowd'. There was an angry verbal confrontation which ended with a white man being thrown to the ground. The *Times* account said:

> Among the whites were a number of young soldiers in khaki and many ex-soldiers. The coloured men were concealed in the darkness of a large railway arch, and cries of 'Charge! Charge!' came from the soldiers. There was a wild rush for the bridge and revolver shots rang out from the ranks of the negroes. A soldier was wounded in the thigh with a revolver bullet. When the coloured men saw the determined character of their opponents' charge and that the revolver shots would not stop it, they ran into the maze of narrow streets abutting on the canal, an area known to Cardiff people as 'Nigger Town.' The whites followed the blacks into their retreat and pandemonium ensued. As trouble had been anticipated extra police had been drafted in but the tone of the whites became more and more angry. They assembled in front of a house where eight negroes were known to reside, and challenges were issued to them to come out. Several colonial (Australian) soldiers constituted themselves the ringleaders of the besieging party, which was largely made up of discharged soldiers. Some of the latter asked: 'Why should these coloured men be able to get work when it is refused to us?' The relations of coloured men with white women were also referred to angrily.[6]

The district included many mixed-race couples and the sight of white men and girls living with black men enraged the mob. A group of whites led by a soldier smashed their way into a black household and found four white girls in their nightdresses. They were roughly treated. When the fire brigade extinguished the flames in another house they rescued a young white woman who was then attacked by other white women. Two black men took refuge in a shop but were dragged out and brutally beaten with sticks and frying pans. The blacks fought back but were generally overwhelmed. A newspaper report described another attack on a house occupied by immigrants:

> The door was battered to splinters. The screams of a woman were heard and revolver shots again rang out. A fleeing negro was sighted and, giving chase, the whites overhauled him and brought him down. A revolver was wrestled from his hand, and he was belaboured with sticks, kicked and struck.

During that night an unidentified black man was beaten to death and an Irishman, John Donovan, was shot through the heart during an attack on an immigrant house. A 20-year-old former soldier, Harold Smart, walked up to a policeman and said that a coloured man had cut his throat. The policeman took him to King Edward's Hospital in a taxi, but he died within minutes of arrival. Men from the 1st Welsh Regiment acted as pallbearers at his funeral the following week. After the service tensions were so fraught that a magistrate read the Riot Act. Smart's ex-comrades were on hand to enforce it.

On 14 June a coffee shop owned by an Arab was stormed by a white crowd in London's Cable Street. Two revolver shots were fired into the crowd. The *Daily Mail* reported:

> The riot arose on a report being spread that some white girls had been seen to enter the house. Soon a crowd of about 3,000 people assembled, and the place was attacked. A few nights later a quarrel over a woman resulted in an arson attack on Chinese-owned premises in Poplar.[7]

Such violence, whoever the instigators, prompted widespread calls for segregation and repatriation. Tensions eased during the interwar years, however, and during the Second World War black and Asian servicemen made an immense contribution to the defeat of Nazism and the Axis powers. After the war, with the steady and well-organised return of demobilised soldiers, Britain's economy recovered and there were manpower shortages, particularly in engineering and service sectors. The overcrowding of the West Indies offered a simple solution. The 1948 Nationality Act guaranteed the right of all British subjects of the colonies and Commonwealth to migrate to Britain without restriction. On 22 June 1948 the freighter *Empire Windrush* arrived in England with 492 Jamaican immigrants. It was the start of an influx of non-whites. No longer were black faces generally confined to Britain's ports.[8] By 1958 an estimated 125,000 immigrants arrived from the West Indies alone. Most early immigrants were men, including many who has served as engineers and ground crew in the RAF. Only later did women and children begin arriving in large numbers. Prior to the war, black faces were rare outside the port areas. That began to change.[9]

The Commonwealth immigrants were in for a shock. They had been taught to respect the 'Mother Country' and their contact with whites had been largely confined to the educated and, generally, benign colonial administrators. What greeted them on arrival was naked bigotry. Despite the labour shortages, many employers and their workforces rejected the newcomers. They were refused lodgings, work and access to pubs, restaurants and other establishments. There was no law against racial discrimination. White workers, fed propaganda by the remnants of Mosley's Blackshirts, believed that the newcomers were unskilled labourers with no job prospects unless they undercut British workers. In fact the opposite was initially true, although later highly-skilled black workers were driven by desperation to accept lower pay. Labour unions colluded with bosses to keep black faces off the factory floor. Reports, some of them undoubtedly true, began to circulate of West Indians living as pimps off the immoral earnings of white prostitutes, or simply claiming state benefits. Such reports were raised at Cabinet level while Conservative backbenchers kept up pressure for immigration curbs, a campaign which fuelled frenzied fears in ignorant minds.

In 1958 Britain was hit by a mild recession and as people began to lose their jobs they looked for scapegoats. Although the unemployment rate amongst West Indians was four times the 2 per cent overall rate, they were blamed for taking jobs away from whites or living off benefits paid for by white taxpayers. Another factor was a shortage of housing. Blacks were forced into poor, crowded, working-class neighbourhoods and landlords quickly discovered they could charge higher rents to immigrants who were not welcome anywhere else.[10] Historian Tim Helbing wrote:

> The first West Indian renters were quite a shock to the white residents of the neighbourhoods. Brought up during the Imperial period, most believed that their 'black brother' were inferior to whites, and that they had to be affectionate and tolerant of their poor relations. But the West Indians did not play their part, refusing to act inferior, which caused resentment and confusion among whites. For the most part the black immigrants were confident, worked hard, and weren't afraid to speak their minds.[11]

The more radical groups of both the right and left were openly racist, and attracted poor, white working-class men. The fear of racial mixing was one of the most common complaints. In their minds it justified political demands for forcible deportations and street violence. Mosley's supporters were behind a 'Keep Britain White' campaign, but many shifted to the League of Empire Loyalists led, among others, by the fascist John Tyndall. Gangs of Teddy Boys set upon blacks with bicycle chains. In London, Kelso Cochrane, a young Antiguan carpenter, was murdered by six white youths. Although fascists openly boasted of their involvement, no one was charged with the killing. Young black ex-servicemen armed themselves with Molotov cocktails against attack. On 18 August the recently launched *West Indian Gazette* received a letter addressed to 'My Dear B Ape'. It went on: 'We, the Ayran Knights, miss nothing. Close attention has been paid to every issue of this rag and I do assure you, the information gleaned has proven of great assistance to the Klan.'[12] The scene was ripe for extreme violence, but the Government tried to maintain a neutral stance, neither encouraging nor discouraging further immigration. Academic Stuart Hall said: '1958 was a big moment. Before that, individuals had endured discrimination. But in that year racism became a mass, collective experience that went beyond that.'[13]

*   *   *

On 23 August rioting broke out in the St Ann's Well district of Nottingham, a slum area with over 2,000 mainly West Indian immigrants. Nine white youths, aged between 17 and 20, from the White City estate, appear to have sparked the violence. After cruising in a car driven by an older man they set upon a black kitchen porter with iron bars and a chair leg as he walked with a white girl. Four other black men were injured in the rampage, three of them seriously. One of the victims was later pushed into a local courthouse in a wheelchair to give evidence despite a chest wound. The attacks aroused a predictable response, and white youths now became the target. One report said: Dozens of people were injured by bottles, knives, razors and stakes. One man had 57 stitches inserted in his throat. No coloured men were taken to hospital. Police, ambulance men and firemen with hoses were quickly sent to the scene and order was restored after several hours.[14]

A week later there was renewed rioting in that city. The reports of the previous weekend's violence inflamed a drunken, white working-class mob. *The Times* reported that a TV cameraman further inflamed a tense situation by lighting a magnesium flare to illuminate what the police regarded as a mock fight between two gangs of white youths. 'By then the crowd had become angry and fighting started', the correspondent filed. 'Although reinforced in some numbers, the police had considerable difficulty in handling the crowds which were uncooperative. Policemen were assaulted, in some cases somewhat viciously.' The cameraman vehemently denied inciting the violence.

A few days later, five men aged between 22 to 44 were sentenced to three months each for violence and affray, and 14 other men and youths were fined between £10 and £30 for related offences. All the defendants were white. When the sentences were read out relatives screamed and shouted from the public gallery. Four policemen were needed to carry out one kicking and screaming woman. Another woman fainted. The presiding magistrate, Arthur Turney, said: 'Lawlessness is not going to be tolerated in this city. We are going to treat it as a threat to the peace of the community and we shall act with the utmost severity that lies in our power.' He said that the coloured population had not contributed to that night of violence, but added that their presence in the city 'has been used as an excuse for lawless rallies to create a violent disturbance'. Referring to others in the Saturday night crowd he said: 'It is despicable that when the police are handling a desperate situation the public can do no better than obstruct them and actually take sides with the rowdies.'[15]

The Nottingham riots were, however, dwarfed by simultaneous events in the broad Notting Hill–Portobello Road area of London. The area between the Wood Lane factories to the west and newly reclaimed upper-middle-class streets on Notting Hill itself, was regarded in contemporary accounts as 'drab at best, squalid at worst'.[16] It contained a mix of clannish gypsy families and Irish labourers alongside up to 3,000 black immigrants who worked on building sites and as London Underground porters. Their white neighbours claimed resentfully that many relied solely on state benefits. Other charges, familiar from elsewhere, were made against the newcomers – that they ran brothels, that they were responsible for the rape of at least one young white girl. A reporter entered one pub and found

a group of men singing 'Bye Bye Blackbird' and punctuating the songs with vicious anti-Negro slogans. The men said that their motto was 'Keep Britain White' and they made all sorts of wild charges against their coloured neighbours. They were very bitter against the Labour Party for 'letting them in.'[17]

But equally there were stories of interracial working-class harmony – of white women looking after black babies when trouble flared, of black stall-holders being protected by white neighbours.

The rioting appears to have been sparked by up to 400 Teddy Boys and fascist youths, many from outside the area, embarking on an extensive 'nigger-hunt'. The White Defence League, launched by Colin Jordan, and John Bean's National Labour Party, came together with elements of Mosley's Union Movement (all three groupings of what would become the National Front).[18] Their first target was Majbritt Morrison, a Swedish woman whom a gang of white youths had seen the previous night arguing with her Jamaican husband Jimmy outside a pub. They followed her, throwing milk bottles and shouting 'Nigger lover! Kill her.' She escaped, wielding an iron bar, but the fuse was lit.

The white mob ran down Bramley Road shouting at policemen: 'We will kill all black bastards. Why don't you send them home?' PC Ian McQueen blocked their way and was told: 'Mind your own business, coppers. Keep out of it. We will settle these niggers our way. We'll murder the bastards.'[19]

Baker Baron, a 33-year-old Jamaican and wartime RAF veteran, recalled: 'They were going around in groups seeking out a coloured and beating him up, fighting, kicking them. Black people were so frightened at the time that they wouldn't leave their homes.' Baron, well-known for campaigning for better housing, helped organise a vigilante force to escort black people to and from their homes, and to protect those homes from attack. When fascists warned that they were coming on the night of the 31st he told the black women to prepare pots, kettles, boiling water and caustic soda to throw if their houses were attacked. The men were armed with Molotov cocktails, iron bars and machetes. Baron said:

> We made preparations at our headquarters for the attack. We had men on the housetop waiting for them. I was standing on the second floor with the lights out as look-out when I saw a massive number of people out there. They say, 'Let's burn the niggers, let's lynch the niggers.' That's the time I gave the order for the gates to open and to throw them back to where they were coming from. I was an ex-serviceman. I knew guerrilla warfare. I knew all about their game. It was very, very effective. I says, 'Start bombing them.' When they saw the Molotov cocktails coming, they start to run. It was a very serious bit of fighting that night. We were determined to use any means, anything at our disposal ... We were not prepared to go down

like dying dogs. We gave them such a whipping they never come back to Notting Hill. The following morning we walked the streets free because we were not going to stand for that type of behaviour.[20]

Police who tried to keep both sides apart came under attack. In one of several later trials the prosecutor said: 'There were running fights continuously between coloured and white people and at times the two opponents were ganging up against the police. The attitude to the police was "Get out and let us get on with our fight."' Some of the officers were knocked down, some kicked in the face and some cut with broken milk bottles. Four or five officers were injured, windows smashed and police cars damaged. PC Raymond McGuire saw an 18-year-old white youth throwing dustbin lids at windows in Walmer Road. 'I went and spoke to him, and he said to the surrounding people, "Come on, let's do him,"' the constable said. 'I was struck several times on the body, back and front, by several youths and the accused kicked me on the right leg and punched me in the stomach.' PC Charles Duthie saw a fellow officer hit on the head with a beer bottle in Bramley Road by a white 23-year-old. 'I went to arrest him. They dragged me to the ground and he kicked me with his right foot once in the throat and once on my right cheek. I lost consciousness.' As Duthie lay on the ground the crowd shouted 'Kill the bastard.' He was rescued by another officer who was himself injured on the head and hand.[21]

A 26-year-old white woman was rescued by foot police from a surging crowd after a voice had cried: 'There she goes, a black man's trollop.' The woman was herself arrested for obstruction when she refused to stay in her house for protection. A house in Blechynden Road became the focus of another confrontation between blacks and whites. The basement was used for 'jungle' dancing, and white youths laid siege. The occupants collected bottles for use as missiles, but serious violence was halted by the police.[22]

Young black men also began to surge through the streets, ready to hit back. Detective Sergeant M. Walters reported a large group walking along Ladbroke Grove: 'What can only be described as a mob were shouting threats and abuse, and variously displaying various most offensive weapons, ranging from iron bars to choppers and open razors.' A man later sentenced to twelve months' imprisonment waved an axe and shouted: 'Come and fight.' Another black man, stopped coming out of Bluey's Club on Talbot Road, was found to have a piece of iron down his left trouser leg, a petrol bomb in his right pocket and an open razor blade in his inside breast pocket. He told the arresting officer: 'I have to protect myself.'

Black student Seymour Manning was chased by a white gang and took refuge in a greengrocer's. The white proprietress barred the door until the police arrived.[23]

The local Labour MP, George Rogers, toured the glass-strewn area and told everyone who would listen: 'I appeal to you for common sense, decency and tolerance in the matter of race relations. I ask you to remain calm, stay indoors in your home tonight, and obey the police.' Police reinforcements poured into the area and the trouble gradually died down.[24]

After three nights of intermittent street-fighting there were 150 arrests. In the first major hearing 30 adults and one juvenile appeared in the local court. Fifteen of them were white youths and eleven were black. Most of the whites were charged with threatening behaviour, and most of the blacks with possessing offensive weapons. In the court room an evidence box was filled to the brim with flick knives, stilettos, razors, two studded leather belts, a bicycle chain, choppers, a club and a carving knife. The West London magistrate, Eric Guest, appealed for a voluntary curfew. He said:

> Now is the time for people of good will to stay indoors in the evening for a day or two to let the police restore order – and above all to keep the children indoors. Then the authorities will be able to see that the streets are clear again, and that if trouble is caused it is not caused by the people of Notting Hill.[25]

Outside the court groups of Teddy Boys gathered on the pavement under the eyes of police officers patrolling in pairs. The only black man seen was a barrister who hurriedly entered the building. He was watched in sullen silence by the onlookers.

*   *   *

Senior Metropolitan Police officers tried to play down the racial aspects of the riots. They were helped by Detective Sergeant Walters who reported to his superiors: 'Whereas there certainly was some ill-feeling between white and coloured residents in this area, it is abundantly clear much of the trouble was caused by ruffians, both coloured and white, who seized on this opportunity to indulge in hooliganism.' But many police witness statements, some of which are quoted above and which were not released by the Home Office until August 2002, show that most of the trouble was caused by whites, including fascists, engaged in 'nigger-bashing'. That was widely recognised at the time, in the press if not by the authorities.

The special correspondent of *The Times* gave his verdict:

> It is no good dismissing the evening pursuits and bottle-throwing and lynch-mobs as the work of Teddy Boys alone. After all some of the young men of the area are Teddy Boys. They get reinforcements from all over the town because these stunted pallid thugs like the chance of violence without dangerous odds. But having listened to what some of the fathers and the little brothers were saying in the day time, one felt that quite a few families must be proud of their teenage sons. Fights between white and coloured people have flared up in this area because it is a rough area, suspicious of strangers and used to settling its differences with fists and knives anyway. Into this miserable breeding ground come the strangers, and some of them behave badly by any standards. Then come the young roughs, hunting in packs, and find the trouble they are looking for.[26]

The London *Evening Standard* reported:

> These were battles in which those who had imbibed fascist propaganda were the aggressors, the persons who threw petrol bombs, stabbed, coshed and marauded as lynch gangs. Where 'coloureds' used violence it was in self-defence, self-defence made necessary by police inaction ...[27]

Something worse than police inaction was also widely suspected – the partisanship of officers. Local officers often clearly sympathised with the Blackshirts, and tolerated fascist meetings and gangs prowling the streets taunting blacks. They took no action against a group of Mosleyites who shouted 'We've no need for half-castes here' at the American entertainer Sammy Davis as he tried to eat in a restaurant. But an anti-fascist who shouted 'Blackshirt bastard' at Oswald Mosley at a public meeting was arrested, fined and bound over for twelve months.

On 3 September, at the Trades Union Congress (TUC) in Bournemouth, Peter Maurice of the Clerical and Administrative Workers' Union said that the union movement had always deplored racial intolerance in other countries. 'Now we have the problem on our own doorsteps', he said.

It is our problem and we should not be satisfied to deplore it and leave it to the police and the Ministry. As trade unionists the best we can do is to try to prevent the conditions arising where this sort of disturbance can happen. We must face the fact that racial prejudice still exists among some of our people; that the activities of a minority of the coloured people may cause antagonism against them in general; that unemployment, bad housing, and inadequate housing is going to make these prejudices and antagonisms come to the surface. Probably the most helpful thing we can do ... is to combat prejudice wherever and whenever it arises and to take whatever steps we can to help coloured people to become integrated into our community and to help their white neighbours to understand and accept them.[28]

The following day the TUC echoed his words in a motion condemning racial discrimination and intolerance. Church leaders in the stricken area put out their appeal for calm and tolerance.

The Home Secretary, R.A. Butler, stressed that all British citizens, regardless of colour, enjoy equality before the law. Speaking in Essex, he said:

We are rightly proud in this country of the fact that racial discrimination has never been part of our life in this country. We have prided ourselves on our hospitality to our fellow beings from Commonwealth and colonial territories who enjoy the right of unrestricted entry to the mother country.[29]

After the riots Conservative MPs and some unions urged a twelve-month moratorium on immigration. The proposal was rejected, but by then the influx was in any case slowing down. Successive administrations would both impose race relations legislation and tighten controls on immigration.

*   *   *

The tensions did not go away. The rule of law was applied relatively fairly and the Teddy Boys who sparked the violence were dealt with. But the riots left a bitter legacy. The second and third generation of young blacks beyond Notting Hill regarded it as a by-word for racism, both institutional and personal. Such resentments, increased by high unemployment, heavy-handed police tactics and drug crime, later exploded in places like Toxteth and Brixton. The sons and grandsons of the Teds became skinheads and National Front bovver-boys. Mutual suspicion and undisguised venom blighted lives, split communities and increased alienation. The 1962 Commonwealth Immigration Act introduced new curbs, but by then immigrants from the Indian sub-continent amounted to by far the largest intake. A further intake of 27,000 Ugandan Asians in the early 1970s brought with them enterprise skills which many young Afro-Caribbeans appeared to have forgotten or ditched. Racial tensions were no longer black and white, but complex webs of ethnic differences exacerbated and exploited by the extreme right.

The annual Notting Hill Carnival celebrating Caribbean roots was set up 1959, as a direct response to the riots, to promote racial harmony and, according to one of its founders, 'to prove that from our ghetto there was a wealth of culture waiting to express itself, to show that we weren't rubbish people'.[30] On August bank holidays it has attracted up to 2 million revellers to Notting Hill, making it Europe's biggest street party. It has also, some years, become a haven for muggers, drug dealers and occasional rioters.

The appeal of the carnival to subsequent generations of Afro-Caribbean Britons was clear. A Metropolitan Police officer said: 'Carnival was their day. For the rest of the year the police would be stopping them in ones and twos on the streets, where they would be a minority. But for one weekend they were the majority, and they took over the streets.' That caused much police resentment, and the carnival also became a target for National Front racists and skinhead gangs. Young blacks reacted with aggression of their own.

In 1976 rioting erupted as gangs of black and white youths hurled bottles. One witness described it as 'like watching a relentless parade of salmon leaping upstream'. The police, like the carnival organisers, were taken by suprise and badly prepared and ill-equipped to restore order. Officers were swamped by the crowd and several were injured. One officer said: 'We were very sore. We had taken a beating and we were determined that it would not happen again. When the next one came around there was some desire for revenge.' That occurred the following year when riot police were briefly deployed during skirmishing. Calls for the carnival's banning were loud, until Prince Charles declared he fully supported the event because 'it's so nice to see so many happy, dancing people with smiles on their faces'. However, there were ongoing concerns about the cost of policing the carnival, and the strain it put on police resources: in 1980 half the entire Metropolitan Police strength, 11,022 officers, were deployed for the event, but only made 53 arrests.[31]

Three months ahead of the 1987 carnival, a police operation was launched against drug dealers in the All Saints Road area of Notting Hill and 16 major dealers were arrested. Attacks on police escalated and fears grew of more anti-police violence at the carnival. Hundreds of officers were drafted in from across London before, during and after the event. There was violence during the carnival – including one murder – but it was less organised than expected. In the 1989 carnival mounted officers and 560 riot police, in groups of 20, cleared the streets. A large area was sealed off and hundreds more police manned a dozen roadblocks. In 2000, two men were murdered at the carnival and the following year the Metropolitan Police deployed 10,000 officers at a cost of £5.6 million, the most expensive operation in the force's history.

Since then, however, better community relations between police and local people, more sensitive policing tactics and improved organisation have prevented serious outbreaks. Crime has been kept to levels below that regarded as normal for an event which attracts between 1 and 2 million people.

The carnival parade was a major feature of the 2002 Golden Jubilee celebrations. The following August it featured all significant ethnic groupings, including participants from Afghanistan, Kurdistan, Bangladesh, the Philippines, Bulgaria, Russia, Brazil and all parts of the Caribbean, Africa, Asia, the Americas and the UK. There was no trouble.

17
From Student Protest to Blair Peach

'may we bring harmony'

In March 1968, *Times* education correspondent Brian MacArthur wrote:

> After black power, student power. Some students in Britain have stopped knocking at university doors and asking politely to see the vice-chancellor. After 10 years of having their requests for a hearing ignored, they have started kicking down the doors and demanded a hearing.[1]

The new student militancy in Britain reflected that on campuses in America and across Europe. Behind the Iron Curtain students were in the forefront of struggles for freedom. Across the Atlantic they opposed racial segregation and the negative aspects of capitalism. In Britain the Campaign for Nuclear Disarmament had attracted many student members, while the TV satire boom had added to the culture of dissent. There was Flower Power, too, mingling with the protest songs of Bob Dylan and with growing drugs experimentation. Authority was questioned on all fronts, in the home, in the workplace, in academia. The times they really were a-changing.

Posters of the Cuban guerrilla Che Guevara appeared in bedsits while students devoured the works of Trotsky, Herbert Marcuse, Rosa Luxemburg and Regis Debray. Such revolutionary thinkers endorsed violence and incited action against repression. A contemporary wrote:

> They made equally suitable heroes for French workers, American negroes, Polish Jews, and any other minority group on the 'out' of society which in 1968 found allies in articulate, reckless students too young to have a stake in society, with nothing to lose from the disruption of that society, and the

optimism to believe that they had everything to gain by the reconstruction of the existing world.[2]

One of the most prominent student leaders was Tariq Ali, a Pakistani journalist and ex-president of the Oxford Union. Small-scale demonstrations erupted across Britain, and he was a speaker, if not organiser, at many of them. The scale of student unrest, however, was small when compared with mainland Europe, in part because student numbers in proportion to population was still relatively low. What youthful protest also lacked was a unifying theme. The horrors of the Vietnam War, replayed nightly on TV screens, provided it. Scenes of a superpower raining bombs on a Third World country to prop up a corrupt puppet regime seemed to epitomise all that was wrong with the world. The Flower Children were growing angry.

The day before MacArthur's article appeared, that anger was expressed outside the United States embassy in Grosvenor Square, West London.

*   *   *

On Sunday 17 March the left-wing actress Vanessa Redgrave addressed a rally of around 10,000 in Trafalgar Square. She and others spoke eloquently against American actions in Vietnam, and the support – though falling short of committing British troops – given by the Labour administration of Harold Wilson. There were mature, veteran protesters on the platforms and in the crowd, but the majority of those who then headed for the US embassy were young and idealistic.

The first clashes came when the police tried to halt the main body of marchers entering Grosvenor Square from Oxford Street. They were brushed aside by a largely good-humoured crowd. A 1,000-strong police cordon around the embassy held, but the crowded wheeled around and faced the main embassy entrance. The mood turned ugly and police without protective gear were pelted with smoke bombs, ball-bearings, cans and fireworks. The police only managed to stem the flow 100 yards from the doors. The siege lasted two hours.

The protesters made numerous charges at the police lines, brandishing placards, poles and branches, and throwing stones and clods of earth from the gardens. Mounted police rode into the crowd, crushing some demonstrators. Thunder flashes and other fireworks were thrown under the hooves and the horses reared, lashing out in panic and adding to both the confusion and the carnage. Some horses were pierced with darts, while others were brought down by marbles rolled under their hooves.

During a lull in the fighting the police regrouped and used the calmed horses to herd people off the gardens and out of the square. The demonstration was broken up, and the wounded were carried away. The St John Ambulance Brigade treated 86 people for injuries and around 50 were taken to hospital. About half were policemen, including one with a serious spinal injury and another with a neck wound.[3]

The graphic violence was broadcast around the world. The sight of students using poles like medieval knights to ram police lines shocked the right. And the spectacle of police lines being stoned was alien in the UK before the outbreak of the Northern Ireland Troubles. But Labour MP Peter Jackson, who had taken part in the demonstration, protested: 'I was particularly outraged by the violent use of police horses, who charged into the crowd even after they had cleared the street in front of the embassy.' And there were public qualms. People who may have applauded pictures of a girl student being publicly spanked by police officers were nevertheless sickened by the sound of hooves and batons thudding into flesh.

The following day 48 people appeared in four magistrates' courts. A 21-year-old unemployed man was sentenced to two months for assaulting a police officer in Duke Street. He said: 'I just sort of got carried away.' A commercial traveller from Lancashire was fined £25 and given a three-month suspended sentence after a police officer testified he dived at his legs in the mêlée. A 24-year-old electronics engineer was fined £30 with costs for assaulting a policeman, damaging his raincoat, and kicking a police horse in the stomach. The court heard: 'The animal was already excited as red paint had been daubed about its head and it had been jabbed several times with darts.' But the majority of the defendants were students and other young people who were given fines ranging from £2 to £25. Three Cambridge University students were charged with possessing offensive weapons after coaches carrying demonstrators were stopped by the police at Hendon. One was found with a glass-cutter in his shoe, another was carrying a bag of marbles, and the third had a can of pepper spray. A German student who had travelled from Berlin with 50 others to take part in the demonstration was found guilty of assaulting a policeman, but was conditionally discharged for three years. A 20-year-old American student studying at Essex University was fined £10 for using threatening words. The words had been: 'Stop the war in Vietnam' and 'Burn the embassy'.[4] Eventually another 56 protesters faced similar charges.

Similar violence was seen at another anti-Vietnam War demonstration in October 1968. Evidence was later produced suggesting that Trotskyist organisers planned a determined assault on the US embassy. A first aid centre for injured demonstrators was set up in advance at the London School of Economics. A crowd of about 25,000 assembled on the Victoria Embankment and marched to a rally in Hyde Park. Once the speeches were over, and the demonstration breaking up, around 5,000 people broke away from the procession and headed for Grosvenor Square. Once again missiles were thrown at the police, but the lines held and the onslaught abandoned.

*   *   *

The 1970s saw dissent spill out from the campuses as student veterans of demonstrations began work in the media, the trade union movement, and single-issue campaigns. Left-wing splinter groups sprang up from disillusionment with mainstream Labour Party policies and the advent of a new Labour government in 1974. The Socialist Workers Party was born out of less effective Trotskyist groupings and became increasingly visible due to its organisation on street demonstrations and its impressive publishing arm. It preached revolution and the destruction of what its members saw as a police state. The police responded with heavy-handed tactics which in some instances mirrored those employed in Northern Ireland. With the end of the Vietnam War attention focused on combating racism and other forms of discrimination. The enemy here was visible and close at hand. The National Front (NF) began making gains in council elections, their racist propaganda encouraged by Tory politician Enoch Powell's infamous 'rivers of blood' speech about mass immigration. NF recruitment soared, amongst skinhead youths, football hooligans, and, it was claimed, among some white police officers angered by positive discrimination in police preferment. The NF picked up votes, although not seats, in both 1974 general elections. When 18-year-old Gurdip Chaggar Singh was fatally stabbed,

NF Chairman Kingsley Read reportedly said: 'One down – a million to go.' Asian communities became the particular targets of racial attacks. Defence groups were formed, and the broad left formed the Anti-Nazi League. Street clashes between the League and the NF became frequent. Police tactics in suppressing disorder, particularly those in London involving the feared Special Patrol Group (SPG), were seen as protecting racists rather than their victims.

Students, various left-wing political groupings, and trade unionists came together during a bitter two-year strike by largely Asian workers at a film processing works in Willesden, London.

During the long, hot summer of 1976 there was huge pressure on the mail order department of Grunwick to send out processed photographs as quickly as possible. The lowest pay rates were £28 for a 40-hour week at a time when the national average was £72. Sackings were frequent and the annual staff turnover was 100 per cent. The plant was non-union and overtime was compulsory. Four young men in the mail order department discussed forming a union branch and operated an unofficial go-slow. One was sacked and the other three walked out in protest. Mrs Jayaben Desai was ordered to work overtime and refused, telling the manager that he was running a zoo rather than a factory. She and her son Sunil joined the four men outside the gates. They demanded union recognition and workers inside began joining the Association of Professional, Executive, Clerical and Computer Staff (APEX). The management took counter action and within a week 137 out of a 480-strong workforce were on strike for the right to be represented by the union. The company, headed by managing director George Ward, sacked all the strikers.[5]

Early in 1977, postal workers, at the request of APEX, began to 'black' Grunwick mail, contrary to a legal decision later overturned. In June trade unionists from across the country mounted a series of mass pickets at the Grunwick factory. They were joined by three Government ministers, including Shirley Williams. The pickets were met by large forces of police charged with ensuring that non-striking workers and supplies got through. On 14 June there were violent clashes and 84 arrests. Heavy-handed police tactics and individual acts of police brutality captured by press cameras briefly boosted support for the strikers. But on 23 June when 2,500 pickets appeared and a policeman was severely injured, the mood shifted. Fifty-three people were arrested.

The Advisory Conciliation and Arbitration Service (ACAS) investigated the strikers' grievances and recommended union recognition. The Grunwick management succeeded in persuading Lord Denning to overturn that in the Court of Appeal. The Government appointed a Court of Inquiry under the future Lord Scarman which late in August recommended that the strikers be reinstated, but left the key question of union recognition for collective bargaining to be decided after a House of Lords decision on an ACAS appeal. The union accepted the report and offered to negotiate, promising in particular not to seek a closed shop. George Ward and his directors flatly rejected it, claiming to be champions of age-old British freedoms. They in turn were championed by the Conservative opposition under Mrs Thatcher. A dispute over workers' rights in a small factory was elevated to a battle of wills over the interpretation of basic constitutional rights.

Meanwhile, the strike continued into its second year. Mrs Desai recalled:

> People all over the country realised what a bad situation it was and came to join us on the picket line. Money came in from everywhere to help us. The police were very abusive towards us and one of them even kicked me in the leg when I was trying to talk to someone who was behind him.[6]

The APEX leadership backed away from any further mass picketing, but the local strike committee did not. They were strongly advised to maintain the pressure by Jack Dromey, secretary of Brent trades council and an efficient and cool-headed organiser. In mid October they vainly tried to persuade repair workers not to make good a breach in Grunwick's water supply. The strike committee decided to mount weekly Monday morning mass pickets. The third, on 7 November 1977, was to turn into a bloody battle.

Grunwick was on two nearby sites, one in Cobbold Road, the other in Chapter Road, and it was at the latter where most trouble was expected. Police lines stretched 80 yards each side of its entrance. Both approaches to Chapter Road were blocked off. The first serious scuffle occurred when pickets from Birmingham's British Leyland car plant tried to force through the cordon. There was more violence when the pickets took control of the outside of the front gate. The police counter-charged with batons and retook the position. By now the pickets had swollen to 8,000 outside the two factories. At 9.40 a.m. the Grunwick bus carrying workers got into the Chapter Road factory through a back gate. The bus was later spotted parked behind a nearby pub and its windows smashed.[7]

Sporadic violence continued, most of it confused as pickets probed for weaknesses but were beaten back. Others involved pickets, trapped in the narrow streets, trying to escape from police horses. Police, including members of the notorious SPG, fought back. On one occasion a senior police officer was reported to have pointed to a gang of thickset men in jeans and T-shirts carrying iron bars and said: 'Look at the thugs we are up against.' He was told: 'No sir, they're ours.' Sheffield MP Martin Flannery said:

> The violence was provoked by the show of force, by the use of mounted police, and by their hostile attitude generally to the pickets.' Dromey said: 'It was as if the police had been let off the leash. They just went in dragging people around by their hair for no reason. I just do not see why they did it. There was nothing to gain and it provoked a lot of further trouble.[8]

With Grunwick operating normally the picket was called off and around 3,000 demonstrators marched to Willesden Green police station to protest about police behaviour. After about an hour, during which Willesden High Street was blocked, they were driven off with more violence.

A total of 243 pickets were treated for injuries, twelve of them for broken bones. Forty-two policemen were hurt, of whom nine required hospital treatment and one was detained for observation of a head wound. Of the 113 pickets arrested, 43 were students, five were social workers, three were engineers and the remainder included journalists, gardeners, trade union officials and unemployed men.[9]

The following month five Law Lords dismissed the ACAS appeal. Lod Diplock ruled that Grunwick had done nothing wrong and that an employer was under no obligation to co-operate with ACAS in a union recognition dispute. Mrs Desai and three others went on hunger strike. Later she recalled: 'One of the girls who was with me became dehydrated and I realised she was someone's daughter and I had a responsibility towards her. So I thought, "Forget them. It's time to stop this."' After more than two years the dispute was finally lost.

The sight of the tiny Mrs Desai surrounded by burly police officers as she continued the battle became a symbol of a police force being used to intimidate both would-be trade unionists and Asian women. It was a propaganda gift to extremist factions on the left who were determined to slug out their differences with the extreme right. The worst clash came on 23 April 1979, and it was fatal.

*　　*　　*

The National Front had booked a meeting in a small room of Southall town hall, in an area with a large Asian immigrant population. When the doors opened only 59 NF member attended to listen to organiser Martin Webster. Outside there were several thousand demonstrators and 5,000 police. The Anti-Nazi League had declared the meeting a provocation, and the demonstration was intended to stop it.

Trouble began as crowds collected in the streets around the town hall five hours before the meeting was due to. There were scuffles and a few people were arrested. Serious violence broke out at about 4.00 p.m. when police reinforcements arrived in coaches and by foot in Southall Broadway. As they formed up they were pelted with stones, bricks and pieces of wood by an increasingly volatile crowd.[10]

The majority of 340 arrests that day were made in the hour after 6.15 p.m. On the Broadway demonstrators smashed shop windows as the police move forward in strength. At Southall railway bridge around 200 Asians who had been holding a peaceful sit-in suddenly began to throw missiles at the police. Thirty minutes before the NF meeting was due to start around 250 mainly ethnic youths and young women tried to storm a police cordon thrown across Uxbridge Road about 100 yards from the town hall. Observers described them jeering, spitting and hurling smoke bombs, flares, milk bottles, bricks and paint. The attack turned into a bloody rout.

The police cordon suddenly parted and ranks of mounted police charged through the gap. Behind them came ranks of foot police with riot shields. Within three minutes the horsemen had cornered about 50 demonstrators. The *Daily Telegraph* reporting team wrote:

> As we watched, several dozen crying, screaming coloured demonstrators were dragged bodily along Park View Road and along the Uxbridge Road to the police station and waiting coaches. Nearly every demonstrator we

saw had blood flowing from some sort of injury. Some were doubled up in pain. Women and men were crying. A coloured woman stopped in her tracks to call the police 'White rough bastards.' She was lifted bodily in the air by policemen themselves bleeding from injuries and with their uniforms in tatters.[11]

Several hundred Asian youths were corralled on the Broadway, the area's main shopping development. They began throwing bottles at an equal number of police. Snatch squads of riot police, directed by officers on the flat roofs of nearby shops, charged into the crowd to arrest missile-throwers. Among those arrested were members of the Socialist Workers Party, the Indian Workers Association and Ealing Community Relations Council. Tariq Ali, the veteran student agitator, was arrested in another clash.

A group of about 50 commandeered and wrecked a London Transport bus. Police boarded it and, with chanting and fighting demonstrators still on board, drove the badly damaged vehicle to the nearest police station.

Blair Peach, a New Zealand-born schoolteacher, a married man with two children who worked in a special school in the East End, was among a small group which clashed head-on with members of the Special Patrol Group. He was struck across the head with either a truncheon or a police radio and staggered, with assistance, to a house in Orchard Road before being taken by ambulance to Ealing Hospital. Amanda Leon, a friend of Peach, saw another man on the ground being struck in a 'systematic manner' by the police. When she walked up to the officers and urged them to stop she was herself hit on the head with a truncheon.

During this mayhem the first small group of NF members arrived for the meeting, under heavy police protection. They gave the Nazi salute from behind the blue ranks. Loudspeakers from shops in the High Street responded with slogans: 'No Nazis in Southall' and 'National Front Out'. The police allowed 50 demonstrators to stand on the pavement opposite the town hall and on the balcony of a nearby Indian restaurant to make their protest as the meeting went on inside.[12]

Shortly before 10.00 p.m. a selected group of NF members stood at the top of the town hall steps chanting abuse at Asian demonstrators while Webster, their hero, was smuggled out a back door. When Webster was clear, policemen tapped the NF chanters on the shoulders and ushered them back inside. Minutes later 40 NF men carrying a Union Jack filed out of a side entrance into a coach and were escorted by police convoy half a mile out of the area. As they left a senior police officer spoke into his pocket radio: 'Right, dismiss the Mounties.'

Sir David McNee, the Commissioner of the Metropolitan Police, issued a statement:

> The disturbances that took place in the streets of Southall were unprovoked acts of violence against police and property by groups of people determined to create an atmosphere of tension and hostility. The Commissioner wishes it to be understood that the role of the police is to preserve the Queen's peace and ensure that people of every political persuasion may pass unmolested. Police have no part to play in the political arena but have a bounden duty to see that the laws of the land pertaining to free speech are enforced.[13]

The National Council of Civil Liberties described police action as 'volatile and extremely aggressive.' Jack Dromey, who attended the demonstration as a union official, reported: 'I have never seen such unrestrained violence against demonstrators or such hatred on both sides.'[14]

About 40 policemen were injured, and 20 were taken to hospital where 15 were released after treatment. PC Terence Laverock was stabbed in the back, but there were reports that he was hurt in a scuffle with skinheads. Up to 40 people were taken to Ealing Hospital and a plan drawn up for major emergencies was put into effect. Normal patients due to have operations the following day were sent home to make room for the injured and extra staff were called in. Staff battled to save the life of Blair Peach, but he died in the hospital several hours after his admission.

His death provoked fury. Peach, who lived in Hackney, had been a passionate opponent of the NF and a dedicated member of the Anti-Nazi League. The League accused the police of excessive brutality. Commander John Cass, head of the Complaints Investigation Bureau, was put in charge of the investigation into Peach's death. While a post mortem was carried out on Peach's body, Southall police station was picketed by League supporters carrying placards declaring 'SPG murderers'. The pathologist confirmed that Peach was killed by a 'single blow to the head' with an instrument that could not have been a police issue truncheon. A subsequent search of suspected SPG lockers found an eight-inch metal cosh encased in leather with a lead weight, a pickaxe handle and other non-regulation items. Forensic examination was unable to put any of them at the death scene, although a police radio was the most likely suspect.

Vishnu Sharma, president of the Indian Workers Association, said: 'If anyone would have liked to see the police state in total operation he should have been in Southall. The National Front was allowed to hold its meeting by Ealing Council with the help of the police force.'[15] James Jardine, chairman of the Police Foundation countered:

> We must ensure that the law on public order is enforced so that genuine, and I mean genuine, public meetings, held under election law, can take place. Many people are now going to meetings not to fight the National Front but to attack the police.[16]

Two nights after the riot the largest police operation ever seen in London's East End was deployed to prevent a repetition. Around 5,000 police were sent to Newham to prevent Anti-Nazi League demonstrators clashing with National Front supporters who were attending an election rally in the town hall. Shops and offices closed early and shopkeepers boarded up their windows. During a tense eight-hour stand-off torrential rain was credited with helping to prevent serious outbreaks of violence, although there were 15 arrests for minor offences. Two thousand police surrounded Newham town hall, another 3,000 were held in readiness nearby, and plain clothes SPG and Special Branch officers mingled with the crowds. The NF's opponents were hemmed in by police cordons. Twenty League members managed to infiltrate the meeting but their heckling did not spark disorder.

Home Secretary Merlyn Rees announced that there would be no public inquiry into the Southall riot, but ordered a special police investigation into complaints of police brutality. Rees said that Commissioner McNee had told him that he had adequate resources to deal with further disturbances. 'I told him of my confidence in the ability of the Metropolitan Police to maintain public order.'[17] The Prime Minister, James Callaghan, announcing a review of the Public Order Act, said that there was some evidence that extremists had gone into Southall from outside to foment violence against the police.

The National Front, meanwhile, saw Southall as a recruiting aid. It prepared to field candidates in 303 seats at the upcoming general election. Its 41,000-word manifesto, longer that the Labour,

Conservative and Liberal manifestos combined, appealed to disgruntled voters. The NF leadership saw immigration as its biggest vote-winner and advocated the compulsory repatriation of all coloured immigrants and their offspring.

The main party leaders also saw race as a potent card. But in the event, months of industrial unrest, labelled the 'Winter of Discontent', had already put the seal on the Callaghan administration. Mrs Thatcher was propelled into Downing Street a few weeks after Southall. The National Front lost their deposits in every seat they contested.

On 4 May 1979, within an hour of taking office, Mrs Thatcher quoted St Francis of Assisi: 'Where there is discord, may we bring harmony; where there is error, may we bring truth; where there is doubt, may we bring faith; where there is despair, may we bring hope.'

*   *   *

No one was held responsible for Blair Peach's death, and no police officer faced disciplinary action. An inquest recorded a verdict of 'death by misadventure' even though eleven witnesses reported seeing Peach being struck by police. The internal Metropolitan Police investigation report by Commander Cass was never published.

Twenty years later, 1,000 people marched past Southall police station demanding justice. Home Office minister Paul Boateng, who as a young lawyer had defended several of the accused after the Southall riot, told a delegation that it was 'time to move on'. The New Labour Government refused to reopen the inquiry.[18]

Blair Peach's former partner, Celia Stubbs, currently campaigns for more anti-racist education in schools.

18
Brixton, Toxteth and Broadwater Farm

'My God, the Blitz must have been like this'

For more than a decade the British TV viewing public had become used to almost nightly scenes of rioting, murder, carnage and destruction on the streets of Northern Ireland. In April 1981 they turned on to familiar pictures of burning buildings and cars, petrol bombs and police behind riot shields. This time it was different. This time it was on the streets of England.

A Metropolitan Police inspector recalled:

> We zoomed down there with our carrier into what looked like World War Three. Cars blazing, people running everywhere. The air was filled with orange smoke. The radios only had two channels and both of them were overloaded with people trying to get through. Then suddenly this hurricane of bricks and bottles and God knows what other shit hits the roof of our van from the flats overhead.[1]

Brixton, he added, was 'a nightmare'.

*   *   *

During the 1970s the police were faced with public distaste at heavy-handed policing during strikes and at demonstrations, a lack of public confidence following large-scale corruption trials, and unease at the misuse of 'sus' laws to stop and search black youths. Some forces, particularly the Met, developed a 'them and us' siege mentality. New recruits were not vigorously vetted for membership of the National

Front and other racist organisations. Many young constables had spent their formative teenage years at punk venues, skinhead gatherings and on the football terraces. They enjoyed a good 'ruck'. Young Afro-Caribbeans, for their part, used their roots as an excuse for drug dealing and intimidation. Tensions between young cops and young blacks grew steadily from the 1977 Notting Hill Carnival. The superior officers of the former and the parents of the latter lost control, and a violent street culture flourished. In some areas young PCs were stopping black youths of their own age or above. Both sides saw it as a question of who controlled the streets. It was gang warfare, with one gang wearing uniforms.

When Mrs Thatcher came to power in 1979 she embraced the police and vilified the urban, black poor. The explosion in drug dealing seen in the early 1980s, together with mass unemployment and alienation, added more fuel to the tinderbox. Black youths were 35 times more likely to be stopped and searched than white youths.

The spark was lit in April 1981 when 110 plain clothes officers of the Special Patrol Group – notorious for its alleged brutality – were sent into Brixton to tackle street crime. Even the name of the operation – 'Swamp 81' – was provocative, echoing the warnings of right-wing politicians that Britain was being 'swamped' by ethnic minorities. Over subsequent days there were 1,000 stop and searches of black youths, 118 arrests and 75 charges, only one of which was for robbery. Police relations with the community were reduced to a shambles and there was no significant impact on crime.

Rioting was triggered on the evening of Friday 10 April when two constables on foot saw a black youth being chased by several others. They stopped him and discovered he was bleeding badly from a four-inch wound between his shoulder blades. He refused to tell them who his attackers were and ran through a crowd which obstructed the officers. He was later traced to a private house and put in a taxi while two other constables followed in a police car. During a stop at traffic lights one officer examined the youth more closely and concluded that a lung was punctured, obstructing breathing, and that it was too dangerous to continue. He ordered the taxi-driver to await an ambulance. A crowd of up to 40 mainly black youths and men surrounded the taxi and the rumour spread that the police were assaulting the bleeding youth. Despite the efforts of the constables to explain, the taxi doors were opened and the youth was carried away. He was put in another car and taken to hospital but three days later he discharged himself and disappeared.[2]

Meanwhile, the first two constables were being pelted with bricks and bottles. They called for assistance and officers arrived from Brixton police station. Passions among the crowd, now swelled to over 100, were clearly aggravated by the Swamp operation. An inspector ordered his men to advance on the crowd and clear the area, even though only three officers were carrying shields. The crowd was broken up into small groups but refused to disperse. Several officers were hurt by missiles. More police were moved into the area and, although motor patrols were reduced, foot patrols were increased. Alleged ringleaders were arrested, more police arrived in riot gear, and the violence died away.[3]

Saturday morning appeared normal with the streets and markets crowded with shoppers, but there was a tension which the extra numbers of police did nothing to dispel. The rumour spread that the youth had died in hospital and that the police were responsible. Early in the afternoon two constables questioning the driver of a parked car about suspected drug dealing were surrounded by a crowd screaming 'Police harassment'. A young black man who tried to shove an officer aside was arrested and as they struggled to hold onto him, the constables radioed for help. More police arrived with a van and the arrestee was bundled inside. The crowd, now about 150, tried to overturn the vehicle and smashed a rear door window. Lord Scarman later wrote: 'The inference is irresistible that many young people, and especially many young black people, were spoiling for a row.'[4]

More police officers and vehicles became hemmed in by an ever-growing and angry crowd. The missiles began to rain down. The local Chief Superintendent appealed urgently for assistance from the whole Metropolitan force. He ordered his officers, in the meantime, to draw their truncheons and clear the immediate front. People fled the charge down sidestreets and connecting roads, the police in pursuit. Shop windows were smashed and extensive looting began. An Inspector and 20 constables came under heavy attack with bricks, bottles and railings used as javelins. As they had no riot shields they picked up dustbin lids. The first petrol bombs were thrown and it quickly became clear that stockpiles had been prepared overnight. Lord Scarman wrote:

'The evidence of a tumultuous, violent crowd determined to execute and executing a common purpose to attack the police with alarming and very dangerous missiles is too plain to be challenged.'[5]

By early evening the riot had engulfed all of central Brixton. The police, still thinly spread, limited their operations to cordoning principal streets to contain the mayhem until reinforcements arrived. Throughout they were under a shower of missiles and petrol bombs. The burning fuel seeped around the police shields and ignited the padding at the back. More and more officers dropped. Houses were fired, police and private cars were fire-bombed and overturned, and a bus was hijacked by teenagers who knocked down the conductor and stole his takings. Ambulance crews and firemen were attacked when they answered 999 calls. A Met inspector with twelve years in the job, said: 'I had bottles and bricks at the Notting Hill Carnival, but this time it was petrol bombs and everything – a lot more organised.' A 30-year-old WPC recalled:

> Somebody said to me, 'My God, the Blitz must have been like this.' At one point, all we could see was orange, everywhere around was smoke. But there wasn't time to stop and think what the hell was going on, because you were so busy. I had nightmares long afterwards.[6]

By mid evening police strength had grown sufficiently to take the offensive. They moved forward from two opposite sides of the riot zone against fierce and continuous resistance. One party was cut off, badly beaten and relieved of their riot shields, but that was an exception. Generally the police tactics were brutally efficient and by 10.00 p.m. the centre of Brixton was cleared. An hour later order was fully restored, although the night was still disturbed by the crackle of burning buildings. The cost was high – 279 police officers injured; 61 private cars and 56 police vehicles damaged or destroyed; 145 buildings damaged, 28 by fire.[7] Lord Scarman reported: 'The police had undergone an experience till then unparalleled on the mainland of the United Kingdom.'[8]

Sunday morning saw the police out in force, and cordons were thrown around the main battle zones as council workers and the emergency services cleared away the smoking rubble and gutted cars. In the afternoon senior officers and community leaders were holding another conference when gangs of black youths again began to congregate.

Police lines were stoned but the disorder was nothing like as bad as the previous day. Stores were looted and individuals robbed, but there was no further arson. Bizarrely, Swamp 81 continued and sparked isolated fury. In one incident a hostile crowd gathered when the police searched and humiliated an innocent black minicab-driver in front of them. But it is all comparative – during Sunday 122 police were injured and 89 vehicles damaged or destroyed.[9]

During 10–12 April there were almost 800 crimes reported, and the police estimated that a third of the rioters were white. Forty-eight civilians and 401 police officers were injured, although many rioters who were hurt did not seek hospital treatment for fear of arrest. There were 257 arrests, of which 172 cases were found guilty. Damage was put at £4.75 million, including the destruction of 20 buildings, 30 private cars destroyed, 61 damaged, four police cars gutted by petrol bombs, and 118 police cars and four ambulances damaged.

The *Annual Register* noted:

> The riots shocked the nation not only by their violence and presumed racial implications but also by their demonstration that police forces could not control or even contain mobs throwing petrol bombs and other lethal missiles and attacking them with petrol bombs, crowbars or the like in confined city streets, even in the metropolis.[10]

* * *

In Liverpool tensions between the long-established West Indian community and the police had also been growing, and for much the same reasons as in London. The black population was largely concentrated in Liverpool 8, a district defined by urban decay and official neglect. Extremist groupings were actively exploiting genuine grievances.

On 3 July 1981, three months after the Brixton Riots, a young motorcyclist, Leroy Cooper, being followed by traffic police turned into Granby Street, in the heart of Toxteth, and fell off. The officers accused him of stealing the bike. A crowd quickly gathered and blocked an arrest. More police were summoned and in the ensuing fight one officer suffered a broken nose and four others were injured. Cooper, who later served a short borstal sentence for assaulting the officers, recalled: 'It was quite scary. It suddenly turned from one type of situation into a completely different one.'[11]

The following morning, a Saturday, police intelligence suggested that youths were preparing for more serious public disorder. At 5.30 p.m. youths stoned police on Upper Parliament Street and sporadic violence sprang up throughout the evening. It got worse when the pubs closed. Shops were burnt and a wine store was ransacked. Shortly after 11.00 p.m. three police columns moved along Upper Parliament Street to confront up to 300 youths. Stones and bricks were hurled at them, to be quickly followed by the first petrol bombs. The youths turned over a workman's generator to use as a barricade. A bus shelter was demolished. Cars who slowed to pass the barricade were pelted with stones. Some drivers were pulled out and beaten up, and watched their vehicles being wrecked.

More police were drafted in and made repeated charges behind plastic shields. The battle raged all night as cars were burned or driven at bus shelters to wreck them and shops were looted. Shopkeeper Bridie Hefferman described how 30 masked youths broke into her premises to steal boxes of tinned goods. They also emptied the contents of freezers on the floor. 'It was sheer vandalism', she said.[12] A BBC television crew ran for cover when another masked gang attacked them with pickaxe handles. A £12,000 camera was snatched and destroyed. Throughout the night police escorted firemen on their way to extinguish burning buildings and cars. At last, at 7.00 a.m. the police baton-charged the mob which then melted away into side alleys and on to the Kingsley housing estate.[13] Sunday dawned on a scene of devastation, but there was much worse to come.

After a relatively quiet Sunday the violence erupted again at eight p.m. when a gang looted the Galleon Wine Lodge at the Smithdown Road end of Upper Parliament Street. Police were drawn up behind riot shields, but the mob broke into the Unigate Dairy depot and started aiming milk floats, their throttles jammed open, at the police lines.[14] By midnight almost half of Upper Parliament Street was ablaze. The famous Rialto Cinema was destroyed, as was the 150-year-old Racquets Club with its collection of art and antique furniture. Local reporter Ian Craig witnessed the club's destruction:

> A signal was given by a motorcyclist and three hooded men threw petrol bombs into the yard. The front doors were blasted open and the windows in the bar were blown out onto the pavement. I saw a portly club member come through the doorway, silhouetted by the flames. He was carrying the stuffed

head of a deer with a full set of antlers. He raised the trophy as a defiant gesture to the arsonists. It was the only thing rescued from the blaze.[15]

Britain's first drive-in bank, a branch of NatWest, was looted and burnt. Ninety-six bewildered and frightened elderly patients were evacuated in their nightclothes from Prince's Park geriatric hospital, which was threatened by flames from nearby houses. Some rioters stopped briefly to help with the evacuation, and the police lines also pulled back.

9   The Toxteth Riots, Liverpool
empics

Looters rampaged down Lodge Lane, smashing every window along their route. Booty included caseloads of spirits, groceries, clothing and electrical goods. Entire families filled up supermarket trolleys with stolen goods as the police watched helplessly from their beleaguered lines. Queues even formed outside shattered shop windows as rioters waited their turn to plunder. A pub was set ablaze along with more shops. Firemen, unprotected by the police, searched the blazing buildings. Some residents were trapped in their homes by the heat and forced to evacuate over back walls.[16] *The Times* reported:

> A pall of smoke rose over the city as rioters, many little more than 15 years old, carried trophies of the fighting. There were police helmets and riot

shields being paraded as cries of 'stone the bastards' echoed through the smoke. Riot shields dropped by the police were seized by advancing rioters who at one point took control of a fire hose the police had been using on them, and turned it on the officers. Faced with a screaming, almost berserk mob, the police were forced to retreat. They faced youths armed with every conceivable weapon, including lengths of scaffolding which they thrust at the walls of riot shields like medieval knights.[17]

By now most of the rioters appeared to be white. Racial tensions within the community's youth were forgotten. The police were the common enemy. A gang commandeered a bulldozer, lifted a police car in the air and smashed it through a block of scaffolding. The police line broke.

One constable recalled:

I saw bobbies getting injured with stones, bricks and all that stuff they were dropping out of the flats – coping stones, railings. I honestly thought one or two lads had snuffed it, the way they took the blow. I realised, standing there with a shield, that people out there wanted me dead. That's a frightening thought.

Another said:

I don't know how you can describe the smoke and the flames and the terror, absolute terror. You're confined to a little space, you're stood behind the shield, there's petrol bombs flying through the air and every now and then someone's on fire who's in the same line as you, or your shield's on fire, or your shoes are on fire. It went on for so long.

Individual police officers seethed at superiors who ordered them to stand in line, like coconuts in a carnival shy, waiting to be knocked down. An Inspector said:

When I was in Northern Ireland I was mortared. On two or three occasions I was shot at, but I was more frightened when I was in the front line down at Toxteth than I ever was in Ulster. Not because of what was happening, but because I was stuck there behind a shield with no chance whatsoever of doing anything to the people who were throwing petrol bombs at me, driving cars at us and trying to set fire to us by pouring diesel down the road. We stood there from 1am to 9am the next morning, taking that lot, and there wasn't one decision taken.

A Chief Inspector said:

On the first night of the riot I stood in the front line for about 12 hours with seven other officers. At the end of that night, one was in hospital with a fractured skull, one was in for about two weeks with complications to his spleen after being hit by a brick, and two other officers were in for two or three days each. It was only myself and two others who returned to duty the next day. It was a bloody disaster.[18]

Eight hundred police were on the streets but much of their equipment was scant protection from petrol bombs and iron bars. There also appears to have been failures in the command structures, with senior officers too far back to judge the extremes of violence at the front. The police had clearly lost control of the situation, if they ever had it in the first place. Reinforcements were requested and sent from Cheshire, Lancashire and Greater Manchester, taking total police numbers to 4,000, but the rioting continued. The police cordon was pushed back to within 200 yards of the Anglican Cathedral. One officer was speared in the head by a spiked six-foot railing thrown by a rioter. As the police retreated they left behind them 'no-go' areas open to a crowd of jubilant rioters, most of them white. David Alton, Liberal Democrat MP for Edge Hill, said as buildings burned behind him: 'Police have abandoned parts of Liverpool to the mob.' An outraged black resident wept as he told reporters: 'This is a conspiracy to rob and nothing more. It has nothing to do with racial matters.' Local councillor Chris Davies complained: 'Every shop, from supermarkets to small corner stores have been smashed and looted. And there is not a policeman in sight.' He claimed that the rioters had leaders:

I've seen them wearing balaclava helmets – just like Belfast – handing out petrol bombs and telling people where to go. There are people standing on street corners with pick-axe handles, looking like hell's preachers, to make sure that no-one interferes with what's going on.[19]

At 2.15 a.m. on the 7 July Merseyside Chief Constable Kenneth Oxford authorised, for the first and last time on the British mainland, the use of CS gas and 25 canisters were fired at the mob. Two people were seriously injured, substantiating allegations that they were fired directly into the crowd, against regulations. Brutal they may have been, but such tactics worked and the streets were cleared. Ian Craig recalled:

I was behind the police lines while Liverpool 8 was ablaze. The police were being beaten back. They had inadequate equipment, shields which melted as molotov cocktails burst all around, totally useless against such a savage assault. I thought the police were going to lose it. Suddenly a police van swerved to a halt and they began pulling out gas canisters. It was all over in what seemed like a matter of minutes, but it must have been longer. The rioters fell back, choking. The police were immediately back in control. The hail of stones and molotov cocktails stopped instantly.

The rest was mopping up and the riot officially ended at 7.00 a.m.[20]

The casualty units at the Royal Liverpool and Broadgreen hospitals were overflowing. The Toxteth community was in turmoil. Parents searched for children held in custody or being treated in hospitals. Black parents took to the streets to call for peace. Sir Trevor Jones, Leader of Liverpool City Council, called for the army to be put on standby. He said: 'It is a legitimate request. If the police cannot cope, as quite clearly they have not been able to, then the military should be available to protect the city centre.'[21] That night rioting flared yet again, but the police, smarting under the criticism, were better prepared.

A television shop in the Park Road area of Toxteth was set ablaze and gutted and several others were looted as several hundred young people rioted briefly. Police in riot gear drove them into the side streets. Police vans swept the streets, followed by foot policemen running at full pace. Reinforcements were swiftly moved in, beating their riot shields with truncheons. More charges were made as groups of youths gathered at street corners. A massive police presence swamped the Toxteth area.

On some estates anger was focused on 'police harassment and provocation'. The Liverpool 8 Defence Committee was formed by families of arrestees, but the general public was sickened by what they had seen on their TV screens. The police counted 355 colleagues injured, of whom 30 were hospitalised and one suffered a fractured skull, and 132 civilians or rioters were also injured. Of the 244 arrests over the four days, 222, or 91 per cent, were white. There were 172 convictions. The cost of the damage was estimated at just over £4.675 million.

In the Commons Home Secretary Willie Whitelaw defended the use of CS gas. He said that the Chief Constable was right to deploy it because of the 'new ferocity of the violence' seen at Toxteth. And he pledged that the police would be issued with better protective headgear and fire-resistant clothing.[22]

Merseyside Police, meantime, were still deeply shocked at their failure to control and subdue a disorganised and not-that-massive mob without using gas. They seethed at the injuries they had taken, at the inadequacies of their superior officers, and at the youths who continued to sneer at them in the streets. Three weeks later Toxteth erupted again, during 26–28 July, and the police took their revenge.

Boiling water and old TV sets were hurled at the police from the upper storeys of tower blocks, but on the ground the police adopted tactics used in Northern Ireland to disperse mobs. They called it 'positive policing'. It simply involved driving armoured Land-Rovers at high speed into the crowd. A PC said:

> When it happened again we were ready for them, at least more so. You have to make the first move, use your vehicles, drive the Land-Rover straight at the bastards. Then they scatter. You deal with the rest with your sticks. No problem. I don't give a f*** about the kids who got hurt. What were they doing on the streets in the first place in the middle of the night?[23]

A 23-year-old disabled man from Wavertree, David Moore, was killed by a police van on waste ground off Upper Parliament street on the night of the 28th. Later, at Mold crown court, two police officers were found not guilty of his unlawful killing on the direction of the judge. Mark Thomas, a young reporter on the *Liverpool Echo*, recalled:

> It was extraordinary and frightening. My journalistic experience up to then was knocking on people's doors. Suddenly I was a war correspondent ... petrol bombs flying through the air, lamp posts being pulled down, blazing cars aimed at police cordons, all set against a background of rumours that things were going to get much worse, that the rioters were arming themselves with guns. At one point there was a WHOOSH and something came low and fast down the road. We thought it was a missile or some kind but when it hit we realised it was a firework. In a funny way the early evening was more scary. I was in a taxi with a photographer when a kid in a balaclava – from his stature he can't have been more than 13 – came strolling towards us with a petrol bomb. We got out of there fast. Later that night it became more formalised, with rioters at one end of Upper Parliament Street and police lines at the other. After a while the police were clearly fed up with being targets. Police vehicles, personnel carriers and Land-Rovers with bull bars, were driven at speed across wasteland whenever groups of people formed. It was alarming and maybe excessive force but I would not condemn them. Tactics were being made up on the spot. They had seen their colleagues beaten, stoned and set on fire. It was a miracle that more people weren't killed or seriously injured.[24]

Early in the new wave of rioting a taxi-driver swerved to avoid a shower of missiles and petrol bombs aimed at police lines and hit a tree, suffering severe skull fractures. The Liverpool taxi union threatened to make Toxteth a no-go area for their members.

On the second night 400 police rushed again to Toxteth as black and white youths threw petrol bombs and other missiles in Upper Parliament Street. Once again several cars were overturned and set on fire. The worst trouble was centred on flats in St Nathaniel Street. A witness said: 'About a hundred police moved in. A television set was thrown from a balcony. It hit a policeman and he fell to the ground.'[25] Pots of boiling water were also poured on the heads of the police. Firemen tried to extinguish a blaze in a workman's hut, but they were driven back. Colleagues called to a fire in a basement were also stoned. Nineteen-year-old Paul Conroy suffered a broken back when he was pinned against a wall by a police Land-Rover. Witnesses claimed he was beaten about the head as he lay injured. As he recovered in hospital his mother said: 'It seems Paul had one drink too many and got caught up in the riots.'[26]

Lady Simey, chairman of Merseyside Police Committee, said that police handling of the riots was 'out of control'. She provoked fury when she added: 'I have been saying for years that conditions (in Toxteth) are not tolerable. I would regard people as apathetic if they didn't riot.'[27]

While the embers in burnt-out shops and homes still glowed, the city's religious leaders stood cassock to cassock. Anglican Bishop David Sheppard and Archbishop Derek Warlock agreed that their churches must take some responsibility for the 'nightmare'. Local author and playwright Alan Bleasdale said:

> The kids we watched on the television screens throwing petrol bombs and driving JCBs at the police, and destroying the very place they live, are defeated. There is nothing down for them. And they know it. They are redundant at 16.[28]

Other commentators were not so sure. On the last night of rioting 26 police officers were hurt badly enough to require hospital treatment. Twenty-one people, eleven of them black, appeared before magistrates facing charges which included throwing a petrol bomb at a police constable. *The Times* said:

> The violence appeared to have been premeditated and arose from a volatile mix of hooliganism, unemployment, frustration, alleged over-intensive

policing and the claim that black people had been provoked by the police. It was not a race riot in the context of Brixton or Southall, but was more the sudden fusing of elements common to black and white youths.[29]

Chief Constable Kenneth Oxford said: 'Race relations leaders tried to maintain some order but failed to quell the riot. The hooligans were hell-bent on attacking the police, who are so readily identified as symbols of law and order. Their fight was with us.' He later acknowledged that racial harassment had taken place in Toxteth and apologised to the black community. But he added: 'Parents have a responsibility to discipline and control the movement and behaviour of their children.'

*　*　*

Further 'copycat' riots broke out the day after David Moore's death marked an end to the Toxteth disorder. The Moss Side district of Manchester was shattered by a mob which attacked the police, smashed windows and looted shops. Hundreds of mainly black youths went on the rampage in Brixton, Southall, Reading, Hull and Preston. In each case a pattern was followed: youths challenged the police, and used the resulting uproar to cover looting in which some older people took part.

At Westminster Labour blamed the Government's hard-nosed economic policies and the resultant high unemployment, plus the failure of successive administrations to tackle the urban rot in which disorder festers. They made the obvious point that unemployment was highest amongst the ethnic 16–20-year-olds in deprived inner-city areas; in public perception at least, the typical rioter. Others blamed the breakdown in family discipline and parental control. Mrs Thatcher declared: 'A free society will survive only if we, its citizens, obey the law and teach our children to do so.' She resisted attempts by the far right to pin the blame exclusively on immigrants, and rejected the Monday Club's call for reparation of 50,000 immigrants each year. She said: 'British citizenship, once granted, cannot be taken away.' Instead she promised a review of public order legislation. Home Secretary Willie Whitelaw outlined plans to allow the courts to require parents to pay fines imposed on their children aged under 17. Some senior police officers accused the hard left, such as the Workers Revolutionary Party, of inciting attacks on the police. But behind the political posturing it was understood that in Brixton at least, the main cause was the two-way hostility between young blacks and the police.

That was the focus of much of the evidence given to the Scarman Inquiry. Ministers recognised that in advance of his report and repealed the 'sus' law, replacing it by the end of August with the Criminal Attempts Law which created an arrestable offence of trying to do that which, if successful, would constitute a crime. There was a consensus within the Cabinet that something must be done to alleviate the urban squalor in which the riots had been bred. A special task force under Environment Secretary Michael Heseltine was sent to Merseyside to investigate the causes of the trouble. Heseltine recommended substantial investment to develop run-down areas. The first evidence that he meant business was the establishment of a Garden Festival site along the river. Later in the year he won an extra £95 million in Treasury grants to the inner cities to improve the environment and create jobs in unemployment blackspots.[30]

Lord Scarman's report into Brixton found that, apart from one or two incidents, the police 'acted wisely, coolly and with commendable restraint in a testing, dangerous and alarming situation'. He added:

> It is a tribute to their restraint that no-one was killed in the suppression of the disorders. Broadly, the police strategy and tactics in handling the disorders are to be commended, not criticised. They stood between our society and a total collapse of law and order in an important part of the capital.[31]

But he was severely critical of Swamp 81, saying it was wrong-headed to saturate an area with officers to combat minor offences. He recommended a police recruitment drive amongst ethnic minorities, improved training, new bodies to oversee complaints against the police, and the sacking of officers found guilty of racially prejudiced conduct.[32]

And his overview of the reasons behind the disturbances made uneasy reading for Mrs Thatcher and her ministers. He said that while the position of ethnic minorities appeared to have improved, they suffered the sharpest deprivation common in all inner cities:

> Unemployment and poor housing bear on them very heavily; and the educational system has not adjusted itself satisfactorily to their needs. Their difficulties are intensified by the sense they have of a concealed discrimination against them, particularly in relation to job opportunities and housing ... The accumulation of these anxieties and frustrations encourages them to

protest on the streets and it is regrettably true that some are tempted by their deprivations into crime, particularly street crime. The recipe for a clash with the police is therefore ready-mixed; and it takes little, or nothing, to persuade them that the police, representing an establishment which they see as insensitive to their plight, are their enemies. None of these features can perhaps be usefully described as a *cause* of the disorders, either in Brixton or elsewhere. But taken together they provide a set of *conditions* which create a predisposition towards violent protest. Moreover, many of them [young blacks in Brixton] believe with justification that violence, though wrong, is a very effective means of protest; for by attracting the attention of the mass media of communication they get their message across to the people as a whole.[33]

* * *

As the 1980s progressed, unemployment breached 3 million, and the contrast between the affluent flaunting their wealth – the 'Loadsamoney' culture – and a growing underclass of the ill-educated and unruly poor fostered more rioting. Few urban areas were completely unscathed, and there was another outbreak in Toxteth in 1985 in which 300 black and white youths were arrested, but the worst were in London, the St Paul's area of Bristol, and Handsworth, Birmingham. As with previous outbursts in areas with a high immigrant population, heavy-handed policing or imagined slights could provoke a savage response.

In Handsworth on 10 September 1985 two traffic policemen attempted to arrest a black man on suspicion of car theft outside a notorious drug-dealing centre. The suspect was rescued by a crowd of black youths who assaulted the officers. Two youths were arrested, and the incident appeared to be over. But two hours later a fire broke out at a disused bingo hall nearby and a fire crew went to the scene. They were told by a group of black men that there would be trouble if they unreeled their hoses. They ignored the threats and were then attacked with stones and petrol bombs thrown from a crowd which swiftly swelled to an estimated 2,000. Police in riot gear drove the mob down an adjoining street and were showered with more petrol and broken paving slabs. Shops along the street, mainly owned by Asian families, were systematically looted and fired.[34] *The Times* reported:

> Some of the looters piled stolen goods onto vans and cars. Others used supermarket trolleys. Parked vehicles in side streets were overturned, petrol

tanks smashed, fuel lines cut and the pouring petrol set ablaze. The burning vehicles scattered at crazy angles across the streets were used as barricades against the police who tried to seal off the area.[35]

The orgy of looting and destruction spread and by midnight consumed much of the centre of Handsworth. The main targets appeared to be the police, firemen and Asian families. Two Asian brothers were beaten up by black youths and left to die in their own burning home. Police reinforcements arrived from across the Midlands. The tactics were becoming more familiar – seal off the riot zone, send in columns of riot police, split up the crowds and clear the streets. At least one senior police officer requested permission to use plastic bullets, but they were forbidden. Order was restored by daybreak, and the clear-up began. Once again millions of pounds worth of damage had been done, a community was even more deeply divided, and two men were dead.[36]

A subsequent report to the Home Office claimed that the riots were orchestrated by drug barons because the police had been too successful in curbing their activities. The West Midlands Chief Constable insisted that the main motivation had been hatred of the police and produced as evidence leaflets providing a step-by-step guide to the making of petrol bombs. That verdict was reinforced by local journalists who covered the riot throughout the night. Bill Jacobs, a young evening paper reporter, said:

> I shall never again walk down a street on the British mainland where both sides were ablaze. It was not a race riot – it was an anti-police riot. The mob was black and white, but predominantly West Indian youngsters. They did not like the fact that the police were interfering with the major local industry of drug dealing. Apart from the police the main targets were Asian shopkeepers but I also remember a West Indian greengrocer berating the rioters. He said he had built up his business over 20 years, only to see it destroyed by his own people. He shouted: 'Why are you doing this. You are not getting at the police or the Government, you are destroying where you live.'[37]

Labour frontbencher Roy Hattersley, MP for a nearby Birmingham seat, visited the scene and was told by community activists that the riot was a product of poverty and alienation. He replied: 'I represent Sparkbrook, one of the most deprived areas of the city with one of the largest ethnic populations, and they don't bloody riot.'

Later that month police and community leaders in Brixton heard rumours that shadowy figures from Handsworth were fomenting more unrest in Brixton. Whatever the truth of that, it took a police blunder to set Brixton aflame once again. Early on 28 September 1985, armed police raided a house in the area looking for someone they regarded as a dangerous, and black, criminal. During the raid a police officer accidentally shot the wanted man's mother, Cherry Groce, leaving her permanently paralysed. Horrified senior officers immediately issued a public apology and pledged a thorough investigation. Words were not enough. By the afternoon a crowd of around 1,500 black youths, many in masks and balaclava helmets, attacked Brixton police station with bricks and petrol bombs. The riot quickly spread and soon eclipsed that of four years earlier: Barricades of burning cars were set up; passing motorists were dragged out of their vehicles, beaten and robbed; homes and shops were broken into and looted. The theft and destruction was indiscriminate. Once again the fire brigade was prevented from putting out the fires which were ignited across the area.

Rioting continued all evening until a large force of police with riot shields and batons finally cleared the streets. A 29-year-old journalist died from a head wound. Ninety-three police officers were injured and the cost of the damage was estimated at over £2 million.

The following month the police suffered their first fatal casualty in the seemingly endless spiral of riots.

*   *   *

The Broadwater Farm estate was a relatively new, soulless, concrete development in London's Tottenham. The residents were 71 per cent of West Indian origin and their children nurtured a deep-seated hatred for the police. The Met, in turn, regarded it as a hot-bed of drug dealing and mugging, a lawless place which needed to be reclaimed. Throughout the summer there were clashes between youths and police every weekend. Attacks on pairs of police on foot patrol, and attacks on police cars, became more common and more violent. Young men in combat gear were seen congregating and but disappeared when challenged down the warren of walkways and alleys. A full petrol bomb was found hidden in a drain. Stockpiles of bottles were collected.

On Saturday 5 October 1985, the police arrested a man and went to conduct a routine search of his mother's home. Mrs Cynthia Jarrett suffered a fatal heart attack when she was knocked over during the police rush into her house. There were reports that she was too tightly restrained when she struggled, but a coroner's jury later recorded a verdict of accidental death. Overnight, however, the story spread that she had died through police brutality. The scene was set for further tragedy.

Early in the evening of the 6th an angry crowd of black youths marched out of the estate brandishing machetes, axes, iron bars, knives and hammers. They formed a barricade of blazing cars at four junctions 400 yards apart. They claimed as their own all the territory within. Shops, houses and cars were looted and fired. Passers-by were mugged. Police with riot shields were repulsed when they tried to knock down the barricades. They came under a barrage of missiles and petrol bombs, and some sniping from one or more firearms aimed from the tower block balconies. A new weapon of choice was plastic bags filled with petrol which exploded on impact. Police units were positioned in vulnerable places and could do little but hold the cordon. Every time they moved they were bombarded from the walkways above.[38]

A Met Superintendent said:

> I'm not given to fear, but I thought, 'We're going to lose this.' Bottles of flaming petrol were coming down, they were getting brazen and running up to the shields, and the blokes are standing there, not quite knowing what to do. We were being pushed back. For the first time in my life I'm frightened. Every entrance to the estate is barricades, with big fires. Just getting into the place is completely impossible.[39]

Two commanding officers were heard arguing furiously on police radio channels about whether to invade the estate. Up to 1,300 officers were available, but only a few hundred were actively deployed. The remainder sat in vans near the estate, listening to radio reports which became increasingly gruesome. The local District Support Unit, a riot-trained team which knew the complex geography of the estate, was sent home. Tactical police firearms units were sent to the scene with authorisation to fire plastic bullets. By the time they arrived, however, things had quietened somewhat and they were not fired, even though by then a policeman had lost his life.[40]

Two Asian shops on the outskirts of the riot zone were torched and the fire brigade feared that the fire would spread to neighbouring homes. Ten firemen with a handful of police officers courageously went forward to fight the fire. They were swiftly surrounded and attacked by a gang of heavily armed black youths and men. PC Keith Blakelock, a 40-year-old married man with three sons, fell in the mêlée and was cut off from his colleagues. They saw machetes rise above the heads of the crowd. Blakelock was hacked to death as he lay helpless on the ground. There was an attempt to sever his head, with the aim, a youth later confessed, of sticking it on a pole. When his colleagues recovered his body the handle of a bread knife was protruding from his neck. The pathologist's report referred to 40 cutting wounds on his head, back, arms and leg. One wound started at the edge of a lip and continued around the back of his neck. The Met superintendent recalled the scene when Blakelock was carried out:

> The firemen were trying to resuscitate him – he was covered in cuts, you couldn't see his face. They turn his head over and there's a knife in his throat. You know he's got to be dead. I can remember blokes from his unit – one bloke saw it and his legs went from under him, he flaked out. The word went round and about three or four blokes just physically went down in the road like that – just couldn't believe it was one of their own mates.[41]

As word of the murder spread, attacks on the police gradually diminished and by midnight the riot was virtually over. A total of 163 police officers were injured, seven by bullets or shotgun pellets, while 17 civilians and one fireman were also hurt. PC Blakelock was in the morgue. Two days later the leader of Haringey Borough Council, Bernie Grant, told a crowd outside Tottenham town hall: 'The police were to blame for what happened on Sunday night and what they got was a bloody good hiding.' His words, which were later to haunt him when he became MP for Tottenham, were greeted by cheers and fist-waving.[42]

Senior Met officers were severely criticised for their handling of the riot. The strongest criticisms came from their own men. An Inspector said:

> Broadwater Farm is a prime example of when no-one was willing to make a decision. They were being shot at. They almost certainly knew an officer had been killed, and they didn't have the bottle to give the order to use plastic bullets.[43]

An independent inquiry – boycotted by the police – found that the police had burst into Cynthia Jarrett's home without warning, using keys taken improperly from her son while he was being held for questioning. No disciplinary action was taken against any officer.

Three men, Winston Silcott, Engin Raghip and Mark Braithwaite, were sentenced to life imprisonment for the murder of Keith Blakelock. In November 1991 Silcott was cleared on appeal after tests showed the police may have fabricated evidence. He stayed in prison, however, for an earlier killing which he insisted was self-defence. Raghip and Braithwaite were freed on bail ahead of the formal quashing of their convictions. Three years later two senior officers were cleared of attempting to pervert the course of justice. And in October 1999 Silcott was awarded £50,000 damages by the Metropolitan Police as compensation for wrongful imprisonment. In October 2003, after serving 18 years, Silcott was released shortly after his eight-foot 'freedom beard' fell off under its own weight. He returned to the community to work with young people, vowing to clear his name and prove his innocence. He said: 'What happened to PC Blakelock was a horrific crime. Instead of solving it, they (the police) rushed it. They had to arrest someone. That someone was me.'[44] In August 2005, with police backing, he was working to keep local youths off the streets at night and in sports venues.

Fourteen witnesses to the killing of PC Blakelock gave statements to the police and a new investigation after Silcott's successful appeal identified a dozen members of the death mob. A dossier was sent to the Crown Prosecution Service. Their lawyers decided there was insufficient evidence to justify charges.

*   *   *

PC Blakelock's brutal murder caused much soul-searching amongst community leaders, while the police and politicians took stock of the chain of riots in areas of ethnic mix. The 1985 Police and Criminal Evidence Act restricted the circumstances in which people could be stopped. 'Community policing' became the new buzz-phrase. Racial discrimination within the police was made a disciplinary offence. At the same time police equipment was updated, riot tactics were reconsidered, and access to plastic bullets and other weaponry was improved. But the decade's rioting was not over.

On 11 September 1985 police moved in force into the St Paul's area of Bristol which, they believed, had become a centre for organised drug trafficking. As they began to make arrests, rioting began. Battles between truncheon-wielding police and hooded youths continued for several hours before order was restored.

The Metropolitan Police and other forces launched a drive to recruit more ethnic minorities. It met with limited success. Organised crime, often linked to the Jamaican Yardies, continued to thrive.

19
The Battle of Orgreave

'Sticks and bladders'

Margeret Thatcher's 1979 pledge to bring harmony became a joke, as we have seen, during the riot-torn 1980s. During the first half of that bloody decade she was also engaged in a battle of wits with her ideological opposite number, a man of equally blinkered vision who, like Thatcher in the other armed camp, was idolised by many of his troops. The outcome was a tragedy for the miners, the coal communities and the country.

* * *

Coal was the backbone of Great Britain. In 1913, after a century in which steam had created and sustained an industrial revolution, there were 3,000 working pits in Britain producing 300 million tonnes annually. Ten years later the industry employed 1,250,000 people. Few realised at the time that it was an all-time peak. The trade began to decline as cheaper overseas coal became available. In 1947 the 958 largest surviving pits were nationalised by Clement Attlee's post-war Labour government. By then output had dropped to 200 million tonnes and manpower was just over 700,000. During the 1950s and 1960s cheaper oil from the Middle East began to flood the market, British Rail switched its trains from steam to diesel, householders changed to oil-fired central heating, North Sea gas was tapped and nuclear power stations were built. In 1969 coal provided 50.4 per cent of the nation's energy needs, the last time it was in a slender majority.

The National Union of Mineworkers (NUM) was born in 1944, at the height of the war effort, and replaced the old, disunited confederation of county associations. Initially the union co-operated with the closure of older pits, provided replacement jobs were found elsewhere. Successive General Secretaries worked smoothly with the National Coal Board (NCB) to ease the period of transition. But the pace of closures accelerated and 264 were shut down between 1957 and 1963. The miners were still regarded as working-class royalty, paid relatively well for hard and dangerous work, but their place at the forefront of the trade union movement was threatened. And miners who had already moved two of three times to different pits began to dig their heels in when more closures were threatened.

That new militancy came to the fore in 1968 when Lawrence Daly, a former Scottish communist, beat the more pragmatic Lancastrian Joe Gormley in the ballot for General Secretary. Daly advocated industrial action to change overall fuel policy and small local groups sprang up across the coalfields to discuss how that could be achieved. One, the Barnsley Miners' Forum, was established by 29-year-old Arthur Scargill, a face worker at Wooley colliery.

The first industrial clashes came in 1969 when unofficial strikes erupted over delays in implementing long-promised pay scales for surface workers. For two weeks 130,000 miners in 140 pits stayed out in the union's first post-war taste of direct industrial action. And the mainly young miners involved learnt that the union's cumbersome disputes procedures could be bypassed. Over the next two years the new Conservative Government of Ted Heath was facing an avalanche of industrial unrest and the NUM was not about to be left out.

Heath was determined on imposing an 8 per cent incomes policy. The miners, embittered by more pit closures and the eroding of their pay differentials, were equally determined to bust it. A ballot of the membership gave the go-ahead for the first national coal strike since 1926 to start on 9 January 1972. It lasted seven weeks, ended in victory, and made Arthur Scargill a national figure.

Scargill was the only son of a hard-line Communist Party member. His activities in the NUM were often confrontational. During the strike he became a passionate advocate of the flying picket as part of a systematic plan to cut off Britain's power supplies. His organisation of the picketing of Saltley Gate, a huge West Midlands cokeworks, made him a hero to union rank and file. He marshalled 12,000 pickets – miners and other supporters – to halt all supplies going in and out, despite the efforts of 1,000 police. Scargill described the turning point when the pickets closed the gates and the police were forced by sheer numbers to stand aside:

> Absolute delirium on the part of the people who were there … Here was the living proof that the working class only had to flex its muscles and it could bring governments, employers, society to a total standstill. I know the fear of Birmingham on the part of the ruling class. The fear was that what happened in Birmingham could happen in every city in Britain.[1]

His dynamic presence on the picket line ensured that his face was broadcast into every home with a TV. In a later interview he described the picketing of Saltley as a military operation: 'I believe in a class war you have to fight with the tools at your disposal … We took the view that we were in a class war, not playing cricket on the village green like they did in 1926. We had to declare war on them … and you don't fight a class war with sticks and bladders.'

By mid February, 1.4 million workers were idle, electricity supplies were reduced to a trickle and twelve major generating stations were shut down. The NCB and the Government caved in. The scale of Heath's humiliation was recognised by one of his junior ministers, Margaret Thatcher.

Two years later the victory was dramatically underlined. An overtime ban to support a pay claim turned into another full-time strike just as the oil sheikhs started to push up prices. Heath put the nation on a three-day week, and called a general election on the question 'Who governs Britain?' The answer the electorate gave was 'Not him' and Labour were returned to office. Scargill believed that his own militancy, and that of the miners, had ousted a Tory Government once and could do so again.

When Mrs Thatcher took over the Tory leadership in 1975 she drew up a blueprint for taking on the miners or any other union prepared to 'hold the country to ransom'. The plan included building up maximum coal stocks, encouraging the recruitment on non-union drivers in haulage firms, cutting off the money supply to strikers and creating large, mobile police units to smash flying pickets. Almost her first decision after taking power in May 1979 was to appoint Willie Whitelaw, her Home Secretary, head of the Civil Contingencies Unit charged with preparing for industrial confrontation. The following year a new Employment Act stripped legal immunity from all pickets except those engaged at their own place of work, and social security rules were amended to strip most strikers of full entitlement to benefits. A revised Coal Industry Act laid down that the NCB must break even, without subsidy, within four years. That meant more pit closures. Scargill, by now leader of the Yorkshire miners, was given an 86 per cent ballot mandate to oppose the closure of any pit by industrial action.

The issue was overtaken in 1981, however, when NCB chairman Sir Derek Ezra signalled at a meeting with Joe Gormley, now President, that around 30 more pits and 30,000 jobs would have to go to meet cash limits on state spending. It later emerged that Ezra's figures were exaggerated, but a furious Gormley, backed for once by both moderates and militants, gave Thatcher an ultimatum: bail out the industry within seven days or face a solid, national strike. Many miners did not bother to wait, but walked out of pits in Yorkshire, Durham and South Wales. The transport workers, seamen, railwaymen and steelworkers pledged their support and another general strike seemed on the cards. Thatcher was not ready for such a trial of strength – coal stocks were not high enough, her civil contingency measures not yet in place. She caved in and all the threatened pits were reprieved.

Scargill was elected president of the NUM while the Thatcher Government stockpiled over 50 million tonnes of coal. In 1983, 70-year-old Ian MacGregor, a Scots-born naturalised American millionaire and an implacable enemy of trade unions, was appointed to run the NCB. He was one of Thatcher's favourite moguls and the NUM knew they had a fight on their hands. Before he began work Thatcher called the June 1983 general election and, largely due to victory in the Falklands War and a divided opposition, won a landslide majority of 144 seats. She was unassailable, and believed she now had the clearest mandate possible to neuter the unions and crush the militants. The glint in her eye was terrifying, her aims obvious. Her long-term agenda was to privatise all the nationalised giants, end union power and use the ever-growing dole queues as a way of keeping down wage demands and discouraging industrial action. She made the moderate Peter Walker Energy Secretary, telling the latter: 'Peter, we are going to have a miners' strike ...'

Scargill, who now had a left-wing majority on the union executive, claimed to have leaked documents showing that a NCB hit-list scheduled 75 more pits for the chop. The NCB admitted that the documents were genuine, but claimed they were no more than a 'working summary'. The annual NUM conference in Perth in July unanimously backed an emergency resolution empowering the executive to hold a ballot on strike action 'at a time deemed most appropriate'.

The NCB announced its last accounts before MacGregor officially took over – a loss of £111 million after receiving £374 million in Government grants and paying £366 million in interest charges. The NUM reluctantly agreed to the closure of two high-cost pits in Scotland and South Wales. MacGregor took control on 1 September and, during a whirlwind tour of the coalfields, told the miners at Bilston Glen: 'Perform, and you have a future; don't, and you have no future; it's as simple as that.' He left a pint of beer behind the bar for each of the pitmen he had addressed. At the end of September he made the NUM a 'first and final' offer of a 5.2 per cent pay rise, well below the 8 per cent already on the table for other public sector workers. He also warned that there could be no slowdown on pit closures, and added five more to the list.

Scargill did not immediately rise to the provocation. He offered to meet MacGregor and ministers for tripartite talks on the future of the industry. And a delegates' meeting in London on 21 October voted to call an overtime ban with effect from the beginning of November. It was rigidly enforced even though it meant lay-offs amongst winding engine operators.[2]

In the early months of 1984 local disputes flared up. The NCB announced that Polmaise colliery near Stirling, which had been mothballed for three years for a £15 million redevelopment, was to close permanently. Bullcliffe Wood near Barnsley was added to the NCB's 'death list' after a picket line dispute. At Manvers Main in South Yorkshire a row over meal times turned ugly. In February MacGregor was knocked to the ground, probably accidentally, during a visit to Ellington colliery in Northumberland. Furious miners protested at the closure of the Bates pit in the same area with the loss of 600 jobs. The overtime ban cut output by 6.5 million tonnes.

The final trigger took both sides by suprise. MacGregor had intended to force a confrontation at a 6 March meeting with all coal industry ministers when he would spell out his further plans for cutting losses. Six days before that a local NCB director jumped the gun and confirmed plans to close the Cortonwood pit in Wath-upon-Dearne, South Yorkshire, which employed 830 miners. Five hundred of them crammed into a small parish hall and vowed to fight the closure. They called on the rest of the Yorkshire miners to take action in support. The other local branches agreed to call a strike from last shift on 9 March 'to stop the action of the NCB to butcher our pits and jobs'.

Meanwhile, MacGregor put his latest plans on the table: to close 20 more mines with the loss of around 20,00 jobs and to reduce capacity by 4 million tonnes. Closures on a similar scale had taken place the previous year, sweetened by early retirement packages for the older pitmen. This time, however, Scargill and his negotiators refused to countenance any deal. By then the strike in South Yorkshire over Cortonwood was solid and fast spreading to other areas. But Nottingham NUM President Ray Chadburn warned that his 29,000 members would do nothing without a formal national strike ballot. Mick McGahey responded that he was not interested in constitutional niceties. 'Area by area will decide,' he said, 'and in my opinion it will have a domino effect.' On 8 March the NUM executive gave the regional strikes against closures its formal blessing.[3]

By the weekend 103,000 men were out, Leicester's 2,500 miners were against the strike, and 76,000 more union members were undecided. The refusal to hold a national ballot was devastating. It robbed the NUM leadership of legitimacy even amongst those who fully sympathised with strike action to save jobs. Labour leader Neil Kinnock later bitterly regretted his failure to pressurise the NUM into holding one. Even in those areas now on strike, there were bitter divisions. Scargill began organising flying pickets from South Yorkshire to harden resolve and cower potential scabs. Such tactics split the union from day one.

Scotland, Yorkshire and Kent areas were solid in support of the strike. Wales, the Midlands, Lancashire, Derbyshire and Cumbria were divided. Miners in Nottinghamshire voted four to one against. Nevertheless, by mid April only 43 out of the 174 pits were working. The dispatch of hundreds of flying pickets was co-ordinated by a national control centre in the London HQ of the National Union of Seamen, later shifted to Sheffield. Violent clashes became a daily occurrence.

In Nottingham the picketing was ferocious, as strikers from Yorkshire and South Wales tried to impose the strike on an area which was clearly against it. The first target, Harworth colliery, closed when 200 pickets turned up, outnumbering the twelve police on duty. The furious Harworth men vowed to go in the following day to defy the 'Yorkshire mob' but changed their minds when 450 pickets streamed down the motorway to their pit gates.

By 14 March six pits were out of action in Nottinghamshire, and North Derbyshire and the Yorkshire flying pickets were pouring into the working areas. The next focus was Ollerton and in the early hours 14 pickets got into the pit-head baths and outbuildings and were cleared out by the police. Bricks and bottles were thrown at the incoming night shift. Later that day 24-year-old David Gareth Jones, from Ackton Hall colliery near Pontefract, was among a contingent of Welsh miners who drove to Ollerton. It was his first time on a picket line. There was later some inconclusive evidence that Jones was crushed up against a car in the general pushing and shoving. He did not complain, however, and joined a major scuffle. Milk and beer bottles were among the missiles rained down on the Ollerton men as the police escorted them miners through the pickets. The word spread to the pickets that their own cars parked in the main Ollerton shopping area were being wrecked by local youths. Jones and others ran to chase them away and were met in turn by a shower of bricks and stones. At around 11.00 p.m. Jones was hit just below the throat by a half-brick. He collapsed unconscious on a grassy verge. An ambulance took him to Mansfield Hospital where he died less than two hours later.[4]

In the first week the picketing was having an impact. Of the 83 pits open at the beginning, only 29 were operating normally. Mrs Thatcher slammed 'fourth-rate' police chiefs who could not uphold the law. Home Secretary Leon Brittan told MPs:

> The legal position is clear. Any attempt to obstruct or intimidate those who wish to go to work is a breach of the criminal law. The mere presence of large numbers of pickets can be intimidating. The police have a duty to prevent obstruction and intimidation.

The National Reporting Centre (NRC) was activated under the command of David Hall, Chief Constable of Humberside. Its role, quite simply, was to mobilise the police. The NRC, which had been set up as a response to the police defeat at Saltley, asked each police force how many men could be spared and moved them around the country in response to flying pickets. Mrs Thatcher was briefed daily.

Thousands of officers were sent into the affected areas to contain the pickets. Three army camps in Nottinghamshire alone were commandeered to billet police reinforcements. In an example of state power never before seen in peacetime, police stopped and held buses, coaches and cars suspected of carrying pickets to distant pits. Even traffic heading through the Dartford Tunnel under the Thames was disrupted. Parts of Nottinghamshire became a virtual no-go zone as visitors were halted at police roadblocks and by spot traffic checks. Nottinghamshire Chief Constable Charles McLachlan reckoned that in the first 27 weeks of the strike, 164,508 'presumed pickets' were prevented from entering the county. The legality of such action was challenged, but upheld by the High Court. Main roads on the Yorkshire and Derbyshire borders were heavily patrolled by police cars and helicopters. Mrs Thatcher had given the police a blank cheque.

On 26 March would-be pickets retaliated by blocking the M1 to prevent supply lorries getting through. Eight police were injured and 21 miners arrested in clashes on the motorway verges and at a demonstration outside the NCB's regional HQ. Nationwide there were 200 arrests that day, as tempers flared. Magistrates gave standardised bail forms to all those arrested for picketing offences with conditions which amounted to virtual house arrest. MI5 mounted covert operations against NUM officials whom they suspected of having links with subversive organisations.

The resolve of the miners was stiffened by the sheer scale of the police operation. They saw it as an occupying army. Officers from across Britain were mobilised on a paramilitary scale with up to 4,000 men accommodated in local barracks. The strike gave them their first chance, outside Northern Ireland, to try out new public order tactics and the riot equipment issued after the Brixton riots. For two years most police forces had sent their men to army camps for drill and some officers admitted to the adrenalin buzz of being in a paramilitary unit with an almost free licence to impose their will on the 'enemy'. Although much of the picketing was peaceful, and friendly contacts – including football matches – were made with the police, when trouble flared up it could quickly get out of hand. Critics claimed that unnecessarily heavy policing increased the violence. The contingents of Metropolitan Police had a particularly unpleasant reputation for bullying and violence. Others from working-class homes had considerable sympathy for the miners and resented being called 'Maggie's boot boys'. But such fellow feelings quickly became stretched as abuse and missiles were heaped upon their heads.

Police overtime pay was excellent, however, while 'front line' conditions varied. Roger Graef wrote:

> For men up from the inner cities of Liverpool, Manchester and London, the strike was a moral no-man's land. It was a break from the pressures of urban policing. No-one knew them and they knew no-one. They had plenty of money, and time: they would finish duty at noon, sleep until six, then drink until the pubs and clubs finally closed. Officers frequently rolled up for duty at two or three a.m. much the worse for wear. The behaviour of some off-duty PCs in these 'foreign parts' was an echo of Vietnam.[5]

The young policemen caused further resentment when they went looking for local girls.

On 19 April another attempt to call a national strike ballot was sidestepped at a delegates' assembly in Sheffield Memorial Hall, which was itself picketed by 7,000 striking miners. Scargill declared:

> I am the custodian of the rule book, and I want to say to my colleagues in the union that there is one rule, above all the rules in the book, and that is that when workers are involved in action you do not cross picket lines in any circumstances.[6]

Lines of police drilled outside and another violent clash was inevitable. Dozens were injured as miners pelted police, cameramen and journalists with bricks, and Bill Stubbs, a Durham member of the national executive, had two ribs crushed in a police charge. At a bitter rally in Mansfield an ITN engineer trying to fix a transmission dish was knocked down and urinated on by a group of demonstrators. Tempers were fraying on all sides, and Scargill was planning to up the ante.

* * *

As the weeks dragged into months the intensity of the picketing – and the police response – increased. Efforts to blockade steel production, inextricably linked with coal, failed largely because other unions would not stomach an attack on a heavy industry fighting for its own life. Targets switched to plants supplying the power stations. Scargill was searching for another Saltley.

Orgreave cokeworks, which supplied the giant BSC steel plant at Scunthorpe, was an obvious choice, to Scargill at least. He saw its stacks pumping out dark smoke every time he drove off the motorway to Sheffield, and it seemed a constant reminder of his inability to bring energy supplies to a standstill. The plant was already a secondary target for Yorkshire pickets turned back from Nottinghamshire. Scargill decided it was to be the focus for mass picketing, a potent symbol of workers' power against that of the state. Other strike leaders were not so sure, seeing it as a diversion which would take valuable manpower away from the main task of picketing open pits and increasing pressure on the Nottingham miners. Their view was later endorsed by Ian MacGregor:

> Orgreave became a cause célèbre for Scargill, a fight he had to win. We were quite encouraged that he thought it so important and did everything we could to help him continue to think so, but in truth it hardly mattered a jot to us – beyond the fact that it kept him out of Nottingham.[7]

The first convoys arrived on 23 May and for three weeks there was mayhem. From the strikers' point of view the main problem was Orgreave's countryside location. Roads approached it from two directions and there were open spaces ideal for parking and assembling vehicles. The main approach was down a lane and over a narrow bridge which the police could easily seal. And the police were there in force. Scargill had made the most basic mistake of generalship. He picked the wrong ground to fight upon.

On 28 May 1,800 pickets confronted 1,500 police. It was a bloody shambles. The police used dogs and horses, baton charges and riot shields. The pickets used every type of missile and spread iron railings across the road to nobble the police horses. Thirty-five lorries arrived at the plant to load up. Pickets charged forward under a covering barrage of missiles and fire-crackers. The police counter-charged with long batons and shields. The convoy got through. When the lorries returned for a second load the police scattered pickets across surrounding fields. Sixty-four people were injured and 84 arrested. An enraged Arthur Scargill complained of 'scenes of unbelieveable brutality reminiscent

of a Latin American state'. The following day 3,000 pickets arrived.
A telegraph pole was used as a crude battering ram against the police.
Wires were stretched across the road to unhorse mounted police. A
portakabin was first used as a barricade, and then torched. Scargill, in
full view of the cameras, led a column of 50 miners towards the plant.
When he was stopped by the police he said: 'No way, no way.' He was
arrested for obstruction and led to a police van, shouting to reporters:
'1984 – Great Britain.'[8] Rotherham magistrates later released him on
unconditional bail. He denied that he had intended to get arrested as
a publicity stunt. His driver and bodyguard Jim Parker has a different
version: 'He was adamant he was going to get arrested to show the
lads he was suffering like them.'

Jack Taylor, President of the Yorkshire miners, described the constant
battles:

> People were saying 'Pickets three, police four.' It was becoming a bit like
> football results. But we were talking about lads in running pumps with no
> shirts on in many cases, and fighting for jobs. On the other side you were
> talking about men in uniforms and big boots, doing it for the money.[9]

Constant skirmishes in which a hut was set on fire, stones were
thrown at police and lorry drivers, a telegraph pole was rolled down
the hill towards police lines, and other tactics were employed to better
effect elsewhere, failed to prevent a single lorry going in or out of
Orgreave. Scargill planned the biggest mass picket of the dispute for
18 June. His entire reputation was staked on it.

The first trouble came at 3.00 a.m. when 50 pickets demolished
walls and threw the bricks into the plant. A scrapyard was ransacked
for materials to build barricades. Hundreds more left their buses in
Sheffield city centre and walked to Orgreave. By 9.00 a.m. there were
10,000 pickets facing 8,000 police officers, more men than belonged
to any mainland force outside London.

When the violence erupted Scargill was found sitting on the ground
by a burning barricade, with his head in his hands, clearly badly shaken.
He was taken from the scene by ambulance to Rotherham District
Hospital. He claimed he was hit by a riot shield, saying: 'All I know is
that these bastards rushed in and this guy hit me on the back of the head
with his shield and I was out.' The police claimed he had slipped and
fallen down a bank. Assistant Chief Constable Tony Clement of South

Yorkshire, in charge of police operations at Orgreave, told reporters: 'He was not near a riot shield. The officers with riot shields did not come within seven or eight yards of him.'[10] Whatever the truth, his injury inflamed feelings dangerously. Scrap cars, boulders and a heavy girder were used to construct a barricade to stop the lorries. Stan Orme, chairman of the Parliamentary Labour Party, said: 'It reminded me of Henry V with the armies ranged up on different sides of the hill.'

For hours the two sides stood their ground, hurling abuse and missiles. The foot police were in full riot gear but largely stationary, the pickets wore light clothing but were mobile. Lines of mounted police both bore and inflicted the brunt of the violence. Repeated mounted charges were met with bricks, bottles, paving stones, petrol bombs and sharpened posts. Clement said: 'It was a miracle no one was killed.' Later he admitted that he would not be 'the slightest troubled' if pickets were trampled by police horses.[11] They were.

A 32-year-old sergeant said:

> Before the horses went in at Orgreave it was bloody chaos. There were smoke bombs, all sorts of missiles. They were up in a field; blokes ripped up bloody palings and were waving them at us. We should have gone in, taken them out, but for some reason we just stood there watching them. We'd had so much bloody aggravation. Like the miners were getting away with murder.[12]

A constable recalled:

> It was late in the afternoon the horses went through. And when they came back we all applauded. I've never been in a situation like it. It was great to see them smashing into all them bastards who'd been giving us grief all day. It was the greatest thing I ever saw.[13]

The heaviest fighting was on the hill overlooking the plant, held by 2,000 striking miners and supporters. Reporter Craig Seton telephoned his copy that night:

> One police line was swamped as the demonstrators moved forward, and mounted police were used three times to drive them back ... Police led by helmeted officers equipped with riot shields began to push them back, and hand-to-hand fighting broke out on open ground. The mounted officers were sent in again, and as the demonstrators retreated to stand their ground by the railway bridge, a cascade of bricks, bottles, iron bars and jagged glass descended on the heads of the advancing policemen. Police stormed across the bridge under a deluge of stones as mounted officers and squads

of policemen with short shields advanced with truncheons drawn, and started making arrests. Police chased miners and demonstrators along the embankment on the far side of the bridge where a garage had been broken into and three vehicles taken and set on fire to form a barricade. The battle of the railway bridge went on for nearly two hours ...[14]

That night the public saw on the TV screens footage of the police charging, lashing out indiscriminately. An ITN crew recorded a policeman repeatedly beating a fallen miner with his truncheon. South Yorkshire Chief Constable Peter Wright, asked whether some officers had lost their tempers, replied: 'A man, whether he is a policeman or a miner, is responsible for his own actions, and no provocation can really justify unnecessary and abusive violence.'

By day's end there were 93 arrests. Seventy-two police officers were injured, but the police estimate of 51 injuries on the other side was a laughable understatement. Over three weeks, 32,500 pickets had gone to Orgreave. The plant had remained open, the coke had got through. For Scargill and his troops it was a painful defeat.

Kim Howells, who had organised 30 coach-loads of pickets from South Wales, said:

Orgreave was a turning point for the strike. It was proof of what we had already suspected, that the police were able to take on any number of pickets. The feeling after 18th June was horrible. We realised it was a disastrous policy. 1972 and Saltley was an age away. It was a government of a completely different order to Heath.[15]

*   *   *

The reaction to the Battle of Orgreave split along predictable lines. Mrs Thatcher declared that there would be no concessions to 'mob rule'. Neil Kinnock said: 'Nothing can excuse the conflict that takes place or the violence that takes place by anyone at any time, but we have a government that is prepared to preside over the causes of that conflict.'[16] Tony Benn, a former Energy Secretary, described the scenes at Orgreave as a pitched battle which smacked of 'civil war'. Ian MacGregor, in his memoirs, wrote: 'The battle proved that Scargill was not infallible. The Cecil B. De Mille treatment of these encounters was designed to show him as the ultimate revolutionary leader. Unfortunately it revealed him merely as a bit of a clown, if a dangerous one.'[17] Scargill said that

Orgreave showed that Britain was in the grip of a 'police state' and accused the police of 'blind hatred' towards the pickets.

After 18 June the weapon of mass pickets was rarely used and attempts to 'invade' Nottingham petered out. The NUM leader appealed to the transport unions to impose a total blockade of coke and coal supplies to the five integrated steel plants. He was whistling in the wind. Scargill switched tack to negotiations. Peace talks were wrecked, however, when the NCB rescinded the industry's NUM closed shop. Mrs Thatcher's presence was felt at the negotiating table: the Iron Lady wanted the miners crushed. Later she was to confirm her antagonism when she referred to 'the enemy within', a slur for which she would never be forgiven.

By August any hopes of a settlement had evaporated. The NCB stepped up efforts to encourage individuals or small groups of miners back to work. Such tactics resulted in more skirmishing and, finally, another outbreak of large-scale violence.

On 21 August a bus containing three working miners drove through a nominal picket at Markham Main colliery in South Yorkshire. A thousand pickets appeared at Silverwood building barracks and set vehicles on fire. Battles at nearby collieries raged throughout the morning. At Armthorpe, a village at the entrance to the main pit, a convoy of vehicles was stoned by 150 pickets and one driver was knocked unconscious. The convoy was halted by a metal workman's hut used as a barricade. Initially the police played a 'softly, softly' role, merely forming a cordon around the besieged convoy. Overnight, however, police reinforcements arrived to deal with sporadic attacks on the colliery by around 30 local youths. At 6.30 a.m. the pickets returned, smashed TV security monitors and commandeered a mobile crane to build a barricade. Two road vehicles were seized and the crane set on fire. Around 1,000 pickets now faced 400 Greater Manchester policemen who ran a gauntlet of stones, bottles and metal bars. The police debussed and charged into the crowd. The pickets broke and the police pursued them into a housing estate and the village centre. Local residents complained that the police rampaged through their homes. Margaret Paul received £105 compensation after the police ran through her house, smashing windows, in pursuit of pickets whom they beat to the ground in the back yard. Betty Tucker let in six pickets and locked the door, but police in riot gear battered their way in and dragged the men outside. Twenty-four arrests were made.

The events at Armthorpe set a pattern for the autumn and early winter. The NCB used every inducement to encourage strikebreaking, the pickets responded with violence which was met in kind by the police. At Cortonwood a local cricket club roller was launched down a hill at the police. Catapults fired ball-bearings. Near Silverwood a convoy of dog handlers was ambushed, two vans were overturned, and one policeman was knocked unconscious. His dog went beserk, attacking both pickets and police. The police began to beat their shields like a Zulu impi as they advanced up village streets. It was quickly banned by police chiefs, but left an enduring and bitter image.

Pickets and their families repeatedly complained of police provocation and the language used against their women. John Cummings, later an MP but then secretary of the local pit mechanics' branch, claimed that at Easington police swore at mothers taking their children to school, and baited pickets about what they could afford to buy their children for Christmas. He said: 'They would show £10 notes and talk about the bicycles they were going to give their children, and then roll ten pence pieces across the road to the pickets.'[18] Many miners' wives accompanied their husbands on marches and demonstrations, and suffered police batterings. Their rough treatment enraged their menfolk, but complaints went unheeded.

On 12 November nearly 2,000 miners returned to work following the NCB's offer of large Christmas payments. At pits across the country returning miners were met with an orgy of violence. Pickets entered colliery buildings, smashed up premises, spread oil on roads, felled trees and lamp-posts, pulled down power cables and torched vehicles. A police report said: 'The mass pickets are over and replaced by intense violence by smaller numbers of pickets and increasing instances of intimidation towards working miners.'[19]

Martin Adeney and John Lloyd wrote:

Travelling through the Yorkshire countryside in the early hours of the morning was an eerie experience. Roads deserted, then sudden convoys of police transit vans headed by motorcycle outriders, their warning lights needlessly flashing. Down pit lanes, more transits spaced at intervals, engines running to keep the men inside warm. A few yards away a picket hut of corrugated iron, its wood and canvas door closed to keep in the heat and fug from a breeze-block stove like some First World War dug-out.[20]

By the end of November, 8,460 arrests had been made, 7,100 people had been charged, and 2,740 had been convicted in the 3,483 cases that had been heard. Scargill was fined £250 plus £750 costs on two charges of obstructing the police. He refused to appeal, saying: 'I have no faith in getting a fair trial.'

Meanwhile, the families of striking miners were suffering the full weight of Mrs Thatcher's vindictiveness. Government adjudicators ruled that the NUM should be paying £15 a week strike pay – which it was not – and even in the most extreme cases hardship benefits were cut accordingly. Over £1 billion was held back in benefit to wives, dependents and children. The aim was clear: to starve them back.

Attacks on individual scabs became more vicious. Michael Fletcher, a working miner in Airedale, West Yorkshire, was chased into his own home by a masked gang and brutally beaten with baseball bats in his living room while his pregnant wife and two young children huddled upstairs listening to his screams. The worst charges, that of murder, were laid after the 30 November killing of David Wilkie, a minicab-driver taking a working miner to Merthyr Vale colliery near Aberfan. A concrete block dropped from a motorway bridge by two strikers smashed through his roof and windscreen. The culprits were convicted of murder and sentenced to 20 years. Scargill, who until then had refused to condemn picket line violence, dissociated the union from the events leading to the death and expressed his own 'deep shock'.[21] That shock was shared by all sides and police noted a 'sobering up' on both sides of the picket lines nationwide.

Wilkie's death also provoked a swing of opinion against the NUM amongst previously sympathetic unions. Engineers began to accept 'black' coal at power stations. By early January 500 lorry-loads a day were getting through and stockpiles topped 200,000 tonnes. Nuclear power workers also turned against the NUM, while the General and Municipal Workers, including many who had been at Saltley, were sickened by the ongoing violence. And the trickle of miners back to work was turning into a river, if not a flood.

MacGregor was playing a waiting game. Throughout the winter there were no coal shortages despite the strike and pickets, and there were no power cuts. In early January the highest demand for electricity ever recorded was met with no trouble. By February over half the 170,000 miners on NCB books had returned to work. On 3 March an NUM delegate conference narrowly agreed to a general return to work two days later without any agreement being reached with the NCB. The strike had lasted a few days short of a year.

*   *   *

By 6 March almost 95 per cent of miners were back at work. Scargill declared: 'We will continue to fight against pit closures and job losses.'[22] But his bravado could not disguise a resounding defeat. MacGregor warned that there would be no pay rises until the overtime ban was lifted. The closure programme would continue. There would be no amnesties for 700 miners dismissed during the strike following picketing offences. Mrs Thatcher rejoiced. 'There would have been neither freedom nor order in Britain if we had given in to violence', she said.

In economic terms the cost to the nation had been high. Chancellor Nigel Lawson revealed that the strike had increased public spending by £2.75 billion, added £1.85 billion to the losses of the NCB, worsened the balance of payments by £4 billion, and cut Britain's economic output by 1 per cent. The cost to other nationalised industries was also heavy: British Steel, £300 million; British Rail, £250 million, and the electricity supply industry, £2.2 billion. Fines and the costs of sequestration and receivership cost the NUM more than £1.4 million.

Policing the strike had cost almost £240 million. Forty million extra police hours had been worked by officers from 42 forces. The average deployment was 3,000 officers a day, rising to 8,000 a day at the height of the strike. Police injuries numbered 1,392, of which 10 per cent resulted in hospital treatment and 85 were classed as serious.

Costs to the NCB continued to pile up after the strike's end as some pits had been damaged by neglect and some would never reopen. MacGregor pressed on relentlessly with his policy of cutting manpower and concentrating on a dwindling number of profitable pits. By mid June 1985 the NCB announced 18,000 pending job losses over two years. When that was added to the 12,000 miners who left the industry during the strike, the total exceeded by 50 per cent the threatened job losses which had sparked the strike. The Board also announced the closure of Cortonwood, the trigger for the strike. There was no active protest.

Mrs Thatcher said during a visit to Singapore: 'Despite cruel intimidation, the working miners insisted on their right to continue to work, and they found they had an employer and a government ready to stand up for them. I hope and believe the lesson will not be lost on others.' She was actively encouraging miners in anti-strike areas to form a breakaway union, and she got it.

Supporters of a new union received a boost when the High Court in August turned down an NUM injunction against them. The leaders of the Nottinghamshire and South Derbyshire miners and the small Durham-based Colliery and Allied Trades' Association (CATA) balloted their members on the formation of a Union of Democratic Miners (UDM). Nottingham and CATA voted overwhelmingly for the new union, and South Derbyshire by a narrower margin. Within a month of its formation the UDM negotiated a fresh pay settlement with the NCB of a 6.9 per cent basic rise plus extra earnings based on productivity. The NUM got nothing.

The NUM received a better deal in the courts. Throughout the strike there were 8,810 arrests but only 4,318 convictions for offences ranging from murder to drunkenness. Of the charges initially laid, 4,107 were for breach of the peace, 1,682 were for obstruction, and 1,019 were for criminal damage. But the prosecution ran into intense problems convincing juries of unlawful behaviour. Thirteen miners charged with riot outside the Yorkshire HQ of the NUM in June 1984 were acquitted by a Sheffield jury. The Crown dropped its case against 14 Yorkshire miners charged with riot and unlawful assembly at Orgreave. The prosecution of a further 87 Yorkshire miners was later dropped. In Nottingham a jury acquitted eight men charged with riotous assembly and affray at Mansfield colliery, and the cases against 135 more were dropped after most agreed to be bound over for a year. It was small consolation.

The closures continued relentlessly. Twelve months after the strike, 70 out of 179 pits closed. The following year a further 50 were shut. But the NUM was a broken force. By 1993, after another wave of butchery under the Prime Minister, John Major, and his axeman Michael Heseltine, there were fewer than 30 left. In July 2002 the closures of the collieries at Clipstone in Nottinghamshire, the Prince of Wales in Yorkshire – the oldest working pit in Britain – and the Selby complex, also in Yorkshire, were announced. The shutdowns left Britain with only eleven deep mines, employing just 10,000 men. The NUM no longer had bargaining rights with the privatised coal owners, and could barely raise a whimper of protest. At the end of the same month Arthur Scargill officially retired as NUM President, although with a £12,000 annual consultancy. During his time in office the union's membership shrank from 260,000 to fewer than 8,000.

Both Scargill and Thatcher were to blame for the destruction of an industry which had once powered Britain and which had provided the working class with innumerable heroes. Both were following their own twisted ideologies with little thought for the human cost, the shattered communities. They created an industrial wasteland. For thousands of families a proud, dignified way of life was destroyed. Many families were torn apart, brother against brother, father against son, and the bitter legacy of those divisions will last for generations. Thatcher's career ultimately ended in tears, but Scargill's failure was the greatest. He began as a champion and ended up a wrecker because of simple, personal arrogance. He committed the aristocrats of the working class to a strike they could not win because he could not stomach being seen as anything other than a firebrand, a class warrior. He apparently did not see that a coal strike which began at the end of winter, with coal mountains already stockpiled, and with no ballot to ensure the unity of the membership, was doomed to failure. If he did, his betrayal was all the greater.

Scargill had already switched his attention to the formation of his own party, the Socialist Labour Party, known as 'Arthur's Barmy Army'. At the 2001 general election he challenged Labour's Peter Mandelson at Hartlepool and polled 2.4 per cent of the vote.

20
The Poll Tax Riot

'They seemed to be enjoying themselves'

Margaret Thatcher was returned to power for the third time on 11 June 1987 with a majority of 101. She appeared unbeatable. Almost exactly three years later she sobbed as she left Downing Street. Her departure was dramatic, and had many causes, but a major factor was her stubbornness in pushing through a hated alternative to local rates.

Her first pledge the morning after her last victory was to tackle the problems of the inner cities after a decade of violent turmoil. It was seen initially as an acknowledgement that her Government should do more to make inroads into traditional Labour heartlands. Instead it spawned the community charge – forever known as the poll tax – which was the centrepiece of the Queen's Speech setting out the legislative framework for that Parliament. Its advocates claimed it was a fairer way of collecting revenue for local services. They had little sense of history. Similar taxes had been tried and scrapped for centuries. At the heart of the problem was that it was based on the size of the household, rather than the property itself. Put at its simplest, the rich man in his castle would pay the same as the labourer in his hovel. Michael Heseltine, the flamboyant figure tipped as a future Leader, branded it a 'Tory tax'.[1] By the following April he was involved in a Tory revolt which saw the Government's majority slump to 25 over a rebel amendment to the Poll Tax Bill which attempted to link it to ability to pay.

The Iron Lady no longer looked bulletproof and her problems intensified. Dissatisfaction over her hard-line stance on Europe from those she dismissed as 'wets' was growing. And in November 1989 she faced a 'stalking horse' challenge to her leadership. The challenger, Sir Anthony Meyer, had no hope and she easily crushed him.[2] But some of those Conservatives who backed her muttered darkly that they would not do so again. Such political strife did not prevent her introducing the poll tax a year ahead of schedule in Scotland. In some parts of Glasgow non-payment rates were over 60 per cent. Prominent left-wingers spearheaded the 'Can't Pay, Won't Pay' campaign, and some were imprisoned in a blaze of publicity. The Anti-Poll Tax Federation was born to orchestrate similar waves of civil disobedience UK-wide. Senior Labour and trade union figures shunned it because of its advocacy of non-payment and, therefore, law-breaking. Leadership of the Federation therefore fell into the hands of the militant tendency, with whom the mainstream Labour Party had been at war for a decade. Labour leader Neil Kinnock disassociated himself from those who defied the law, branding them 'toytown revolutionaries', and the party's national executive withdrew their endorsement for three adopted candidates in upcoming Haringey council elections because of their support for non-setting of the poll tax. Similar action was taken against candidates in Liverpool and Swansea.[3]

At the end of February 1990 the 1922 Committee of backbench Tory MPs heard that the poll tax was a 'political cyanide pill' for the party. The following month there were violent town hall demonstrations, and Labour overturned a 14,000 Tory majority in Mid Staffordshire.[4] Many of Mrs Thatcher's natural supporters were in negative equity due to a slump in house prices. That, and a rise to 15.4 per cent in mortgage rates were factors, but the campaign against her revolved around the poll tax. Hatred of the community charge, it appeared, was not merely confined to inner city Labour strongholds. The Federation, building on their experience in opposing the tax in Scotland, offered advice and organisation to non-payers on, for example, how to avoid the seizure of property in lieu of payment. Both the Tory and Labour Leaderships, however, were slow to realise that demonstrations in such true-blue strongholds as Maidenhead showed that anti-poll tax campaigners came from across the political spectrum.[5]

Then on Saturday 31 March 1990 the heart of London was turned into a war zone.

Coaches poured into London from all parts of the country for what was billed as a peaceful demonstration against the hated tax. There was a carnival atmosphere as a crowd of over 145,000 assembled at Kennington Park. The police, forewarned about the intentions of some anarchist groups, donned riot gear out of sight. Any tension was caused more by confusion as ill-prepared stewards milled about awaiting instructions which, if they came at all, were contradictory. Federation organisers were anxious to avoid trouble – in one instance they suggested that the police cordon off Conservative Central Office – but they were incapable of handling such huge numbers. Requests for experienced stewards from the trade unions were turned down or ignored because of the Federation's policy of encouraging illegal non-payment. Some stewards were militant or Socialist Workers Party (SWP) activists who appeared more interested in selling copies of their party newspapers. The result was chaotic, but still good-natured. One senior steward told a later inquiry:

> The only problem we had at the start of the march was that stewards on coaches that missed the main dropping off point didn't get instructions or jackets, and so were hard to call on later when they were needed. Also, the paper jackets fell off very easily and almost immediately on entering a crowd.[6]

Shortly before 1.00 p.m. the march began heading for Trafalgar Square, a destination far too cramped for a crowd of such size. The Federations had requested permission to gather in the far larger Hyde Park, but that was turned down by the Department of the Environment on the grounds that the application did not meet the seven-day notification deadline. A woman protester from Stoke Newington, children in tow, said: 'We marched along as part of a very cheerful crowd. The police presence on the way was fairly relaxed.'[7]

The first arrest were made when police seized an anarchist flag and objects were thrown into the Palace Yard of the House of Commons. At 3.00 p.m. the head of the march reached Whitehall. By arrangement around 75 people sat down in front of Downing Street's wrought-iron gates in a peaceful if boisterous protest. Also by prior arrangement the police and stewards diverted the march around the sit-down and along the eastern side of Whitehall. There was much shouting and jeering, and some drink cans were hurled, but all sides agreed that at that point the majority of marchers were co-operative. Again as previously planned, police and stewards closed off Whitehall to divert the remaining body of the march via Bridge Street and the Embankment. Many demonstrators claimed, however, that the new police lines cut them off from the main body, while stewards later admitted that instructions to the crowd were unclear. There was an uneasy stand-off between marchers and the police lines. Two men who tried to break through were arrested by six officers. So too was a passing cyclist and there were reports of police punching bystanders.

Accounts differ as to what turned a large, but generally peaceful, demonstration into a riot. The police insisted they used only reasonable force and standard tactics of containment. Protesters point to the first mounted police charge against those marchers still inside the Whitehall cordon. They clattered from Richmond Terrace at 3.30 p.m. in a pincer movement aimed at a group of about 1,500 demonstrators. The aim was to sweep them from Whitehall and the green outside the Ministry of Defence and up towards Trafalgar Square, apparently unaware that the route was blocked by other police lines. Those on the green included a number of parents with children in pushchairs. A Coventry protester later gave evidence: 'Two women were in front of a row of mounted police, clutching each other and looking shocked and terrified.' A BBC employee wrote to his MP:

> Fifty men, myself included, sat down spontaneously in the road in front of the horses. The horses kept coming and we scattered. Up till that moment only one missile had been thrown, a small Lucozade bottle which sailed over my head and smashed harmlessly on the empty road just after the horses arrived.

Another steward recalled:

> The horses were brought in from below Downing Street and charged into the crowd. I asked the police why ... and was told to mind my own business. They indiscriminately waded into the crowd causing terror and striking people at will. This caused a huge crush against the barriers including people with pushchairs. Many rank and file police were obviously shocked at the tactics being used and, alongside the stewards, attempted to rescue the trapped people.[8]

As panic swept through the demonstration, the mounted police were followed by lines on foot in riot gear. They moved determinedly against a small group rallying around a black anarchist flag, and the Downing Street sit-down protesters. A demonstrator said:

The police tried to push us from both sides in Whitehall. People were in a panic. There were young children there, and old people, but the horses were stepping on anybody. Everyone was terrified. The police looked as though they were enjoying it. It's no suprise that some people started throwing bottles and cans.

There was general mayhem and reports of fights between official stewards and ultra-left demonstrators. There were also reports of police agent provocateurs. The senior steward recalled four days later:

Our stewards came under attack from groups within the demo. The most worrying report was that 10 or so men in plain clothes ran from the side of Whitehall that the police were in control of, crossed the barriers and had gone into the crowd, just prior to the disturbance, and left just before the riot police moved in. If these were indeed agent provocateurs, their job was made extremely easy by the antics of the SWP, the anarchists and other such groups who, despite the directions of the stewards, insisted on taunting the police. The most disgusting antics of these ultra-Lefts were the attacks on the stewards. There was kicking, spitting, punches and missiles thrown.[9]

Raoul de Vaux, a former policeman and landlord of the Red Lion pub across Whitehall from the Downing Street gates, had a grandstand view:

It really seemed to be a peaceful, family occasion until I saw some black flags go up and then all hell broke loose. There was definitely an element in the crowd who were only there for trouble, but the police tactics suprised me. There does appear to have been a breakdown in communications.[10]

WPC Fiona Roberts was hit by a missile during the storming of the Downing Street gates. She collapsed and suffered a temporary loss of sight in one eye. PC Robert Huntley was trapped with his sergeant in a police car. 'A piece of scaffolding came through the window and a no-entry sign was thrown at us', he said.[11]

Eventually the marchers trapped in Whitehall escaped down side streets and joined the main march on the Embankment. At the top of Northumberland Avenue there was a crush as police attempted to limit marchers entering the Square to three abreast, a tried and tested police tactic known as a 'throttle point'. The crush became dangerous as marchers behind were unaware of the bottleneck due to the lack of working loud-hailers by both stewards and the police. Some demonstrators cried out 'Hillsborough' to the police, a reference to the earlier football tragedy in which fans were crushed to death against barriers.[12]

Press photographers climbed up scaffolding at the corner of Northumberland Avenue to picture the scene, but were followed by demonstrators who began hurling missiles at the police blockade below. One onlooker said: 'They were punky youngsters who looked like kids clambering on a climbing frame.' The police lines opened and a van sped into the crowd, causing many to scatter. At around 4.30 p.m. the chief stewards decided to call off the rally and some demonstrators attempted to leave the Square but were told by police that Charing Cross Underground was closed and that all exits from the Square were blocked.

Tony Wilson, from Manchester, said:

> I was just standing next to the National Gallery when a brick hit me in the eye. I was thrown onto my back. I couldn't get up and a copper had to drag me to an ambulance. Once the trouble had started, I saw many people bashed over their head with truncheons and toppled backwards by police. They were lashing out at everybody, even women and children.[13]

Shortly afterwards three police personnel mini-vans drove at reasonable speed down the Strand towards the Square and stopped at its crowded entrance. They were surrounded by a smallish crowd who began throwing drink cartons and placard sticks. Stewards who tried to maintain calm were threatened by both sides. The vans reversed slowly back down the Strand and window protection shields were fitted and riot gear donned. They returned and, according to numerous witnesses, began to act as snatch squads, accelerating into the crowd. One man was caught up by a van and dragged 60 yards. The vans were surrounded and scaffold poles were thrust at the windows, but without serious injury. The hail of missiles became more intense, but most bounced off the heads of other demonstrators. A steward reported:

> A policeman, flatcapped, was kneeling over somebody lying injured on the ground, possibly hit by a van. A white youth, with a green jacket and dreadlocked hair, ran forward with a stick and hit the policeman. Within seconds riot police appeared ...[14]

One van was immobilised in the centre of the crowd and all the officers inside could do was lock the doors and await rescue. A scaffolding pole was thrust through a window like an outsized javelin, missing the radio operator and piercing the roof. PC David Nield said: 'We could not move. I was very scared.' Sergeant Paul Irvine said that the attackers were like 'baying hounds out for blood'. The van's driver managed to manoeuvre the vehicle out of a trap of mobile barriers. Such incidents appeared to enrage the police. Anna Goodhind, from Bath, said:

> Police were going mad. When they charged towards me everyone ran back. I was grabbed by one and thrown to the floor. I curled in a little ball but one hit me with a truncheon across the head and some kicked me.[15]

Another mounted charge was launched from the Strand, pushing people up against a solid wall of police shields at St Martin-in-the-Fields. The chief steward said: 'The police horses galloped through the crowd, followed by riot police, scattering women and children, picking on anyone they felt like.' Journalist Keith Pannell, who was standing outside the South African embassy, said: 'I fell over a barrier and as I was getting up I saw this policeman coming at me. I heard him say "You'll do" and then he hit me with his baton. I put my arm up and he hit my forearm, breaking it.' One witness said: 'I saw the horses charge up the Steps of St Martin, where young children had been taken supposedly out of harm's way. They had made no attempt to disperse the crowd peacefully. They just came charging in.' Another said: 'To charge on horseback into a dense crowd is not going to encourage it to be non-violent. Indeed it is difficult to see what they could have hoped to achieve by doing this, other than to cause mass panic.'[16]

Yet another witness claimed excessive police force:

> People were running up behind me out of the Square. I turned to see a police cavalry charge galloping uphill towards us. As the cavalry regrouped at the top of the road, people around me were livid. Some had families with them and had been trying to make their way out of the Square as the stewards had advised. Several times the police cavalry charged up and down the St Martin's Lane side. After the first charge they were followed by a squad of running riot police. The crowd shouted abuse at them because there had been no trouble near us and there was no justification for what the police were doing. Some of them taunted us by pulling faces and blowing mock kisses from behind their visors. They seemed to be enjoying themselves. I saw two of them veer towards the crowd. The first one truncheoned a young woman near me to the ground, the second one kicked her in the back as she lay there.[17]

The demonstration swiftly turned into a series of running battles across Trafalgar Square and its approaches. Police batoned demonstrators.

10   The Poll Tax Riot, London
empics

Police vehicles were attacked and a building site's portakabins in a south corner of the Square were set ablaze. The senior steward recalled:

> We decided at this stage to pull out the stewards as the situation was now completely beyond our control, and besides coming under attack from some angry youths, the stewards were also being attacked by the police. We watched helpless as the police ran amok, the thing exploded. Anything people could get their hands on was thrown at the police.

Police charged yet again on horseback at a group of about 150 on the forecourt of Charing Cross station. The people took cover on the station concourse, which was then sealed off. A Cambridge medical student recorded:

> The police used their shields to push and hit the people closest to them. It seemed they were taking out their anger against unruly elements on everyone. A couple were plainly enjoying it, laughing and pinpointing individuals.[18]

A witness reported one incident in Trafalgar Square:

> The line of mounted police started to advance at a walk towards seated demonstrators. I watched in horror as the one on our end steered his horse away from me, and walked his horse coldly and deliberately over the man

seated to my left. The man had one hoof on his right thigh and one on his left shoulder, reeling under the combined weight of policeman and horse, and screaming in agony, but the policeman continued to try to advance. It took a lot of angry people, tugging at the policeman, his baton holster, the saddle and the harness, to pull the horse away. They hung on to him, shouting 'Get the bastard', as others rushed in to help the crushed man. Eventually, with the help of other police, the culprit got away.[19]

A woman from Welwyn Garden City tried to leave the Square after receiving directions from 'ordinary' police officers. She wrote:

We walked away and hadn't got very far when suddenly the crowd were stampeding towards us from behind with riot and mounted police charging them. The riot police were hitting out indiscriminately with truncheons, and pushing those of us clinging to the railings into the path of the mounted police. When they tried pushing myself and one of my daughters into the path of the horses I must admit I became extremely angry, and protective of my daughter. As the riot policeman lifted his truncheon to us I kicked him in the goolies and he soon retreated.[20]

A passing motorist was dragged out of his Jaguar and beaten as the mob set his car alight. A barmaid who saw the incident said: 'There was a girl who appeared to be high on drugs shouting "Come on, come on."'[21]

The rioting spread outwards in the fashionable shopping areas of the West End, and turned into indiscriminate looting and vandalism. The windows of a car showroom were smashed and every new vehicle inside was damaged. About 60 tourists took refuge in a tailor's next door while the owner's car burned outside. Some of the most exclusive shops in London were targeted – Burberry's, Mappin and Webb and the Scotch House – but Garrads, the royal jewellers, escaped. There were surreal moments amid the carnage. A coach of French tourists stopped to take photographs of the rioting outside a Renault showroom. An American tourist, Louis Zeiman of Phoenix, Arizona, pointed his camera at a wrecked tie shop and told a reporter: 'Gee, this is great. I can tell the folks back home that I came to Britain and saw a riot. We thought you simply didn't do that sort of thing.'

Demonstrators were pursued by police to Piccadilly. One person leapt across the roofs of buses caught in a traffic jam to escape them. Riot police formed a wedge, pushing pedestrians towards other police lines. Sporadic fighting, arrests, criminal damage and looting continued for several hours across the West End. In Oxford Street armoured police vans cruised behind knots of marchers, snatching some and dragging them into their vehicles. Over 400 protesters and bystanders were left injured. The police claimed 374 casualties.[22]

*   *   *

The relatively small number of anarchists and trouble-makers on the march were demonised in Parliament and the press. Left-wing MPs and union leaders joined Tory ministers in blaming 'hooligans' for the violence. Mrs Thatcher voiced her 'absolute horror' at the violence. She added: 'People have a right to demonstrate peacefully. This was taken over by some extreme groups who used violence with no consideration for others or their property.'[23]

Many demonstrators gave evidence that the police were provoked not by members of organised parties, such as militants or the SWP, but by 'apolitical disaffected anarchists or the avowedly violent Class War supporters'. Indeed, a Class War spokesman said that their aim was to give the police a 'well-deserved beating'. But the police tactics also came under scrutiny.

One demonstrator, Clare Prout, told Channel Four:

> There may well have been troublemakers there, people who were waiting for some incident they could turn into a riot. But there was no incident until that first police charge, when panic, and finally anger at the unnecessary show of force incited everyone, not just Militant idiots, to show their strength of feeling.[24]

But Superintendent Malcolm Eidmans, who was involved in the subsequent police inquiry, saw it very differently:

> I was lucky in that none of my men were seriously injured, but a lot were very badly shaken by the sheer level of the violence they experienced. Some had to retreat, to hide, take cover, which is something they never experienced before in the job. A lot openly admitted that they were frightened for their own safety. We knew beforehand that there would be a group within the march who would attempt to disrupt it. Trouble-makers were identified and cordoned off, but no-one expected that level of violence, especially with so many families and children and, shall we say, respectable people on the march.[25]

Home Secretary David Waddington rejected demands for a public inquiry into the serious disorder and police tactics. The Poll Tax Bill became law the day after the riot. Heseltine, still sniping from the wilderness, swiftly unveiled a plan to reform it, while Environment Secretary Chris Patten secured an extra £2.5 million from the Treasury to keep bills down.[26] But for Margaret Thatcher, the nightmare was not over.

While Saddam Hussein was invading Kuwait and the West began marshalling their military forces against him, the Conservative Party was again engulfed by internal warfare. An EC summit in Rome set a 1994 deadline for the second stage of monetary union and Mrs Thatcher went ballistic. It was all too much for Sir Geoffrey Howe, her Foreign Secretary, who quit and then delivered an extraordinary resignation speech, saying: 'The time has come for others to consider their response to the tragic conflict of loyalties with which I have myself wrestled for so long.' It was the firing pistol for another leadership challenge.

Heseltine, after some dithering, joined Howe in the contest. Mrs Thatcher won the first round, but by an insufficient margin under party rules. Speaking from a Paris summit, she declared: 'I fight on, I fight to win.' But on her return a succession of Cabinet ministers trooped in to tell her it was all over. On 22 November the Prime Minister, sniffling through tears and a head cold, left Number 10. The subsequent contest, dominated by a 'Stop Heseltine' campaign, saw John Major replace her.[27]

It remains difficult to judge how much the poll tax fiasco and the violence it sparked was to blame for her downfall. The Tory civil war over Europe, monetary union and the economy were certainly the biggest factors, along with the personality clashes which, ultimately, left her isolated. But, equally certainly, her bull-headedness over the poll tax, her refusal to face up to its unpopularity in the country, convinced many previous loyalists on the Conservative benches that she had lost her magic touch. A decade of mass unemployment and civil unrest was not seen as a price worth paying for her failed experiment in monetarism.

The day after his victory, Major brought Heseltine back as Environment Secretary. His first task was to scrap the poll tax.

21
The Return of Race Riots

'Ferocity and sheer carnage'

Rioting did not end with the downfall of Margaret Thatcher or the return of a Labour Government in 1997, but it was mainly confined to low-level disorder, drug turf wars and drunken battles after last orders. There were large attempts to 'Seize the City' by anarchists operating under the Class War banner, and anti-capitalist demonstrations generally contained by the police. The petrol bomb and police cavalry charges were widely seen as a spectacle of the past. But the ongoing influx of asylum-seekers from Kosovo, Eastern Europe, Iraq, Afghanistan and elsewhere, however, exposed the fragile nature of that relative peace. In summer 2001 the ugly face of race riots returned to Britain's northern towns and cities.

On 5 May 2001, 16 people were arrested when the National Front defied a Home Office ban on political marches after a build-up of racial tensions in the Glodwick area of Oldham, Greater Manchester, which has a large Asian population. Earlier in the year a 15-year-old Asian boy was charged with a racially motivated assault on a white pensioner and war veteran. The NF spent several weeks leafleting the area and holding meetings in pubs ahead of forthcoming local elections. Individual Asians and their shop premises were attacked. In the early evening of Saturday 25 May four people were arrested after an attack by white youths on houses belonging to Asian immigrants. A brick was thrown through a window into the flat of a pregnant Asian woman, and a mother with four children, including a six-month-old baby, was racially abused as she fled home. Soon afterwards a gang of around 100 young Asian men attacked the Live and Let Live public house following a fight between an Asian and a white teenager. Landlord Paul Barrow said: 'The first of them got through the door and attacked the customers with whatever they could get their hands on, bottles, stools and glasses.' He and 40 customers were trapped in his living quarters overnight. For seven hours up to 500 Asian youths battled with white youths and police in riot gear. Part of the crowd returned to the Live and Let Live and threw petrol bombs at the windows, and torched parked cars. Four shots were fired and a handgun, later found to be blank-firing, was later recovered. Officers carrying full-length shields fought back, charged the crowd and plucked individual missile-throwers from the mob. Chief Superintendent Eric Hewitt said that he was shocked by the 'ferocity and sheer carnage' of the rioting.[1]

A dozen white men and youths rushed to the area in three taxis and emerged with sticks. More Asian women were threatened, bricks thrown through windows, cars vandalised. An Asian shopkeeper fled through his back door as his front windows were smashed. A man was attacked with an iron bar, while another was chased by a white gang as he tried to get his daughter to safety.

The following sporadic fighting escalated as more than 100 riot police struggled to keep control. A gang fire-bombed the offices of the *Oldham Evening Chronicle*, but did little damage. A barricade of furniture and tyres was set alight in Ward Street. Riot police in body armour and long shields sealed off the main road approaches as a police helicopter circled overhead, illuminating the mob with its powerful spotlight. Another public house, The Jolly Carter, was bombarded with bricks by a crowd of 40. Two hundred Asian youths milled around Hardy Street and were dispersed by police. So too were 30 white men who walked from pub to pub chanting racist slogans and songs.[2] Fifteen police officers suffered minor injuries and 17 people were arrested for public order offences. Twelve whites, including a 17-year-old girl, were later jailed for nine months each after Judge Jonathan Geake told them that they provided the spark which ignited the long night of rioting. He added: 'It was hardly suprising that Asian males resolved to defend their area and hardly suprising it resulted in a major public disorder.' The court gallery was packed with British National Party (BNP) members who shouted abuse.

Ashid Ali, leader of the Bangladesh Youth Association, also insisted that the young Asians were provoked by racist incomers, and had not intended to attack the police. He added: 'It's very difficult to control a crowd when there's so much anger and distress.' He added:

> Right-wing extremists and members of the National Front have been trying to stir trouble every Saturday for five weeks, and for the main part the police response was adequate. But when a gang of white people came into Asian areas and began assaulting people and smashing up homes and businesses, the Asian youths felt they had to protect their community. We had tried to avoid trouble but when it came to our doorsteps people defended themselves and the police were extremely heavy-handed.[3]

A few days later the arrest of a young Asian in Leeds sparked similar mayhem. The rumour swept through the mixed-race Harehills area that the teenager had been kicked and sprayed in the face with CS gas by the police. Officers were drawn into the area by a bogus report of a fire-bomb incident. They were attacked by several hundred Asian youths throwing bricks, bottles and wooden crates. Two police officers and two journalists were slightly injured in the apparent ambush.[4] Casualties in Oldham and Leeds were relatively light, but the scenes of rioting shocked politicians, community leaders and the police. They feared another spiral of racial violence. Their fears quickly came true.

At the 7 June general election the BNP won 16.4 per cent of the vote in Oldham and 11.2 per cent in the Lancashire town of Burnley. The latter has pockets of intense poverty and townspeople were divided by claims that immigrant families were given priority on the council housing ladder. On Saturday 23 June several seemingly unrelated incidents in different parts of the town resulted in widespread rioting over two nights.

An Asian family complained about an all-night party in a semi-derelict house next door in Daneshouse, one of the most deprived wards in England. A van arrived which Asian residents claimed had been used by the BNP during the election campaign. Asian youths began to arrive and a running fight broke out, leaving a trail of damage from the house to the nearby Duke of York pub, an alleged meeting place for white racists. The pub was fire-bombed while the police were kept at a distance by a crowd of 200–300. Meanwhile, a white crowd was seen marching on the predominantly-Asian Stoneyholme estate. And in another part of the town a white gang wielding hammers attacked an Asian taxi driver, breaking his cheekbone. Asian community leaders claimed that the police were slow to respond to the incident, so others took action instead. For several hours there was the increasingly familiar scene of riot police struggling to win control. Another pub, the Baltic, was also attacked by Asian youths, cars were torched, a sex shop was gutted and an Asian newsagents shop in a white neighbourhood was set on fire. Seven people were arrested and a police officer injured.[5]

West Yorkshire Police were the next to be faced with mass disorder. This was to be the worst yet, with 326 officers injured out of 1,000 deployed. On Friday 4 July BNP leader Nick Griffin addressed a small band of supporters in Bradford, scene of earlier, small-scale racial clashes. The following day a planned march by the National Front was banned, but 20 supporters and several hundred counter-demonstrators of the Anti-Nazi League turned up anyway. A tense crowd built up in Centenary Square as police in riot gear began to arrive. Five NF supporters were turned away at the railway station, but trouble was inevitable. It erupted when a group of white men came out of a city-centre pub and began shouting racial insults. A crowd of mainly Asian youths charged up Westgate and began brawling with the taunters. The police made the decision to push the youths away from the centre into the Manningham area, home to many of the area's 55,000-strong population with Pakistani roots. Here the police lines were overwhelmed by bricks and fire-bombs. Burning barricades were set up in Whiteabbey Road. Two white men were stabbed, not fatally. Mounted police were brought in, and a police helicopter clattered overhead.[6]

For several hours Asian and white gangs battled each other and the police. As the main bodies were broken up, the riot turned into sporadic fights and indiscriminate arson and looting. Five pubs and two clubs were torched, as were numerous cars and two garage showrooms. Shops, including a DIY store and a delicatessen, were looted. An attack was launched on Lawcroft House police station and a number of parked police vehicles were damaged. Of the police injuries, two-thirds resulted from assaults and the rest were caused by falls, strained backs and exhaustion.

As the embers smouldered on the Monday morning, Tony Blair's official spokesman said that the disturbances were simply 'thuggery' and that violent protesters had ended up 'destroying their own community'.[7] But the Anti-Fascist Action Group accused politicians of inflaming tensions by concentrating on immigration and asylum-seekers. A spokesman said:

Home Secretary David Blunkett and his colleagues have been posturing over their tough stance on immigration, fuelling the far-Right and further alienating minority communities across the country. Terms like 'bogus asylum seekers' have a very real impact on the ground.[8]

Older Asian community leaders were shocked by the behaviour of younger Asians. But Martin Wainwright of the *Guardian* said: 'Second- and third-generation Asians are not prepared to take what the previous generation took.' But a long-standing white Oldham resident said that youngsters of all ethnic backgrounds had to learn to share their town:

There's white people round here as well as Asian people and we've got to live together. We're the same blood. Their fathers fought in the war just the same as everybody else. We've got to make a community. We've got to have peace.[9]

Over six weeks rioting in northern areas had cost many millions, led to a total of 150 arrests, and left a simmering legacy of increased racial strife. During the inevitable post mortems on the violence, extremist outsiders were blamed, alongside youthful hooliganism. But there were deeper reasons. Most of the riot areas were in towns which built their industrial base on textiles and where ethnic minorities arrived as semi-skilled immigrant labour for an industry which has since collapsed. Immigrant ghettoes, which began out of a natural need for self-protection and mutual support, swelled and took over deprived areas abandoned by the more prosperous whites. The result was immigrant communities which lived together, worked together, went to school together, worshipped together, played together and wed each other with little or no contact with the wider community. Integration never happened, and the result was mutual suspicion and hostility.

That was graphically highlighted the following December in a report compiled by a Home Office inquiry team under Nottingham chief executive Ted Cantle, Chairman of the Community Cohesion review team. Its executive summary concluded:

Whilst the physical segregation of housing estates and inner cities comes as no suprise, the team was particularly struck by the depth of polarisation in our towns and cities. The physical segregation is compounded by so many other aspects of our daily lives: separate education, community and voluntary bodies, employment, places of worship, language and social and cultural networks. It means that communities operate on a series of parallel lives. They do not seem to touch at any point, let alone overlap and promote any meaningful interchange.

A Muslim with a Pakistani family background told the inquiry: 'When I leave this meeting with you, I will not see another white face until I come back here next week.' A white resident said: 'I have never known anybody on my estate who does not come from around here.'

The report concluded: 'Little wonder that the ignorance about each other's communities can grow into fear, especially when extremist groups are determined to undermine community harmony.'[10]

The review made 67 recommendations covering such areas as housing, education, leisure facilities and regeneration cash. Controversially, it criticised the Government's policy of encouraging single-faith schools, saying they deepened social divisions, and demanded an 'open and honest debate' about multiculturalism in Britain. And it suggested that immigrants could take an oath of allegiance setting out a 'clear primary loyalty to this nation'. An independent review into the Oldham riots led by senior civil servant David Ritchie blamed years of 'deep-rooted' segregation, although another by the Burnley Task Force found that disturbances in their town were due to a war between Asian and white drug gangs. Yet another report by Home Office minister John Denham found that trouble occurred in areas which had experienced months of racial attacks and infiltration by far-right groups.[11]

In November 2002 the Audit Commission blamed management weaknesses within Oldham council for failing to promote race relations. Council leader Richard Knowles responded:

> There is a need for greater emphasis on community cohesion ... However, the fundamental changes required take time. It is impossible to reverse a legacy of social and economic problems going back 25 years, particularly against the backdrop of the civil disturbances.[12]

Criminologist Colin Webster was among several academics who traced other influences, including a determination amongst young Asians to copy the motivations of white gangs to reclaim 'their' streets and protect their own turf. During the 1970s and 1980s, the Asian Youth Movement, which grew in such places as Bradford and Southall, forged alliances with mainly white anti-fascist groups to keep out the far right. But many such veterans moved on and the generation left behind were second and third generation British Muslims whose

Pakistani and Bangladeshi parents were hit by the collapse of the UK textile industries in the late 1980s. They attended the worst schools, lived in unemployed households and competed with whites for scarce jobs and housing, an ages-old recipe for racial tension.

Dr Webster wrote:

> As racist violence, abuse and low-level harassment dramatically increased, Asian young people retaliated. Unlike in the 1970s, a pattern was formed whereby territory was defended or extended using ad hoc, loosely organised self-defence groups that reacted to racist events and threats as they occurred. ... Throughout the 1990s this increased confidence and solidarity on the street involved retaliation against known violent white racists, and some who were not. The disorders constitute a search for respect and recognition from real and perceived adversaries, whether white young people or the police. In poor areas respect is won through the ability to stand your ground and fight. Ironically, some young Asians have adopted and adapted a white working class street culture of violence and retaliation, and turned it around to defend themselves. Evidence from both Bradford and Oldham suggests that residential and social segregation is increasing, through whites leaving areas and schools perceived as Asian. This 'colour coding' of areas becomes reinforced as Asians and whites defend 'their' territories.

And increasingly the battles are between Asians and Afro-Caribbean blacks. On 22 October 2005 rumours that a 14-year-old black girl had been gang-raped by Asians resulted in 100 hooded youths attacking motorists with baseball bats.[13] One man was stabbed to death and a policeman was shot in the leg by a ball-bearing gun. Asians and blacks fought each other and once again riot police were called to the Lozells area of Birmingham, close to the scene of the 1985 Handsworth riot. The rape rumours were spread by a local pirate radio station amid warnings of an impending 'race war'. Blacks claimed that Asian shopkeepers were not treating them with sufficient 'respect', although there were also claims that tensions were due to Asian shops selling African foods and beauty products, hitting the trade of black businesses.[14]

The increased alienation of Asian youth also, it is now clear, made them easy prey for Islamic fundamentalist clerics who preached hatred of Britain. A minority became recruits for the suicide bombing campaign which further polarised Britain's ethnic communities and allowed the Blair administration to introduce draconian legislation to curb freedoms of speech, travel and faith. The profile of the suicide bomber as Asian or black, young and defiant, saw the return of 'sus' police practices on station concourses. Given the severity of the threat, few mainstream politicians objected. But disquiet grew over the summer and autumn of 2005 over attempts to outlaw the 'glorification' of Islamic terrorism – a potential legal minefield – and the extension of police powers to detain terrorist suspects for up to 90 days without charge. The latter culminated in Tony Blair's first Commons defeat, with left and right joining to ditch the measure. Despite that setback, the power of the state is growing again, and few can realistically expect peaceful times ahead.

In October–November 2005, anxious eyes were cast across the Channel as French towns, suburbs and cities erupted in an orgy of violence after two youths were electrocuted while fleeing the police. The riots, which started with the torching of 19 cars in a Paris suburb, spread from Lille to Nice and from Bordeaux to Strasbourg. Night after night for almost three weeks cars and buses were targeted with fire-bombs; police with rocks, petrol-bombs and shotguns. A 61-year-old man died after being beaten while trying to extinguish a fire outside his home. Over 2,000 vehicles were destroyed as the French government struggled to regain control. Although poor whites were clearly involved, the explosion of rage was classified as a national race rising. France has 7 million immigrants in a population of just under 60 million, and the great majority are Muslims from Algeria and elsewhere in North Africa. The question was whether the conditions were ripe for similar eruptions to be repeated in Britain. Despite initial panicky reports, there was no evidence of any connection to Islamic fundamentalism; rather the ongoing legacy of the brutal colonialism of Algeria and France's bloody pull-out. The French *maghrebins* – many the sons and grandsons of Arabs who had fought for France – were motivated by decades of post-colonial racism, contempt and marginalisation. France has also never encouraged multiculturalism and always insisted on total assimilation. The result was a generation without hope whose only expression was to be found in torching their own meagre possessions and those of their equally poor and isolated neighbours.

The lesson for Britain is to remain on a multicultural path, however difficult that might appear to readers of the *Daily Mail* and despite the well-intentioned recommendations of the Cantle Report.

22
G8 and Stop the War

'Smash kapital'

The growth of the Web, first harnessed by rave party organisers and anarchists, encouraged a new form of international protest under the loose and ill-defined banner of anti-globalisation. For the first time mass demonstrations were both organised undercover and fully co-ordinated with fellow-thinkers across the world. London's financial district was an obvious target in June 1999 for a 'carnival against capitalism'. More than 4,000 people headed into the City in a demonstration timed to coincide with a G8 summit in Cologne and to protest over the debt burden imposed by the richest nations on the poorest. Among them were 300 banner-waving cyclists who rode slowly to disrupt traffic.

The peaceful, if noisy, gathering turned violent when a small group of anarchists smashed windows in the Liffe Building, part of the Stock Exchange. A small number broke into the premises, but a safety shield prevented them reaching the trading floor. Outside stones and bottles were thrown and four police officers injured. At least 42 demonstrators were hurt, including one woman hospitalised with concussion and a broken leg after she was hit by a police van. Sixteen people were arrested for offences including criminal damage and assault.[1] Home Secretary Jack Straw condemned 'the deplorable outbreak of public disorder and violence'.[2] But a blueprint of sorts had been drawn for future protests. UK anti-capitalists, or at least those who could afford it, became globetrotters.

In December 1999, 100,000, including many Britons, marched on the World Trade Organization's (WTOs) ministerial summit in Seattle. For three days activists battled with riot police as WTO delegates

failed to reach an agreement on international trade agreements. A
state of civil emergency was declared, a curfew was imposed for two
nights, and plastic bullets, water cannon, tear-gas and pepper-spray was
used against the crowds. Over 500 people were arrested and damage
and business losses were estimated at £13 million. The BBC World
Service reported:

> Most demonstrations were peaceful, but there was a hardcore of anarchists
> seeking confrontation with the police. The authorities dealt severely even with
> peaceful protesters who interfered with the running of the conference.[3]

It became a familiar pattern of reportage, as charges of intimidation
were levelled at both sides.

In April 2000, around 10,000 protesters in Washington DC failed to
halt meetings of the World Bank and the International Monetary Fund
(IMF). Most protest was good-natured and there was little violence, but
that did not stop the police making 1,300 arrests.[4] The British police
were less heavy handed in London's May Day rally, despite hours of
running battles through the centre of the capital. Just 95 people were
arrested and nine officers were injured. The Cenotaph was defaced and
a McDonald's fast-food outlet was ransacked. But the defining image of
that day was Winston Churchill's statue in Parliament Square wearing
a Mohican hairstyle made of turf. The day had started peacefully with
the police looking on as demonstrators dug up the green in the square
and planted seed as part of their 'guerrilla gardening' drive to return
urban London to nature. About 1,000 peeled off for Trafalgar Square
and attacked the McDonald's in the Strand, smashing every window. A
policeman was hurt by a flying brick. Police cordoned off the area and
opened a narrow corridor to allow the demonstrators to leave. Violence
flared again as a minority threw bottles, iron bars and scaffolding.
Police holiday leave had been cancelled and more than 5,000 officers
were deployed in the biggest operation of its kind in London for 30
years, with 100 officers in Scotland Yard's control centre monitoring
CCTV cameras and radioing intelligence to police on the ground. By
their standards it was a success, but Tony Blair condemned actions by
demonstrators which 'have nothing to do with conviction and belief
and everything to do with mindless thuggery'.[5] There was also some
public outrage at the defacement of the Cenotaph, the memorial to
wartime dead, and of Churchill's statue (a former soldier was sentenced

to 30 days' imprisonment and ordered to pay £250 compensation). Such outrage prompted a review of future procedures. The police were criticised for being too lenient and strategists for being too cautious. It was not something they could be accused of a year later.

But in the meantime, the international protests continued. In Prague that September demonstrators did manage to close the annual meetings of the World Bank and the IMF 24 hours early after two days of violence. Molotov cocktails and paving stones were thrown against police lines and demonstrators tried to storm a hotel where many delegates were staying. The police deployed tear-gas, water cannon, helicopters and marksmen in balaclavas, making over 400 arrests. In January 2001 the target was the World Economic Forum's annual meeting in the Swiss resort town of Davos. Around 500 people disguised as skiers defied a ban on demonstrations and were dispersed with water cannon with no reported arrests. In April 2001 it was the turn of Quebec City, host of the Summit of the Americas. Petrol-bombs were thrown and 400 arrests were made.[6]

In London on May Day 2001, over 6,000 London police used tactics never before employed, effectively turning Oxford Circus into a pen which held 4,000 people for up to six hours.

As previously, the day began peacefully with a surreal air of carnival. Five hundred cyclists made their go-slow protest until many were corralled in a sidestreet. Organised pigeon-feeding in Trafalgar Square was notable for the police outnumbering the demonstrators. A picket of the Queen's bank, Coutts, also passed quietly. But in and around Oxford Street stores were targeted and there were violent clashes. Fifteen activists in balaclavas stormed a Sainsbury's chanting anti-capitalist slogans. Concrete slabs were hurled at the police, and officers exchanged blows. A sit-down protest was ridiculed by anarchists and elsewhere fights broke out amongst different protest factions. But largely it was a day of minor scuffles and tense stand-offs. The police then took the unprecedented step of corralling the protesters and some bystanders in a narrow space, and keeping them there for hours in crushed conditions. A court later heard that there were fears of another Hillsborough, the 1989 football tragedy in which 96 Liverpool fans were crushed to death. Geoffrey Saxby, who sued the Met for breach of human rights, said that he had initially been unaware of a demonstration and had been merely watching some Oxford Circus street entertainers.

'There was no trouble from the crowd or any indication of trouble arising', he said.

> I looked around and saw the police lined up in a human chain across Regents Street. They started to push the crowd back for no reason at all and seemingly without any concern for our safety. A woman in the crowd screamed at the police at the top of her voice 'remember Hillsborough' which drew home to me the danger that I was in.

Another claimant, Lois Austin, was a veteran demonstrator but insisted she had not seen any major disorder. She had intended to only stay a few hours to protest 'peacefully against globilisation and capitalism'. She was not allowed to leave to collect her eleven-month-old daughter from a childminder and described the police as 'rude and aggressive'. She told the court: 'I was subjected to unfair and humiliating treatment and the policing of the event was completely disproportionate to the behaviour and size of the crowd.'[7]

Another witness, however, saw things differently. Dominic Casciani said:

> In footballing terms, the Met played a blinder. They'd allowed the protesters in – but they weren't going to let them out. Two lines of riot-gear-clad officers and a buffer zone of vans at each exit were making that clear. Fluffies [the anti-violence protesters] played volleyball and banged their drums and unfurled left-wing banners. Spikers [those bent on violence] were in evidence but small in number and biding their time. Two middle-aged women who'd clearly seen years of hippy-inspired demonstrating, declared it 'a fluffy day not a spikey day'. However, it was not long before tension began to rise. Those who had come to fight didn't seem to be able to work out how to start it. The fluffies expressed frustration, predicting police tactics would provoke violence by treating everyone as criminals. Monopoly money had been handed out as part of the game. But someone had forgotten the Get Out of Jail Free cards.[8]

Police loudspeakers told the crowd that they were not going anywhere because of the threat to property. Voices within the crowd complained they were the victims of an illegal mass arrest. Bottles thrown at the Niketown store bounced off its plastic riot-proof windows. Spikies mounted sporadic attacks on the police lines but bounced off the riot shields. Rain drenched much of their ardour and frustration turned into sullen acquiscence. After six hours the crowd were allowed to disperse in small batches. Throughout the day 92 people were arrested and 50 were injured. Extra policing costs amounted to £150,000 while lost business in London's premier shopping area was estimated at £20 million.

Civil liberties groups and protesters accused the police of overreacting. Liberty director John Wadham said: 'This year, unfortunately, the police caved in to political pressure. The containment of thousands of people was unnecessary and unlawful.' But Met Assistant Commissioner Mike Todd said that there had been a real threat of widespread violence and criminal damage, and that people had been warned to stay away. And London Mayor Ken Livingstone, a hero to many protesters, condemned a rampage by some of them in Tottenham Court Road on their way home. 'This appalling vandalism shows the decision to contain the protesters was right', he said. 'The immediate turn to violence on dispersal indicates that this was the core objective of the organisers.'[9]

In June 2001, police in Gothenburg shot three protesters outside a summit of European leaders gathered to discuss the expansion of the EU. Swedish police were caught unprepared and dozens were injured, including mounted officers pulled off their horses. Around 500 arrests were made after a botched operation which contrasted strongly with the tactics used in London.

The George Bush–Tony Blair-led 'war on terror' following the September 11 suicide blitz on New York and Washington provided a new focus. On 13 October 20,000 marched through London in a demonstration against the US bombing of Afghanistan. They chanted 'No War', blew whistles and banged drums but there was no violence. The event had originally been planned by the Campaign for Nuclear Disarmament (CND), but switched focus after six successive nights of bombing. Green London Assembly member Darren Johnson told the rally in Trafalgar Square: 'There are thousands and thousands of us here today for peace and justice.' The modern, fragmented, protest movement was discovering a new cohesion and a wider appeal.

The following year's May Day rally in Trafalgar Square, organised by the Trades Union Congress (TUC), drew trade unionists, students and the middle class. Black-clad anarchists were kept to the sidelines and meekly followed police instructions after a brief stand-off. Once again the event attracted disparate groups, including Critical Mass cyclists and the animal rights group London Animal Action, and the more militant group Shac, under surveillance for its direct action against Huntingdon Life Sciences for its laboratory tests on animals.

Meanwhile, the invasion of Afghanistan messily completed, Bush and Blair began their helter-skelter journey towards an invasion of Iraq to topple Saddam Hussein and destroy his supposed arsenal of weapons of mass destruction. The issue polarised the nation and was a rallying call for protest.

Sunday 15 February 2003 saw Britain's biggest ever demonstration with a million pairs of feet marching in the capital. The event was co-ordinated with other anti-war protests in Glasgow and Belfast, part of a weekend of hundreds of similar events in up to 60 countries. A three and a half hour march organised by the Stop the War Coalition, CND and the Muslim Association of Britain began early as police fretted at the huge numbers gathering. Two streams of cheering, chanting, singing people converged in Picadilly Circus and moved on to Hyde Park. Organiser John Rees said: 'It's fantastic. The atmosphere is electric, but it is also very serious and determined.'[10] Every conceivable grouping was represented, from Socialist Workers to the Women's Institute. Rich and poor, Christians and Muslims, trade unionists and small businessmen, rubbed shoulders, united in their condemnation of what they perceived as an impeding and wholly unnecessary conflict. There were even some who less than four months earlier had marched in the 400,000-strong Countryside Alliance protest against the proposed ban on fox-hunting. The Home Counties twin-set brigade made common cause with the sons and daughters of the Angry Brigade. The speeches from the platform were ferocious, with contributions from writer Tariq Ali, former Northern Ireland Secretary Mo Mowlam, Ken Livingstone, actress Vanessa Redgrave, Bianca Jagger, Hollywood Oscar-winner Tim Robbins, Tony Benn, former US presidential hopeful Jesse Jackson, and playwright Harold Pinter, who described Blair as a 'hired Christian thug'. It was the march of the 'luvvies'. Unfortunately, Blair wasn't interested in theatricals. As the million gathered he said: 'I do not seek unpopularity as a badge of honour, but sometimes it is the price of leadership and the cost of conviction.'

Once again, all police leave was cancelled across the capital, but Scotland Yard reported that the day passed off 'almost without incident'. A handful of arrests were made for minor public order offences, including four picked up at a sit-down protest in Piccadilly

Circus. Andy Todd, Assistant Deputy Commissioner of the Met, said that the crowd had been tolerant and patient.

That patience was wasted. Blair ignored such a large, well-behaved and well-ordered expression of public opinion. Within weeks the bombardment began and US and British forces swept into Iraq. Veteran campaigners were unsurprised, the new, middle class recruits to mass protests were astonished. Demonstrations became deeply personal. On 20 March, schoolchildren mounted a raucous sit-down outside the House of Commons. A 14-year-old girl said: 'We are a peaceful movement. We are not here to cause a riot, but we don't think children are listened to.' One man was arrested for breach of the peace outside Foreign Secretary Jack Straw's home. Others blocked roads near his house, stopping him going to work for all of 30 minutes. Twenty pupils in St Just, Cornwall, were suspended for walking to a Penzance rally.

As the killing began in earnest in Iraq, peace campaigners again co-ordinated their efforts for 22 March. In Brussels, water cannon were used on a splinter group who threw rocks at the US embassy. In New York, around 100,000 people filled 20 city blocks in a lunch-time march. In Wellington, New Zealand, protesters shouting 'No blood for oil' threw fake food into the American embassy compound. The Australian cities of Hobart and Brisbane were brought to a halt. There was a general strike in Bangladesh; Buddhist monks struck giant drums to console the spirits of the war dead in Seoul; and further protests swept Indonesia, Malaysia, South Korea and India. Around 10,000 marched through Naples towards the NATO base at Bagnoli. They were ignored.

The Stop the War coalition tried to disrupt Budget Day, fearful that Chancellor Gordon Brown would double the £3 billion already allocated for the war effort. Council workers protested outside town halls across the country demanding 'Welfare, not warfare'. A minute's silence was observed to remember Iraqi civilians and members of all military forces killed so far. Another march through the streets of central London as American tanks entered Baghdad drew up to 200,000, although the total was hotly disputed. Former Pakistan cricket captain Imran Khan said: 'It doesn't matter how many people turn out. It's about registering a protest that a principle has been violated, international law has been violated and everyone who cares must register a protest.'[11] Marchers laid wreaths, flowers and cards at the gates of Downing Street. The mood was sombre, a change from the jubilation felt at those rallies before the start of the war. Anas Altikriti, of the Muslim Association of Britain, said: 'People are now more angry that we have committed what they see as a crime, an illegal occupation, and that people continue to suffer away from the media spotlight.' But the protesters faced some dissent, not least from Labour MPs loyal to Blair. David Winnick said: 'I don't doubt the sincerity of most of the peace marchers who marched before and those who, for some reason, march today. But the fact remains that there are a number of leading organisers whose commitment to Parliamentary democracy is very remote indeed.'

The apparent end to the war, symbolised by the toppling of Saddam's giant statue in Baghdad, changed little. A year on, with the occupation of Iraq and widespread insurgency, the focus switched to both efforts to pull troops out and to punish Blair, a Prime Minister battered by the lack of weapons of mass destruction, the death of arms inspector David Kelly and the exposure of the 'dodgy dossier' used by Number 10 as an excuse for going to war. Despite March downpours, thousands once again gathered in London to mark the first anniversary of the conflict. The following October they were joined by the parents of slain British soldiers. There were emotional scenes as mothers and fathers spoke of their children dying for Blair, or being sent into war zones unprepared for the grim reality. General election fever was mounting. Former Labour MP George Galloway, who formed his own Respect party, and whose record of heaping praise on Saddam when he was in power was well-reported, predicted that Blair was in 'big trouble'. He was applauded for labelling both Bush and Blair 'war criminals'. Paul Bigley, whose brother Ken was taken hostage in Iraq and beheaded after three weeks in captivity, also publicly blamed Blair.[12]

However, in the subsequent May 2005 general election Blair and his administration won a historic third term. Their overall majority was cut to 66 seats, but it remained a stunning achievement against such widespread ill-will over the war, the countryside, the immigration and asylum question, ministerial sleaze, student fees and the backdoor privatisation of public services. How much a part the anti-war movement played in slashing that majority will continue to be an issue for debate. But it is a fair bet that the lack of a coherent, respected and electable mainstream opposition party played a bigger part. The Stop the War coalition failed in its aims, and failed to take effective revenge.

As Blair began his third term, the focus of protest switched to scheduled meetings in Britain of G8. Ahead of the planned summit in Scotland, the anti-globalisation set targeted a meeting of justice ministers in Sheffield. The police reported only minor disturbances and there were a handful of arrests. Events two weeks later were not so sedate.

On Monday 4 July, organisers mounted a Carnival for Full Enjoyment in Edinburgh as the G8 leaders headed for their summit in Gleneagles 40 miles away. It was the third demo in as many days, following a Make Poverty History march and a smaller Stop the War event at the weekend. Much of the city centre was shuttered, whilst those stores which did open hired extra security staff. Samba drums and whistles marked the beginning of a short march. Police, mounted and on foot, kept pace with protesters dressed as clowns. The closest to a clash came when one anarchist climbed onto a building and threatened to urinate on the police, but he settled for 'mooning' at the crowd. Slogans threatening to 'Smash kapital' were spray-painted on walls, and some black-masked anarchists tried to engage the police, but the city-centre operation was largely good-natured. Trouble erupted at a splinter march to the Scott monument. Demonstrators were met by riot police and some missiles were thrown. Scots Secretary Alistair Darling condemned a 'mindless minority responsible for the violence'.[13]

Meanwhile, a massive security ring, 18 months in preparation, was being thrown around Gleneagles, the famous golfing resort. Miles of steel fencing and wire were erected, and the operation was designed, at all costs it seemed, to keep protesters well away from Blair, Bush and other world leaders preparing an aid package for Africa. Only a small G8 Alternative protest was to be allowed anywhere near the hotel. On the Wednesday Edinburgh was again brought to a standstill when anti-G8 factions on three buses bound for Gleneagles were halted. Hundreds of others were refused access to more vehicles. They marched down Prince's Street chanting 'Whose streets? Our streets.' The police contingents made that debatable and the march, swelled to around 500, turned into a slow shuffle and then a cat and mouse game with the constabulary. There was sporadic violence, but torrential rain proved as effective a dispersal agent as the police.[14]

Closer to Gleneagles it was a different picture. There were running battles on the streets of Stirling and Bannockburn and at the summit security fence near Auchterarder. Sit-down protests briefly blocked surrounding roads, and some small towns were cut off for a few hours. Most of 65 arrests involved attempted roadblocks and smashed car windows. One of the worse affected towns was Dunblane, the scene of the primary school massacre in 1996 in which 16 children died. One Edinburgh resident told the BBC: 'I marched with my family for Make Poverty History, but what is today supposed to be about? It seems like a complete waste of time to me.'[15]

Inevitably, there were conflicting views of the demonstrations and the police operation. Dee Coombes, a 'justice fairy' involved in the attempted road blockade, said: 'Pressure builds up because people become very frightened when they're hemmed in and that's been a problem this whole week. We were searched illegally, and there's a lot of harassment going on.' Chief Constable Peter Wilson said:

> There were clearly some people who were there for peaceful purpose but there were also clearly many who came with intent to cause trouble. We are there to respond robustly when necessary but we are also keen to ensure that it's peaceful policing.[16]

During the week there were 358 arrests, most of them involving protesters from England, Germany and Belgium. Over 10,000 police officers were drafted in from across the UK. Twenty police officers and two police horses were injured and there were 21 complaints about police tactics.[17]

On the morning of 7 July the summit was indeed interrupted, but not by the demonstrators. News filtered in of the terrorist bomb blitz on London's transport system. A clearly shaken Blair spoke of his horror and flew back to the capital. On his return the following day, the G8 summit agreed to boost aid for developing countries by £28.8 billion. Much of the package, as is the nature of such deals, had been agreed beforehand, including cancelling the debt of Africa's poorest nations and agreeing to cut subsidies and tariffs which penalise the Third World. But Bush vetoed serious action to tackle global warming, and the overall reaction was mixed. Kumi Naidoo, chair of the Global Call to Action Against Poverty, said: 'The people have roared but the G8 has whispered.' But Irish rocker Bob Geldof, who had organised the pre-summit Live 8 concert, aimed at influencing the G8 leaders' decisions on reducing Third World debt, welcomed the deal. He said:

> Never have so many people forced a change of policy onto a global agenda. If anyone had said eight weeks ago we will get a doubling of aid, we will get a deal on debt, people would have said 'no'.

But the inferences of such figures that the world's richest nations had been influenced by either street demonstrations or a pop concert seem decidedly shaky. Global factors, including the 'war on terror' were ultimately the key. Anti-globalisation and Stop the War protesters may feel that they scored debating points, but their protests were ultimately futile.

Conclusions

'Revenge for unwanted punishments'

There is an obvious difficulty in drawing a seamless line from the martyrs of Peterloo and Chartism to drug-fuelled hooliganism in Handsworth, looting in Toxteth and the elements of class hatred witnessed in recent riots. The brick and the petrol-bomb should, ideally, never be a substitute for legitimate protest or Parliamentary democracy. But neither can the truncheon or the hooves of police horses be a legitimate tool of governance.

However, rioting has been an engine of beneficial social change. Even in 2003 Clive Bloom could write:

> Rioting is a Londoner's political birthright, central to the democratic system as a safety valve and as a means to effect social change. Sometimes we need to smash windows in Whitehall just to make a point to modern politicians, who have retreated from public encounters behind a screen of orchestrated photo opportunities.

The mob, with its ugly face, has imposed some constraint on the ruling classes, whether the 'oppressors' have worn epaulettes or designer suits. The riot has been a manifestation of social inequality and political impotence. It is an uncomfortable fact that the street thug with an iron bar stands shoulder to shoulder with the dispossessed, and will continue to do so given the disappointments and disillusionment engendered by New Labour.

Abroad, the last two centuries have seen the assassination of Archdukes, Tsars and Presidents, pogroms, military dictatorships and revolutions for good or evil. Britain did not magically escape that turmoil, but its impact was slow rather than instant. The nation did not escape revolution, and some of the uprisings chronicled in this book were indeed putative revolutions, but adapted to revolutionary ideas until they became the norm. Votes for men and women, workplace rights, the forging and dismantlement of an empire, the stresses and benefits of immigration, youth culture, industrial change, the lessening – if not eradication – of rule by a hereditary elite, the rise of socialism and fascism, all played a part in forging our nation. But without the ever-present threat of violence, today's Britain may not have enjoyed the benefits of trade unions, universal suffrage, a welfare state, the National Health Service and an imperfect system of Parliamentary scrutiny and Government accountability. Nor, ironically, would it have avoided the more violent forms of revolution seen elsewhere during those two tumultuous centuries. As we have seen, such gains were hard won from ruling classes empowered by military machinery.

The machine-breaking Luddites responded to the cruelties of a free market magnified by the dizzying speed of technological change. The Establishment reacted with a savagery which quelled the immediate uprising but deepened the burning sense of outrage felt by the emerging industrial working class. That savagery reached a terrifying crossroads with the Peterloo Massacre. Here was a riot by the forces of law and order, not by the protesters. Horses hooves and flashing sabres deployed against a peaceful meeting legitimised, to a degree, future violence when used by the many against the strong. The growth of literacy and newspapers encouraged that trend, with journalists making their reputations through radical rhetoric coupled with melodrama. As Charles Dickens recognised, the nineteenth-century public loved tales of ragged orphans, abused women and brutalised men. The reports of correspondents – lurid, sensational and often accurate – proved a powerful force in at least the recognition of society's injustices.

The rulers continued to respond with repressions – curbs on the press, on assembly, on seditious oratory, on the right to a fair trial and on basic civil liberties – which often went against their own liberal and progressive instincts. Then, as now during the 'war on terror', they salved their consciences with the argument that state security was paramount and that sometimes the only way to uphold the rule of law is to subvert it themselves. That mentality saw habeas corpus suspended, detention without trial and the intervention of the military in civil matters. Not too different from the current political climate exploiting the fear of suicide bombers, with Labour Cabinet ministers excusing continuous crackdowns with the general compliance of the judiciary.

While violence was playing its part in the establishment of seething, crowded and sooty industrial towns and cities, the Swing Riots by workers treated no better than medieval peasants turned much of Britain's countryside into a war zone. William Cobbett wrote of the indignation felt by agricultural workers engaged in orchestrated vandalism: 'It is no temporary cause, it is no new feeling of discontent that is at work; it is a deep sense of grievous wrongs; it is an accumulation of revenge for unwarranted punishment ...' The hangings and mass deportations which followed ensured the further radicalisation of both rural and factory workers. That radicalisation in turn gave new impetus to the rebirth of the electoral reform movement previously cowed by Peterloo. All those sections of society clamouring for change to tackle poverty and inequality saw that there was no chance of building a fairer society without radical changes in the way the country was governed. The Battle of Bristol, two days of far greater carnage than that seen at Peterloo, badly shook the established order. Although the riot quickly deteriorated into drunken looting, the immense damage to property rather than persons of little value gave the rulers a glimpse of their own vulnerability.

Their response was the modest concessions of the 1832 Reform Act which abolished many rotten boroughs but left the vast majority of working men without the vote. Such crumbs dropped from the tables of the elite may have averted a revolution of the kind then erupting in Continental Europe. But the narrowness of the Act created the Chartist Movement, born out of resentment that while the working classes had suffered most during the Reform Riots and the repression that followed them, they, though not their propertied and articulate former leaders, remained powerless. Such movements were fuelled by periodic manufacturing and trade slumps and economic depressions which saw workers' wages and living conditions – and the prospects of their children – going into reverse once again during the glory years of Queen Victoria's empire. The outcome was the Newport Insurrection, the Plug Plot Riots, violent disturbances in virtually every corner of the nation ... and the second Reform Act of 1867 by which a million more people were enfranchised. Successive Governments learnt that modest concessions were better than the prospect of armed revolution. They also began to realise that the wider voting base could be manipulated to enhance, rather than undermine, their own power. Embracing the supposed will of the people, whether from a Whig or Tory starting point, was the best way to knock out your political opponent. As a result, hustings maintained their own levels of violence and intimidation. The Cotton Famine in Lancashire, although not the Stalybridge Riot which was seen as an aberration, resulted in widespread public indignation over the plight of starving families during an era in which Britons would allegedly never, never, never be slaves. In this case it was the stoicism and search for self-betterment, rather than riotous vandalism, which kick-started a change in social attitudes. The fight for social justice and patriotism became linked, while the growing understanding that charity alone was not enough to create a proper Christian community led to the concept of a welfare state.

But concessions inevitably led to further demands. To the chagrin of the rulers, the newly enfranchised were not satisfied with their limited voting rights. They wanted real social change and that passionate desire saw a surge in socialist idealism, the growth of the trade union movement, the Labour Party and the Suffragettes. The right to organise in the workplace, a movement which had refused to be crushed by the treatment of the Tolpuddle Martyrs and many others, was the most dominant and its influence can be seen on every other manifestation of protest against the status quo. What ensued was a variety of violent confrontation epitomised by the Featherstone colliery riot, Bloody Sunday in Trafalgar Square and Black Friday outside Parliament. In each case military tactics by the established order heightened dissent rather than crushing it. Social reform, including the introduction of pensions and welfare payments, were won. So too was a good measure of electoral justice, although it was the demands of industrialised warfare which won the vote for women, rather than civil disruption.

But as the twentieth century progressed the biggest power struggles were between the forces of capital and those of organised labour. The trade unions, supported patchily by the Labour Party, flexed their muscles, while the established order responded with troops and police occupations. The first national or 'general' strike of 1911 brought together miners, dockers and transport workers and the spectre of a nation paralysed by violent, direct action resulted in significant improvements to pay and conditions. It was, however, a convoluted struggle in which workers too often took one step forward and two steps back. The police strike of 1919 – which saw the deployment of gunships and the perception that society's structures were very fragile indeed – failed in its attempt to form a police union opposed to their use as an arm of political control. The social and industrial history of the latter part of that century might have been very different if it had succeeded. The peaceful 1926 General Strike ended in abject failure when its leaders, rather than its foot soldiers, caved in to police and civil militia and the organisational skills of the state.

The rise in fascism and the post-war surge in immigration provided new targets for working-class fury, for good and ill. The riot as a political tool reverted to its eighteenth-century manifestation as a focus of fragmented discontent, and as such became increasingly ineffective. Oswald Mosley and his Blackshirts were marginalised and defeated because of public distaste at his devotion to Mussolini and Hitler, rather than by the Battle of Cable Street. Mosleyite Teddy Boys on 'nigger-bashing' sprees failed to curb the influx of immigrants needed to rebuild post-war Britain. They did, however, contribute to the climate of hate, fear and alienation which erupted so violently in immigrant communities 30 years later. More beneficially, the Notting Hill Riots did force the white trade union movement to make common cause with their ethnic comrades.

Student protest against the Vietnam War during the 1960s was kicking at an open door as Harold Wilson consistently rejected American pressure to join that conflict. Across the Atlantic, in any case, it was not student protest which ended the war but economics, mainstream political changes and a military defeat. In Britain large-scale violent demonstrations owed more to the trendy counter-cultures exported from America than to clearly defined social objectives. During the 1970s youthful energies switched to anti-fascist rallies to combat the resurgent National Front and its bastard children. That had an effect, although a limited one, in softening public perceptions regarding immigrants and exposing the excesses of right-wing thuggery. But the emergence of the Socialist Workers Party, the militant tendency and Trotskyist offspring split the radical left and the unions and fatally damaged a Labour administration, culminating in the Winter of Discontent and a new Conservative Government.

Thatcherism saw Britain transformed into the riot capital of the Western world. The Iron Lady polarised the nation, dismantled hard-won trade union rights, encouraged a 'them and us' mentality and embraced a monetarist economic theory which destroyed such traditional heavy industries as coal, steel and shipbuilding and which accepted 3 million unemployed as a price worth paying. It also came close to destroying the economy of the country, with North Sea oil revenues eaten up by the huge benefit bill of her own creation. Brixton, Toxteth and other inner-city riots pitted disaffected young black men against aggressive young white men in uniforms, with no side the winner and the wider community the loser. Those so-called race riots did achieve some measure of investment in deprived inner-city areas, together with the scrapping of the racially perceived police powers of 'stop and search', but such victories have proved short-lived. The miners strike saw the militarisation of the police with swathes of Britain turned into armed camps or no-go areas. The miners were crushed by a combination of military tactics, internal divisions which led to breakaway coalfields, fatigue, a rising death toll which shamed all sides, and the arrant failings of their industrial and political leaders. The Battle of Orgreave showed that the rawest form of industrial muscle, no matter how brave and determined, is no match for riot shields and cavalry charges. Such industrial warfare and riots which disfigured or burnt out many a town or city centre did little to dent the Iron Lady's armour. Too often genuine grievances were muddled up with drug wars, hooliganism and intimidation. And the violence involved in the marathon Wapping dispute allowed Thatcher and Rupert Murdoch to destroy the print unions and eject the closed shop in the newspaper industry. That has given control of the media to a handful of robber barons who enjoy successive Governments fawning at their feet. The newspaper-reading public, and the concept of democratic debate, has suffered as a result.

What finally did for Mrs Thatcher was, as a contributory factor at least, a riot which was a focus of widespread public distaste for the poll tax, an ancient cause of social friction. This was an issue which crossed social boundaries and united disparate groups in its palpable unfairness. Such disapproval led to a 1990 version of a nineteenth-century 'monster rally'. A minority of anarchists and over-zealous police officers turned Trafalgar Square and Whitehall into a battleground, but it was the steady tramp of all classes united in opposition to a tax which offended their sense of common decency and justice which finally pierced her carapace. In that sense the Poll Tax Riot followed the tradition of the Reformists who fell at Peterloo.

Since then there has been another reversal to single issue public protest such as the million-strong demonstration against the Iraq war or the 400,000-strong Countryside Alliance march against the scrapping of hunting with hounds. In both cases the issues were so broadly defined, and attracted such a disparate range of supporters, that the effect was diluted and the demos had little or no impact. Some anarchists found common cause with both the above, and could be found at the anti-capitalist events, loosely organised through the internet, aimed at bringing down the City or disrupting the meetings of the leaders of the world's richest nations. With unintended irony, many such bedsit Bolsheviks dressed as clowns to further their cause, or lack of one. Such clowns claim to be involved in a process of self-empowerment or 'DIY culture' to oppose the commodification of everyday life. That is used to justify squatting in other people's homes and the disruption of mainstream political processes, including protest. But the confusing, loose and sometimes conflicting aims are seeing the anarchists themselves being unwittingly infiltrated. 'Dave', a May Day protester, told the BBC:

> I've been to Cambridge University but I don't buy into the capitalist system. I want to get a squat in London with some anarchists. I'm not an anarchist myself – I don't believe one group has all the answers to our problems. This is one of my protest T-shirts.

The problem with the Stop the War protests, and the reason they could be safely ignored by the Government, was that they were so broad-based and the objectives so ill-defined. Home Counties matrons marched alongside SWP agitators, fox-hunting Tories found common cause with Marxist trade unionists. Such a coalition worked against the poll tax, but that was a simpler issue to unravel than a war to which thousands of British troops were committed. The very broadness of the protest in this instance neutered it. Objectives ranged from immediate withdrawal, to a phased pull-out, to open support for Islamic Jihadists. And claims that the 'war on terror' was bogus, manufactured by the Governments of Britain and America to justify state repression, looked very silly indeed after the 7 July 2005 suicide bomb blitz on the London transport network. At the other end of the protest spectrum, the Countryside Alliance's efforts to block a hunting ban proved ineffective for similar reasons. The organisers aimed to pull in the biggest crowds by broadening its appeal to include those suffering the effects of Post Office and village school closures, lost bus services and low-flying jets. Again, the protest was so broad, diffuse and ill-defined it could be safely ignored. It is, in any case, harder to hear the echo of Peterloo in such demonstrations. Unlike the great campaigns for social justice and suffrage, common cause was for a day or two only, and disintegrated once the litter had been cleared up.

Britain's rulers over the last 200 years have been helped by the divided nature of their opponents. It took a long while for working-class agitation over famine and poverty to make common cause with Parliamentary reformers. The livelihoods of most workers depended, as they saw it, on the prosperity of their bosses. Those who fought the Corn Laws in the towns found little support in the countryside. Reasonably well-paid artisans insisted on pay differentials to labourers. Patriotism was a rallying cry deployed by all sides. The Establishment never faced an overwhelming coalition of opponents with the unity to pull it down. And the mob's cause was not always just, as witnessed by the Rebecca Riots in South Wales which targeted isolated homesteads, and more widespread mob attacks on Catholics, Jews, immigrants of all colours, and, during the First World War, on those – apart from the Royal Family – with German-sounding names. Corrupt working practices, envy, greed, drunkenness and racial hatred have been common features. As has the desire to loot the brewery rather than the arsenal. In more recent years, Blair Peach may have been a victim, but so too was PC Keith Blakelock.

Furthermore, in the long war for social justice, the working classes have been badly let down by most of their self-appointed leaders, from the bombastic orators who fled at the sound of trotting hooves to the vainglorious inconoclasts who see personal advantage in urging others to man the barricades. Even one of the best, Robert Cunninghame Graham, was later haunted by feelings of failure and described his life's work to improve the lot of working people as 'ploughing sand'. His sincerity cannot be doubted. The motivations of some of today's 'heroes' who disguise their personal wealth or backgrounds is less clear. Honourable social movements have some place for drawing-room revolutionaries, but it is the man or woman in the street who most often changes history. Too often they have been less articulate, educated or cultured, but more genuine, passionate and effective. Often those energies are channelled through trade unionism or local government or pressure groups or even Parliament, but sometimes, as we have seen, there has been no option other than taking to the streets. The brickbat may not be cricket, but Britain would be a different place without it. Riots are ugly, but so are wars. Soldiers have murdered, raped and looted off the battlefield, and been killed or maimed fighting for patriotism and the ideals which society imposes on them. So too have those civilians who have taken on the might of the Establishment. Like the soldier, a social and political reformer might be standing shoulder to shoulder with a drunkard or a thief, but that does not diminish his or her courage or the righteousness of their cause.

That was certainly true of much of the period covered by this book, but becomes more difficult to argue as we come closer to the present day. Riot as a weapon against degrees of poverty and exploitation which could and did kill the body became an expression of rage against a poverty of expectation which can kill the spirit. Whether violence can be justified in that ongoing struggle remains debatable. The closeness of history makes it ever more uncomfortable.

Notes

Introduction

1. Ian Gilmour, *Riots, Risings and Revolution*, p16.
2. Ibid, pp342–70.
3. Mike Jay, *The Unfortunate Colonel Despard*, p10.
4. Richard Holmes, *Redcoat*, pp74–5.
5. Jay, *The Unfortunate Colonel Despard*, p320.

1   Luddites and Blanketeers

1. Robert Reid, *The Peterloo Massacre*, pp15–18.
2. W. Napier, *The Life and Opinions of General Sir Charles Napier*, pp56–7.
3. *The Times*, 24 August 1819.
4. Lord Byron, speech to the House of Lords, 27 February 1812.
5. Robert Reid, *Land of Lost Content*, pp134–7.
6. Ibid, pp241–44.
7. *Leeds Mercury*, 22 April 1812.
8. Archibald Prentice, *Personal Recollections of Manchester*, April 1812 (extracts, BBC History online).
9. *Manchester Chronicle*, April 1812 (exact date unknown).
10. Reid, *The Peterloo Massacre*, p31.
11. Ibid, pp21–2.
12. <http://spartacus.co.uk/PRnadim.htm>.
13. Samuel Bamford, *Passages in the Life of a Radical*, 1843 (extracts, BBC History online).
14. Reid, *The Peterloo Massacre*, p26.
15. G. Pellew, *Right Honorable Henry Addington*, p165.
16. Lord Sidmouth, speech to the House of Lords, 24 February 1817.
17. Home Office extracts of inclosures to Lord Sidmouth, 25 January 1817.
18. Reid, *The Peterloo Massacre*, pp1–4.
19. Home Office paper 42, 3 March 1817.
20. *Manchester Mercury*, 1 April 1817.
21. Home Office correspondence, Byng to Beckett, 15 March 1817.
22. *The Times*, 11 March 1817.
23. John Livesey, Home Office deposition, 3 April 1817.
24. *Manchester Chronicle*, 15 April 1817.
25. Home Office correspondence, Byng to Sidmouth, 15 March 1817.
26. Reid, *The Peterloo Massacre*, pp67–8.

2 The Road to Peterloo

1. Robert Reid, *The Peterloo Massacre*, p101.
2. Ibid, p105.
3. *Dictionary of National Biography*, pp266–8.
4. Home Office paper (henceforth 'Ho') 42.189.
5. HO 42.191.
6. Reid, *The Peterloo Massacre*, p129.

3 The Massacre

1. Samuel Bamford, *Passages in the Life of a Radical*, Vol 2, pp150–60.
2. Robert Reid, *The Peterloo Massacre*, pp148–9.
3. *The Times*, 19 April 1819.
4. *Reports of State Trials*, p1179.
5. Reid, *The Peterloo Massacre*, p168.
6. *Annual Register*.
7. *The Times*, 19 April 1819.
8. *Reports of State Trials*, p1195.
9. Donald Reid, *Peterloo*, p133.
10. *The Times*, 19 April 1819.
11. Ibid.
12. Ibid.
13. Bamford, *Passages in the Life of a Radical*, Vol. 2, pp209.
14. *The Times*, 19 April 1819.
15. *Reports of State Trials*, p256.
16. Reid, *The Peterloo Massacre*, p176.
17. Sidmouth Papers (Devon Record Office) for 11 April 1845.
18. *Reports of State Trials*, p1195.
19. Henry Hunt, *Memoirs*, Vol 3, p618.
20. *Reports of State Trials*, p1102–3.
21. *Manchester Guardian*, 19 August 1819.
22. Sidmouth Papers, 11 April 1845.
23. Bamford, *Passages in the Life of a Radical*, Vol 1, p208.
24. HO 42.192.

4 The Reckoning

1. Sidmouth Papers (Devon Record Office).
2. Home Office Paper 42.193.
3. *Manchester Observer*, 19 August 1819.
4. *The Times*, 21 August 1819.
5. Relief List, Accounts Book (University Library of Manchester).
6. Robert Reid, *The Peterloo Massacre*, p199.
7. Ibid, p204.
8. Ibid, p224.
9. J.E. Taylor, *Peterloo Massacre*, p124.

5   Captain Swing and the Rural War

1. Eric Hobsbawm and G. Rude, *Captain Swing*, quoting HO 52/9, p156.
2. The Peel Web, 'Rural Unrest in the 1830s', <http://dialspace.dial.pipex.com/peel/swing.htm> p2.
3. Clara Kinwardstone, 'The Swing Riots Around Burbage', <http://www.kinwardstone.clara.net/histroric/swing.html>.
4. Hobsbawm and Rude, *Captain Swing*.
5. Kinwardstone, 'The Swing Riots', p5.
6. Ibid, p4.
7. Ibid, p8.
8. Cyril Coffin, *Captain Swing in Dorset*, The Dorset Page, <http://www.thedorsetpage.com.history>, pp3–5.
9. Ibid, p4.
10. 'Rural Unrest in the 1830s', p5.
11. *Annual Register*, Chronicle, November 1830, pp199–201.
12. Geoffrey Sharman, 'Tasmania', rootsweb.
13. William Cobbett, *Political Register*, May 27 1830.

6   The Reform Riots and the Battle of Bristol

1. William Cobbett, *Political Register*, 27 May 1830.
2. Wellington, letter to Miss Arbuthnot, 1 May 1831, <http://www.spartacus.schoolnet.co.uk/Prreformriots.htm>.
3. Bristol Homepage, <http://www.brisray.co.uk/bristol/briot.htm>.
4. *Annual Register*, Chronicle, November 1831, pp171–7.
5. Ibid.
6. Ibid.
7. Ibid.
8. Ibid.
9. Charles Greville, *Journal*, 11 November 1831.
10. J.L. Jackson, letter to C.B. Wollaston, 1 November 1831, <http://www.spartacus.schoolnet.co.uk/Prreformriots.htm>.
11. Greville, *Journal*, 11 November 1831.
12. Letter to the Duke of Wellington, 19 November 1831, <http://www.spartacus.schoolnet.co.uk/Prreformriots.htm>.

7   The Merthyr Rising:

1. 'The Great Rising', chap 16 in *A Brief History of Wales*, <http://www.britannia.com/wales/whist.16.html>.
2. *The Times*, 6 May 1831.
3. *Annual Register*, Chronicle, June 1831.
4. *Annual Register*, June 1831, pp84–5.
5. *Cambrian*, 3 May 1831.
6. 'The Great Rising'.
7. *The Times*, 11 July 1831.

8. 'The Great Rising'.
9. Mrs Arbuthnot's *Diary*, June 1831.
10. Official Report, House of Commons, 10 July 1831.

8   The Chartists and the Newport Insurrection

1. Robert Gammage, *History of the Chartist Movement*.
2. *Chartist*, 12 March 1839.
3. Teaching History Online, 'Physical Force Chartists', <http://www.spartacus. schoolnet.co.uk/Chphysical.htm>.
4. Marjorie Bloy, *The Causes of Chartism*, p2.
5. Ibid.
6. William Lovett, *Life and Struggles*.
7. *Western Vindicator*, April 1839.
8. The Peel Web, 'The Great Rising', chap 16, <http://dialspace.dial.pipex.com/ peel/greatrising.htm>.
9. *Cambrian*, 11 May 1839.
10. Ibid.
11. Dorothy Thompson, *The Chartists*, pp 282–98.
12. *Annual Register*, Law Cases 1839, pp214–17.
13. *Annual Register*, Chronicle, November 1839, pp221–3.
14. *Annual Register*, Chronicle, January 1840.
15. *Cambrian*, November 10 1839.
16. *Annual Register*, Chronicle, December 1839, p249.
17. The Peel Web, 'The Newport Rising', p2, <http://dialspace.dial.pipex.com/ newport.htm>.
18. 'John Frost', <http://www.spartacus.schoolnet.co.uk/Chfrost.htm>.
19. Lovett, *Life and Struggles*.

9   The Chartists and the Plug Plot Riots

1. Robert Gammage, *The History of the Chartist Movement*.
2. Dorothy Thompson, *The Chartists*, pp282–98.
3. F.C. Mather, *The General Strike of 1842*, pp115–38.
4. Thompson, *The Chartists*, p291.
5. Ibid, p296.
6. Ibid, p 291.
7. Ibid, p292.
8. F.H. Grundy, Journal, 16 August 1842, quoted in Thompson, *The Chartists*, p290.
9. Thompson, *The Chartists*, p295.
10. Mather, *The General Strike of 1842*, p115.
11. Lt. Col. Maberley, quoted in ibid.
12. *Annual Register*, Chronicle, pp133–4.
13. Thomas Cooper, *The Life of Thomas Cooper*, (1872).
14. *Annual Register*, Chronicle, October 1842, p162.
15. Ibid.

16. Sir James Graham, letter to Peel, 30 September 1842, <http://www.spartacus. schoolnet.co.uk/Chplug.htm>.
17. *Annual Register*, Chronicle, October 1842, pp157–9.
18. Ibid, p161.
19. Feargus O'Connor, 10 April 1848, <http://spartacus.schoolnet.co.uk/ Choconnor.htm>.
20. Marjorie Bloy, *The Causes of Chartism*, p4.
21. Mather, *The General Strike of 1842*, p135.
22. The Peel Web, 'Feargus O'Connor and the Land Plan', <http://dialspace.dial. pipex.com/peel/oconnor.htm>.

10   Cunninghame Graham and Bloody Sunday

1.   Teaching History Online, 'Cunninghame Graham', <http://www.spartacus. schoolnet.co.uk/Tucunninghame.htm>.
2.   *The Times*, 23 June 1887.
3.   Herbert Faulkner West, *Cunninghame Graham*, pp65–8.
4.   Sir Charles Warren, Letters, 22 October 1887, quoted in Cedric Watts and Laurence Davies, *Cunninghame Graham*, p66.
5.   *The Times*, 14 November 1887.
6.   West, *Cunninghame Graham*, p70.
7.   Ibid, p71.
8.   A.F. Tschiffely, *Don Roberto*, p217.
9.   Ibid, p218.
10. Edward Carpenter, *My Days and Dreams*.
11. Tschiffely, *Don Roberto*, p217.
12. Ibid, p219.
13. The Times, 15 November 1887.
14. *Reynolds News*, 14 November 1187.
15. Watts and Davies, *Cunninghame Graham*, p68.
16. Ibid, p73.
17. *The Times*, 21 November 1887.
18. Tschiffely, *Don Roberto*, p231.
19. West, *Cunninghame Graham*, p77.
20. Teaching History Online, John Burns, <http://www.spartacus.schoolnet.co.uk/ Reburns.htm>.
21. West, *Cunninghame Graham*, pp78–9.
22. Tschiffely, *Don Roberto*.
23. *Annual Register*, 1936 Obituaries, p124.

11   The Featherstone Riot

1.   Maureen Tomison, *The English Sickness*, pp112–13.
2.   Michael Rosen and David Widgery (eds), *The Vintage Book of Dissent*, p38.
3.   Anthony Babington, *Military Intervention in Britain*, pp124–30.
4.   *The Times*, 9 September 1892.

5. *Annual Register* 1893, p236.
6. *The Times*, 9 September 1893.
7. Ibid.
8. Walter Hampson, *Normanton Past and Present* (1928), <http://www.wakegield.org.uk>.
9. *Annual Register* 1893, p294.
10. Babington, *Military Intervention in Britain*, p133.
11. Hansard, 15 November 1893.

12   The Suffragettes and Black Friday

1. Extracts from Emmeline Pankhurst's *My Own Story* and from Emily Pankhurst's *My Own Life* quoted by Teaching History Online, <http://www.spartacus.schoolnet.co.uk/WpankhurstE.htm>.
2. Teresa Billington-Greig, *The Non-Violent Militant*.
3. Annie Kennedy, *Memoirs of a Militant*, p163.
4. <http://cjbooks.demon.co.uk/suffrage.htm>.
5. Melanie Phillips, *The Ascent of Women*, pp269–70.
6. Antonia Raeburn, *The Militant Suffragettes*, p129.
7. Ibid, p153.
8. Ibid, pp154–5.
9. Braisford and Murray, *Treatment of the Women's Deputation by the Metropolitan Police*, p6.
10. Raeburn, *The Militant Suffragettes*, p155.
11. Ibid, p156.
12. *Daily Telegraph*, 2 March 1912.
13. *The Times*, 22 March 1912.
14. *Suffragette*, 20 June 1913, p594.
15. Phillips, *The Ascent of Women*, pp195–6.

13   Churchill and the Troops

1. Randolph S. Churchill, *Winston S. Churchill, Vol II: Young Statesman*, p368.
2. Ibid, p369.
3. Ibid, pp371–2.
4. Ibid, p373.
5. Chartwell Papers, 10 November 1910.
6. South Wales *Daily News*, 9 November 1910.
7. London *Standard*, 9 November 1910.
8. South Wales *Daily News*, 9 November 1910.
9. Churchill, *Winston S. Churchill*, p376.
10. *The Times*, 9 November 1910.
11. Churchill, *Winston S. Churchill*, pp373–5.
12. Manchester *Guardian*, 10 November 1910.
13. Churchill, *Winston S. Churchill*, p378.

14. Gareth Williams, 'A Tribute to the Rhondda', <http://www.therhondda.co.uk/tonypandy>.
15. Ibid.
16. Chartwell Papers, undated minute, July–August 1911, cited in Churchill, *Winston S. Churchill*, pp368–75.
17. Churchill, *Winston S. Churchill*, pp281–2.
18. Chartwell Papers, telegram, 16 August 1911, cited in Churchill, *Winston S. Churchill*.
19. Churchill, *Winston S. Churchill*, p384.
20. Geoffrey Best, *Churchill – A Study in Greatness*, pp40–1.

14   The Police Strike

1. Clive Emsley, *The English Police*, pp119–23.
2. Gerald Reynolds and Anthony Judge, *The Night the Police Went on Strike*, ch3.
3. Ibid.
4. Home Office papers, 21 September 1918.
5. West Midlands Superintendent's Reports 1901–25 f.505.
6. *Annual Register*, May 1919, p62.
7. *The Times*, 7 June 1919.
8. *The Times*, 19 July 1919.
9. Emsley, *The English Police*, p127.
10. *The Times*, 4 August 1919.
11. Ibid.
12. *The Times*, 5 August 1919.
13. Ibid.
14. *Liverpool Echo*, 11 August 1919.
15. *The Times*, 5 August 1919.
16. *The Times*, 8 August.

15   Mosley and the Battle of Cable Street

1. James Johnston, *A Hundred Commoners*, pp124–6.
2. Piers Brandon, *The Dark Valley*, p169.
3. *Daily Mirror*, 22 January 1934.
4. Brandon, *The Dark Valley*, p169.
5. Ibid, p170.
6. David Low, *A Life in Cartoons*.
7. Brandon, *The Dark Valley*, p171.
8. *The Times*, 8 June 1934.
9. *Daily Telegraph*, 8 June 1934.
10. *The Times*, 8 June 1934.
11. Public Records Office, Kew, HO 144/21060/316.
12. *The Times*, 8 June 1934.
13. *Annual Register* 1936, Chronicle, May, pp96–7.
14. Jennie Lee, *My Life with Nye*.

16   The Notting Hill Race Riots

1. *The Times*, 28 January 1919.
2. *Liverpool Echo*, 7 June 1919.
3. *Liverpool Echo*, 11 June 1919.
4. *The Times*, 9 June 1919.
5. *Morning Post*, 9 June 1919.
6. *The Times*, 11 June 1919.
7. *Daily Mail*, 16 June 1919.
8. Michael Banton, 'Recent Immigration', p10.
9. Tim Helbing, *The Notting Hill Race Riots and British National Identity*, <http://www.portowebbo.co.uk/nottinghilltv/revealed8.htm>, p4.
10. J.P.W. Mallalieu, *New Statesman*, 13 September 1958.
11. Helbing, *The Notting Hill Race Riots*.
12. *West Indian Gazette*, August 1958.
13. *Guardian Weekend* supplement, 17 August 2002.
14. *The Times*, 25 August 1958.
15. *The Times*, 21 August 1958.
16. *Annual Register* 1958, p45.
17. *The Times*, 6 September 1958.
18. Clive Bloom, *Violent London – 2000 Years of Riots, Rebels and Revolts*, p379.
19. *The Times*, 6 September 1958.
20. Baker Baron, 'Beating Back Moseley', <http://www.geocities.com/londonriots/nottinghill>.
21. *The Times*, 6 September 1958.
22. Ibid.
23. Ibid.
24. *The Times*, 2 September 1958.
25. *The Times*, 6 September 1958.
26. Ibid.
27. London *Evening Standard*, 4 August 1958.
28. *The Times*, 4 September 1958.
29. Statement issued by Downing Street, 3 September 1958.
30. *Guardian Weekend* supplement, 17 August 2002.
31. Ibid.

17   From Student Protest to Blair Peach

1. *The Times*, 18 March 1968.
2. *Annual Register* 1968, Economics and Unrest, pp489–93.
3. *The Times*, 18 March 1969.
4. *The Times*, 19 March 1968.
5. Brent Council Online, 'Secret History – Rough Justice', <http://www.brent.gov.uk>.
6. Author's contemporary reportage, various publications, various dates, via Central Press, Westminster Press Gallery, House of Commons.
7. Ibid.

8. *Guardian*, 8 November 1977.
9. Ibid.
10. *The Times*, 24 April 1979.
11. *Daily Telegraph*, 24 April 1979.
12. Ibid.
13. *The Times*, 24 April 1979.
14. Ibid.
15. *Daily Telegraph*, 24 April 1979.
16. Ibid.
17. *Daily Telegraph*, 25 April 1979.
18. BBC News Online, 24 April 1999, <http://news.bbc.co.uk>.

18   Brixton, Toxteth and Broadwater Farm

1. Roger Graef, *Talking Blues*, p51.
2. Anthony Babington, *Military Intervention in Britain*, pp181–2.
3. Ibid, p183.
4. Lord Scarman, *The Brixton Disorders*, 10–12 April 1981, command paper 8423.
5. Ibid.
6. Graef, *Talking Blues*, p52.
7. Babington, *Military Intervention in Britain*, p184.
8. Scarman, *The Brixton Disorders*.
9. *The Times*, 13 April 1981.
10. *Annual Register*, chap 2, p9.
11. Lew Baxter, *Liverpool Daily Post*, <http://www.liverpool.co.uk>.
12. Mark Thomas and Philippa Bellis, '20 Years On – Urban Unrest', *Liverpool Echo* website, <http://icliverpool.icnetwork.co.uk>.
13. *Liverpool Echo*, 6 July 1981.
14. Ibid.
15. Interview with author, June 2002.
16. *Liverpool Echo*, 6 July 1981.
17. *The Times*, 6 July 1981.
18. Graef, *Talking Blues*, pp53–5.
19. *Liverpool Daily Post*, 7 July 1981.
20. Interview with author, June 2002.
21. *Liverpool Echo*, 7 July 1981.
22. Hansard, 8 July 1981.
23. Graef, *Talking Blues*, p58.
24. Interview with author, July 2003.
25. Thomas and Bellis, '20 Years On'.
26. *The Times*, 30 July 1981.
27. *Liverpool Echo*, 30 July 1981.
28. Baxter, *Liverpool Daily Post*.
29. *The Times*, 30 July 1981.
30. *Annual Register* 1981, pp11–3.
31. Scarman, *The Brixton Disorders*, pp73–4.
32. Ibid, pp126–31.

33. Ibid, pp10–11.
34. Babington, *Military Intervention in Britain*, pp192–3.
35. *The Times*, 11 September 1985.
36. *Annual Register* 1985, p35.
37. Interview with author, June 2003.
38. Babington, *Military Intervention in Britain*, pp194–5.
39. Graef, *Talking Blues*, p79.
40. Babington, *Military Intervention in Britain*, pp194–5.
41. Graef, *Talking Blues*, p79.
42. *The Times*, 9 October 1985.
43. Graef, *Talking Blues*, p80.
44. *Daily Mirror*, 22 August 2005.

19   The Battle of Orgreave

1.   Paul Routledge, *Scargill – The Unauthorised Biography*, pp72–3.
2.   *The Times*, 22 October 1983.
3.   *Guardian*, 9 March 1984.
4.   *Daily Telegraph*, 16 March 1984.
5.   Roger Graef, *Talking Blues*, p60.
6.   *Daily Telegraph*, 20 April 1984.
7.   Ian MacGregor, *The Enemies Within*, p205.
8.   *Daily Telegraph*, 29 May 1984.
9.   Martin Adeney and John Lloyd, *The Miners' Strike*, p115.
10. *Daily Telegraph*, 19 June 1984.
11. Ibid.
12. Graef, *Talking Blues*, p73.
13. Ibid, p74.
14. *Daily Telegraph*, 19 June 1984.
15. Adeney and Lloyd, *The Miners' Strike*, p113.
16. Hansard, 20 June 1984.
17. MacGregor, *The Enemies Within*, pp208–4.
18. Peter Wilsher, with Donald MacIntyre, Michael Jones and the Sunday Times Insight Team, *Strike: Thatcher, Scargill and the Miners*, p126.
19. *Daily Telegraph*, 13 November 1984.
20. Adeney and Lloyd, *The Miners' Strike*.
21. *The Times*, 1 December 1984.
22. *Guardian*, 7 March 1985.

20   The Poll Tax Riot

1.   Philip Webster, *The Times Guide to the Commons*, p26.
2.   Ibid, pp27–8.
3.   *Liverpool Echo*, February 1990, various days.
4.   *Annual Register* 1990, p15.
5.   Webster, *Times Guide to the Commons*, pp25–8.

6. Anti-Poll Tax Federation unpublished internal inquiry, July–September 1990, witness evidence provided to author on condition of anonymity.
7. Ibid.
8. Ibid.
9. Ibid.
10. Interview with author, July 2002.
11. *The Times*, 2 April 1990.
12. Ibid.
13. Anti-Poll Tax Federation unpublished internal inquiry.
14. Ibid.
15. Ibid.
16. Ibid.
17. Ibid.
18. Ibid.
19. Ibid.
20. Ibid.
21. *The Times*, 2 April 1990.
22. *Annual Register* 1990, p16.
23. *Daily Telegraph*, 2 April 1990.
24. Channel Four News, 1 April 1990.
25. Interview with author, July 2002.
26. *Annual Register* 1990, p22.
27. Webster, *Times Guide to the Commons*, p28.

21   The Return of Race Riots

1. *The Times*, 6 May 2001.
2. *Guardian*, 6 May 2001.
3. BBC News, 7 May 2001.
4. BBC News Online, <http://news.bbc.co.uk/leeds.riots>, 28 May 2001.
5. BBC News Online, <http://news.bbc.co.uk/burnley.riots>, 24 June 2002.
6. *The Times*, 7 July 2001.
7. Author's contemporary reportage, various publications, various dates, via Central Press, Westminster Press Gallery, House of Commons.
8. BBC News, 7 July 2001.
9. BBC News Online, 27 May 2001, <http://news.bbc.co.uk>.
10. *Guardian*, 11 December 2001.
11. BBC News, 11 December 2001.
12. *Guardian*, 21 November 2002.
13. *Sunday Times/Observer*, 23 October 2005.
14. *Guardian*, 24 October 2005.

22   G8 and Stop the War

1. BBC News Online, <http://news.bbc.co.uk>, 19 June 1999.
2. Ibid.
3. Tony Smith, BBC World Service, 18 December 1999.

4. Ibid.
5. Downing Street, 2 May 2000.
6. BBC News Online, <http://news.bbc.co.uk>, 6 April 2000.
7. *Guardian*, 2 May 2001.
8. Dominic Casciani, BBC News Online, <http://news.bbc.co.uk>, 1 May 2001.
9. *The Times*, 3 May 2001.
10. BBC News Online, <http://news.bbc.co.uk>, 15 February 2003.
11. ITN, 12 April 2003.
12. *Liverpool Echo*, 18 October 2004.
13. Hansard, 5 July 2005.
14. BBC News Online, <http://news.bbc.co.uk>, 6 July 2005.
15. Ibid.
16. BBC News, 7 July 2005.
17. BBC News, 9 July 2005.

Bibliography

Adeney, Martin, and Lloyd, John, *The Miners' Strike 1984 – Loss Without Limit* (Routledge and Kegan Paul, London, 1986)

Alison, Archibald, *The Chartists and Universal Suffrage* (Blackwoods Magazine, 1839)

Annual Register, various years (Law and Gilbert, London)

Arbuthnot, Mrs, *Diary* (1831)

Arnold, Sir Arthur, *History of the Cotton Famine* (1864)

Atkinson, Diane, *The Suffragettes in Pictures* (Sutton Publishing, Stroud, 1996)

Babington, Anthony, *Military Intervention in Britain – From the Gordon Riots to the Gibraltar Incident* (Routledge, London and New York, 1990)

Bamford, Samuel, *Passages in the Life of a Radical* (Cass, London,1843)

Banton, Michael, 'Recent Immigration', *Population Studies*, July 1953

Barlee, Ellen, *A Visit to Lancashire in December 1862* (1863)

Baron, Baker 'Beating Back Mosely' (2002), <http://www.geocities.com/londonriots/nottinghill>

Baxter, Lew, *Liverpool Daily Post*, <http://www.liverpool.co.uk>

BBC News Online, various dates, <http://news.bbc.co.uk>

Best, Geoffrey, *Churchill – A Study in Greatness* (Hambledon, London and New York, 2001)

Billington-Greig, Teresa, *Towards Women's Liberty* (Garden City Press, Letchworth, 1907)

Billington-Greig, Teresa, *The Non-Violent Militant, Selected Writings* (Routledge, London, 1987)

Bloom, Clive, *Violent London: 2,000 Years of Riots, Rebels and Revolts* (Sidgwick and Jackson, London, 2003)

Bloy, Marjorie, *The Causes of Chartism* (The Victorian Web, 2000)

Braisford and Murray, *Treatment of the Women's Deputation by the Metropolitan Police* (The Women's Press, London, 1911)

Brandon, Piers, *The Dark Valley – A Panorama of the 1930s* (Jonathan Cape, London, 2000)

Brent Council Online, 'Secret History – Rough Justice', <http://www.brent.gov.uk>

Bristol Homepage, <http://www.brisray.co.uk/bristol/briot/htm>

Carpenter, Edward, *My Days and Dreams* (Allen & Unwin, London, 1888)

Churchill, Randolph S., *Winston S. Churchill, Vol II: Young Statesman* (Heinemann, London, 1967)

Cobbett, William, *Political Register* (Richard Bradshaw, 1818)

Cobbett, William, *Rural Rides* (Penguin, London, 1967)

Coffin, Cyril, *Captain Swing in Dorset* (1999), The Dorset Page, <http://www.thedorsetpage.com.history>

Colby, Charles W., *Selections from the Sources of English History* (Longman, London, 1920)

Cooper, Thomas, *The Life of Thomas Cooper* (1872) (reprinted Leicester University Press, Leicester, 1971)

Critchley, T.A., *A History of Police in England and Wales* (Constable, London, 1967)

Cunninghame Graham, Robert, *Sursum Corda, a Sketch in Success* (Heinemann, London, 1900)

Dalley, Jane, *Diana Mosley – A Life* (Faber and Faber, London, 1999)

Darvall, F., *Popular Disturbances and Public Order in Regency Britain* (Oxford University Press, Oxford, 1934)

Dictionary of National Biography

Ellenborough, Lord, *Diary* (1831)

Emsley, Clive, *The English Police – A Political and Social History* (St Martin's Press, New York, 1991)

Fielding, Nigel G., *The Police and Social Conflict – Rhetoric and Reality* (Athlone Press, London and New Jersey, 1991)

Fyfe, Henry Hamilton, *My Seven Selves* (London, 1935)

Gammage, Robert, *History of the Chartist Movement* (1894)

Gaskell, P., *The Manufacturing Population of England* (Baldwin and Craddock, London, 1833)

Gilmour, Ian, *Riots, Risings and Revolution* (Hutchinson, London, 1992)

Graef, Roger, *Talking Blues – The Police in Their Own Words* (Collins Harvill, London, 1989)

'The Great Rising', *A Brief History of Wales*, <http://www.britannia.com/wales/whist.16.html>

Greville, Charles, *Journal* (1832) (reprinted Macmillan, London)

Hammond, J.L., and Hammond, B., *The Village Labourer* (1911) (reprinted Nonsuch, Stroud, 2005)

Hammond, J.L., and Hammond, B., *The Skilled Labourer, 1760–1831* (1919)

Hampson, Walter, *Normanton Past and Present* (1928), <http://www.wakefield.org.uk>

Helbing, Tim, *The Notting Hill Race Riots and British National Identity* (Indiana University Press, 2002), <http://www.portowebbo.co.uk/nottinghilltv/revealed8.htm>

Hobhouse, Henry, *Hobhouse Memoirs* (Wessex Press, 1927)

Hobsbawm, Eric, and Rude, G., *Captain Swing* (Lawrence & Wishart, London, 1969)

Holmes, Richard, *Redcoat – The British Soldier in the Age of Horse and Musket* (HarperCollins, London, 2001)

Hudson, Ray, and Williams, Allan M., *Divided Britain* (Belhaven Press, London, 1989)

Hughes, Robert, *The Fatal Shore – A History of the Transportation of Convicts to Australia 1787–1868* (Guild Publishing, London, 1986)

Hunt, Henry, *Memoirs* (three vols) (Dolby, London, 1820)

Jackson, Jamie, Interview, *Observer Magazine*, 2003

Jay, Mike, *The Unfortunate Colonel Despard* (Bantam Press, London, 2004)

Johnston, James, *A Hundred Commoners* (Herbert Joseph, London, 1931)

Jones, David J.V., *Rebecca's Children – A Study of Rural Society, Crime and Protest* (Clarendon Press, Oxford, 1989)

Judge, Tony, *The Force of Persuasion – The Story of the Police Federation* (Police Federation, Surbiton, 1994)

Kennedy, Annie, *Memoirs of a Militant* (1924)

Killingray, David, *Africans in Britain* (Frank Cass, London, 1994)

Kinwardstone, Clara, 'The Swing Riots Around Burbage', <http://www.kinwardstone.clara.net/historic/swing>

Lansbury, Carol, *The Old Brown Dog: Women, Workers and Vivisection in Edwardian England* (University of Wisconsin Press, 1985)

Lee, Jennie, *My Life with Nye* (Jonathan Cape, London, 1980)

Levy, Geoffrey, article in *Daily Mail* (2003)

Longmate, Norman, *The Hungry Mills* (Temple Smith, London, 1978)

Longmate, Norman, *The Breadstealers – The Fight Against the Corn Laws 1836–46* (St Martin's Press, London, 1984)

Loveless, George, *Victims of Whiggery* (1839)

Lovett, William, *Life and Struggles* (London, 1876) (reprinted McGibbon and Kee, 1967)

Low, David, *A Life in Cartoons* (Gollancz, London, 1986)

MacGregor, Ian, *The Enemies Within – The Story of the Miners' Strike 1984–5* (Collins, London, 1986)

Marlow, Joyce, *The Peterloo Massacre* (Rapp and Whiting, London, 1969)

Mather, F.C., *Public Order in the Age of the Chartists* (1959) (reprinted Allen & Unwin, London, 1974)

Mather, F.C., *The General Strike of 1842, from Popular Protest and Public Order: Six Studies in British History* (Allen and Unwin, London, 1974)

Napier, W., *The Life and Opinions of General Sir Charles Napier* (John Murray, London, 1857)

O'Connell, Dee, Interview, *Observer Magazine*, 2003

Okokon, Susan, *Black Londoners* (Sutton Publishing, Stroud, 1998)

Ottey, Roy, *The Strike – An Insider's Story* (Sidgwick and Jackson, London, 1985)

Pankhurst, Emmeline, *My Own Life* (1914), Teaching History Online, <http://www.spartacus.schoolnet.co.uk/WpankhurstE.htm>

Pankhurst, Emmeline, *My Own Story* (Eveleigh Nash, London, 1924), Teaching History Online, <http://www.spartacus.schoolnet.co.uk/WpankhurstE.htm>

Pankhurst, Sylvia, *The Suffragette Movement* (Longman, London, 1931)

Parker, M. St J., and Rid, D.J., *The British Revolution 1750–1970* (Blandford Press, London, 1972)

The Peel Web, 'Feargus O'Connor and the Land Plan', <http://dialspace.dial.pipex.com/peel/oconnor.htm>

The Peel Web, 'The Great Rising', <http://dialspace.dial.pipex.com/peel/greatrising.htm>

The Peel Web, 'The Newport Rising', <http://dialspace.dial.pipex.com/peel/newport.htm>

The Peel Web, 'Rural Unrest in the 1830s', <http://dialspace.dial.pipex.com/peel/swing.htm>

Pellew, G., *The Life and Correspondence of the Right Honourable Henry Addington, First Viscount Sidmouth* (John Murray, London, 1847)

Pelling, Henry, *A History of British Trade Unionism* (Penguin, London, 1963)

Phillips, Melanie, *The Ascent of Women* (Little, Brown, London, 2003)

Pitkin, Margot, article in *Daily Telegraph*, Sydney, 1997

Prentice, Archibald, *Historical Sketches and Personal Recollections of Manchester* (1851) (reprinted Frank Cass, London, 1970)

Raeburn, Antonia, *The Militant Suffragettes* (Michael Joseph, London, 1973)

Reid, Donald, *Peterloo* (Manchester University Press, Manchester, 1958)

Reid, Robert, *Land of Lost Content – The Luddite Revolt 1812* (Heinemann, London, 1986)

Reid, Robert, *The Peterloo Massacre* (Heinemann, London, 1989)

Relief List, Accounts Book, University Library of Manchester

Reports of State Trials, Volume 1 (HMSO, London, 1888)

Reynolds, Gerald, and Judge, Anthony, *The Night the Police Went on Strike* (Weidenfeld and Nicolson, London, 1968)

Rosen, Michael, and Widgery, David, *The Vintage Book of Dissent* (Random House, London, 1991)

Routledge, Paul, *Scargill – The Unauthorised Biography* (HarperCollins, London, 1993)

Scarman, Lord, *The Brixton Disorders*, 10–12 April 1981, command paper 8423

Sharman, Geoffrey, 'Tasmania', rootsweb

Shelley, Percy Bysshe, *The Mask of Anarchy* (1819) (London, 1832)

Sidmouth Papers (Devon Record Office), various dates

Smith, John Owen, *One Monday in November – The Story of the Selborne and Headley Workhouse Riots* (self-published Selborne, 2001)

Spartacus.schoolnet, 'John Frost', <http://www.spartacus.schoolnet.co.uk/Chfrost.htm>

Spencer, Ian R.G., *British Immigration Policy Since 1939* (Routledge, London and New York, 1997)

Stevenson, John, *Popular Disturbances in England 1700–1832* (Longman, London, 1979)

Swiney, Frances, *The Cosmic Procession* (1906)

Taylor, A.J.P., *English History 1914–1945* (Oxford University Press, Oxford, 1965)

Taylor, J.E., *Peterloo Massacre* (n.p., published 1819)

Teaching History Online, 'Cunninghame Graham', <http://www.spartacus.schoolnet.co.uk/Tucunninghame.htm>

Teaching History Online, 'John Burns', <http://www.spartacus.schoolnet.co.uk/Reburns.htm>

Teaching History Online, 'Physical Force Chartists', <http://www.spartacus.schoolnet.co.uk/Chphysical.htm>

Thomas, Mark, and Bellis, Philippa, '20 Years On – Urban Unrest', *Liverpool Echo*, <http://www.icliverpool.icnetwork.co.uk>

Thompson, Dorothy, *The Chartists* (Temple Smith, London, 1984)

Tomison, Maureen, *The English Sickness – The Rise of Trade Union Political Power* (Tom Stacey, London, 1972)

Tschiffely, A.F., *Don Roberto* (William Heinemann, London, 1937)

Ure, A., *The Philosophy of Manufacturers* (Charles Knight, London, 1835)

Watts, Cedric, and Davies, Laurence, *Cunninghame Graham – A Critical Biography* (Cambridge University Press, Cambridge, 1979)

Watts, John, *The Facts of the Cotton Famine* (1866)

Wearmouth, R.F., *Some Working Class Movements of the Nineteenth Century* (London, 1948)

Webster, Philip, *The Times Guide to the Commons* (Times Books, London, 1992)

West, Herbert Faulkner, *A Modern Conquistador: Robert Bontine Cunninghame Graham – His Life and Works* (Cranley and Day, London, 1932)

West Midlands Superintendent's Reports, 1901–25

Wilkinson, George Theodore, *An Authentic History of the Cato Street Conspiracy* (London, 1820) (reprinted Wordsworth Editions, Ware, 1997)

Williams, Gareth, 'A Tribute to the Rhondda', <http://www.therhondda.co.uk/tonypandy>

Williams, Gwyne A., *The Merthyr Rising* (Croom Helm, London, 1978)

Williams, Peter N., *The Long Struggle for Identity – The Story of Wales and its People* (Britannia Wales, Cardiff, 2000)

Wilsher, Peter, with Donald MacIntyre, Michael Jones and the Sunday Times Insight Team, Strike – *Thatcher, Scargill and the Miners* (Andre Deutsch, London, 1985)

Winder, Robert, *Bloody Foreigners – The Story of Immigration to Britain* (Little, Brown, London, 2004)

Woodward, Sir Llewellyn, *The Age of Reform 1815–1870, The Oxford History of England* (Clarenden Press, Oxford, 1962)

Younge, Gary, 'The Politics of Partying', *Guardian Weekend*, 2002

Ziegler, P., *Addington* (Collins, London, 1965)

Index